The Cry of a Lonely Planet

Rising from this troubled planet like incense of despair is the persistent question—
WHY?

Books by the Author

The Day the Cat Jumped
A Day to Remember
Destination Life
Hammers in the Fire
How to Burn Your Candle
How to Live With a Tiger
The Impersonation Game
Is Anybody Listening?
Lady, I'm Tired Too
Look! No Doomsday
Planet in Rebellion
Psychic Roulette
Sail Your Own Seas
Showdown in the Middle East
The Stuff of Survival
Touch and Live
Tying Down the Sun

The Cry of a Lonely Planet

George E. Vandeman

Pacific Press Publishing Association
Mountain View, California

The Book That You Hold in Your Hand Will Tell You—

why God hasn't stepped in to stop the war and crime and sickness and disaster that seem to be out of control—

why a strange, cosmic war—in which not a shot was fired, and in which not one participant died—concerns you personally—

why you need to know what happens after death—

why any prediction of the precise time for the world's end is sure to be wrong—

why and how you can be sure that Jesus of Nazareth was who He claimed to be—

why the psychics sometimes possess information that is known to no living person but you—

why it is not possible to successfully counterfeit the second coming of Christ—

why the Bible prophets used such strange symbols—and how you can understand them—

why and how a false prophet can be easily recognized—

why hell is not burning now—and why it will not burn eternally—

why this lonely planet is full of tears—and what God intends to do about it—

Dedication

If a book is destined to be universally helpful, I believe it must spring from the crucible of life. And life involves the family.

Therefore I dedicate these pages to my family. To Nellie, a loving and faithful companion in a lifelong commitment to service for others. To three fine sons—George, Ronald, and Robert. And to a lovely daughter, Connie. All these have helped to keep me humble, human, and happy. I owe much to my family.

And I owe much to my office family as well—a skilled and faithful team of workers who live and breathe the ministry to which we're all committed. Outstanding among these is Marjorie Lewis Lloyd, always an able writer and researcher, who for twenty-five years has assisted in the production of the "It Is Written" program. She has been tireless in the preparation of this manuscript as well.

To all these I owe very much indeed. But to the Unseen One—my *Friend*—goes the eternal credit for the vastly more important dimension that will make this book live in the hearts of all who read it. Thank You, Lord, for putting it all together!

George E. Vandeman

Contents

And Now Before You Turn the Page

If you want to understand the strange things that are happening, if you would like to make sense out of the play and counterplay of the past, if you would like to view an inspired, authentic, and hope-filled panorama of a future that now appears so frightening, this book is for you.

In these pages you step inside the unseen world and see a cosmic conflict speeding toward its final showdown. And you are not a spectator but an actor in this drama that is being watched with breathless interest by all the universe. This planet is where the action is. And control is the name of the game.

You will recoil with horror at the ruthlessness of hate. You will be shocked as you see how subtle and lying propaganda has swept the world. You will be stunned as you see how closely you have unwittingly brushed against it.

But only as you understand the subtle strategy of rebellion, the dark dilemma of a rebel race, do you begin to understand the incredible wonder of a Creator's love. A Creator whose heart was broken by our guilt—and by our tears. A Creator who forged an incomparable hope out of a planet's despair!

Please, God, Be Careful!

An American president, speaking to an audience of women, read a letter that he had received from the mother of a U. S. serviceman. This is what it said:

"A week ago my son was still enrolled in the college of his choice. Tonight he's in a strange motel somewhere. Tomorrow he steps onto an airplane which will take him far away. He enlisted in a branch of the U. S. armed forces.

"During these past weeks I've sensed and seen him . . . in the process of pulling away, cutting the cord, getting ready to leave the nest. I saw him bequeath some valuable possessions, like his penny collection and his baseball cards. They went to a couple of small boys in his Pied Piper following on the block."

The mother said she had watched him wax his new car. And he had told her she was a great cook. And she wrote, "So I now take my place among the thousands of other mothers who through the years have watched as their feelings were not so different from mine tonight.

"Actually," she said, "it's all quite appropriate. This is a guy who grew up in a room wallpapered with flags and muskets and drums. He regularly ran Old Glory up the flagpole in the backyard before breakfast in those days. He and his big brother had G. I. Joe uniforms sizes 4 and 6."

She went on, "I remember seeing them sneak up the little hill in the neighbor lady's backyard on their stomachs. I wonder how many times I've picked up little plastic army men from under the furniture. All those toys and memories have been packed away for years, but I feel the need to bring them out and handle them tonight.

"He has examined the options, as I suggested. The choices he's made are taking him far away from me. He believes there are opportunities for him in education, travel and experience. No doubt there are.

"He thinks he's getting a good deal. No doubt he is.

"Personally, I'm inclined to believe the country is getting a good deal. In exchange for all their provisions, they're getting one tall, tanned fellow with summer-bleached hair, a sharp young mind and more potential and possibilities than I have space to describe."

And then she concluded, "Thank you for taking the time from running the nation to listen to the passions of a mother's heart. And, please, will you be especially careful with the country right now?"

The president replied solemnly, "I will be very careful with the country just now."

A mother's letter to an American president. And there were tears all over the audience. The first lady, sitting on the platform near her husband, had big tears running down her cheeks.

It's good that he was speaking to an audience of women, for men might have cried too. And men try not to cry—except when it's very dark and very still and no one is listening but God.

There's so much that is wrong with our world right now—so much that technology can't fix. It seems to be so fragile. It trembles and quakes and convulses as if about to break up. Solid earth isn't so solid anymore. It slides into the sea. It sinks into the mud. It washes away in the floods that follow the fires. It blows away. Stronger hands than those of even our best leaders are needed now.

It is no wonder that from uncounted hearts there rises like incense the silent, unspoken cry, "Please, God, be very careful with our little world!"

And with good reason. For our world really is little— so little that it seems it would never be missed if suddenly it should disappear.

Mark Twain, in his story *Captain Stormfield's Visit to Heaven,* shared a tale that was obviously intended to be completely absurd. Captain Stormfield, the story goes, had died and was on his way to heaven, but was unable to resist the temptation to race with a comet. He ended up way off course, in a sort of heavenly "missing persons bureau." An angel, wanting to help, went up in a balloon alongside a huge map of the universe, hoping to locate our solar system. The map was about the size of the whole state of Rhode Island. Three days later the angel came back down to report that he might have found our solar system, but he couldn't be sure. It might have been just flyspecks!

Just an absurd piece of exaggeration. Never intended to be taken seriously. But we know now that Mark Twain may not have been so far off. We *are* like a tiny cinder on the edge of the universe. Could the Creator ever be concerned with us? Does He even know that we are here?

It was David who wrote, "When I consider your heavens, the work of your fingers, the moon and the stars, which you have set in place, what is man that you are mindful of him, the son of man that you care for him?" Psalm 8:3, 4, NIV.

Some believe that visitors from outer space are circling the earth, looking us over, wondering about us. But the astronomer Carl Sagan discounts such an idea. He says there's nothing very interesting, nothing special about our planet. He describes it as "where the action isn't."

But our little world is so important, and so frightening, to *us*. It's so full of trouble and confusion and hate. And it's hurtling so fast—somewhere. We have a feeling that something is very wrong. We live in the atmosphere of expected crisis. Are we about to collide with something—or burn up—or explode—or perhaps be sucked into one of those black holes they talk about? What if God should drop one of those black holes? What if He should drop us?

Years ago a popular song was pleading, "Stop the world! I want to get off!" It was a clever title. Some took it seriously even then. Today we all do. If only there were some escape—somewhere to go—somewhere safe—before the planet we're riding goes up in smoke.

God said through the prophet Isaiah, "The earth will wear out like a garment." Isaiah 51:6, NIV.

And do you recall these words from the book of Revelation? "The time has come for . . . destroying those who destroy the earth." Revelation 11:18, NIV.

Does God know the trouble we're in? Does He know we're on this speeding, careening planet—and does He care? Are we on a collision course with doomsday? Can God correct our course the way NASA corrects the path of its spacecraft? And if He can, does He intend to—and in the nick of time?

NASA's *Voyager 2,* after a four-year journey from earth, reached its closest encounter with Saturn's rings right on time— almost on time. It was 2.7 seconds early! We marvel, and rightly, at such precision.

But if NASA can work such technological miracles, if NASA can boost a vehicle from here to Saturn's rings—what about the One who *made* Saturn and the incredible beauty of its rings? Is His power less than that of the people He has made?

That's another question that will have to be settled before we can sleep well at night. Did God create Saturn—and this world— and us? In the very first ten words of the Bible, the ancient and indestructible Book that claims to be the Word of God—in those very first words it says, "In the beginning God created the heavens and the earth." Genesis 1:1, NIV.

Did He—or didn't He? If He did, then we have nothing to fear. But if He didn't, then the Bible is a Book not to be trusted—and we'd better forget the idea of its being even a good book. If the Book is not what it claims to be, then it is the work of the worst impostor the world has ever known.

Yet impostor or not, the Author of the Bible puts its most incredible claim right up front, in the first ten words, making Himself vulnerable, as if to invite challenge. God stands or falls, and so does our personal security along with that of the universe, with the credibility of those ten words. For who of us can sleep peacefully tonight, believing that our future is in the hands of blind, bungling chance? Chance that, according to all the laws of probability, never created anything and never will.

This is something that has to be settled before we can face the future with any confidence at all. Do we, or do we not, have a Creator? Were we made in the image of God, as the Book says? Or are we the hapless children of some cosmic accident, of some long-buried mystery that fizzled?

How can we pray to a God who lied to us in His first ten words—if He did? Our cry is lost before it gets through the ceiling if there is no one listening. It is mockery to pray to One we have written off as myth, as dead, or as a liar.

"Please, God, be very careful with our little world!" Such a prayer makes sense only as we believe that He is there, that He is listening, and that He really does hold this frightened, wobbly world in His hands!

Remember the song—the old spiritual that we all love? "He's got the whole world in His hands. . . . He's got the little tiny baby in His hands. . . . He's got everybody in His hands." Remember?

But did you know that this world, and the whole human race, trembled in His hands once—for a few moments? And not a soul knew!

It was a Thursday evening. Jesus and His closest friends—eleven of them—were on their way out of the city. Eleven of them, not twelve, for one had left the group a little while earlier. Jesus had sent him on an errand, they thought. But the errand was his own. He had gone to finalize a project he had been thinking about—the betrayal of his Lord. And only Jesus knew!

It was a beautiful spring evening. The moon was bright. But something was wrong. Something was wrong with Jesus. He seemed troubled, weighted down with some terrible problem that they could not understand. He must be very tired.

Leaving the others, He took three of His men deep into the garden. He needed them to share His terrible ordeal. He needed to know that they were waiting and praying nearby. But they understood not at all what was happening. How could the Messiah, the Son of God, need their prayers? Besides, they were exhausted. Twice He came back and found them asleep.

So Jesus went on alone. And His unseen enemy was there waiting. This was his chance.

Try to forget the paintings of Gethsemane that you have seen. Jesus kneeling by a carefully chosen rock. His robe flawlessly draped. Every hair in place. Ready for the camera. No. It wasn't like that at all. Jesus was carrying the sins of the whole world that night. And the Father, though it caused Him exquisite pain to do it, must withdraw His presence from His Son. I picture Jesus falling prostrate on the cold ground, digging His fingers into the dirt as if to keep from being drawn still farther from His Father.

Jesus had come to this planet to give His life for a lost race. All His life His footsteps had been leading straight to this hour. But now it loomed like a monster before Him. Was there no other way to save men? The tempter saw His human weakness and pressed his strongest arguments. Why should He die for a world that didn't even want to be saved? Why not call for a legion of angels to sweep Him back to heaven? Let men pay for their own sins!

The fate of the whole human race trembled in the balance as Jesus wrestled with the temptation to turn back. But no. The cry of a lost and lonely planet was ringing in His ears. He would go through with the decision that had brought Him to this world. And when Judas came with the cruel mob in search of Him, He stood tall and straight, ready for the cross that now in only hours would overtake Him.

And that's why you—and I—are safe in His hands. That's why we can sleep tonight unafraid, knowing that He will be very, very careful with our little world!

Robots Don't Fight

Imagine, if you will, that you are a boy of five again, playing with toy soldiers, parading them across the floor in perfect rank. They take orders patiently, and carry them out without protest. Toy soldiers are such fun.

But tell me, little boy. What if those toy soldiers should suddenly come alive? What if suddenly they were real? Your eyes light up at the thought! Real soldiers! And they would be such good soldiers! They would still do everything you tell them. But they would be real. As real as your dog. As real as you. They could even salute you when they pass by. Not toys anymore!

But, what if it doesn't work out that way? What if one of those soldiers decides he is going to rebel? What if he sullenly refuses to march when you tell him to march? What if he wrenches his painted face into an ugly snarl and calls you a dictator?

What if those come-alive soldiers start fighting with each other, and then killing each other, until you have a full-scale war on your hands? What would you do about it?

Even at five years old you're bigger than they are. You could cuff them and force them back into line. That would prove you are still in charge.

Yes, it would prove you're in charge. But it would also prove you didn't really want them to come alive after all. You really wanted toys!

Even a child can understand that if you let your toys come alive, you take a big risk!

Now you understand God's problem! He didn't want toys that He could manipulate and control. He didn't want robots. He didn't want windup angels or battery-powered people. He didn't want His vast kingdom filled with electronic subjects that didn't even know they were being controlled. He wanted real live angels that He could love—and who could love Him back. He wanted people who were free to choose, to love Him or not love Him—even if it meant that one of them, or all of them, should rebel.

If that should happen, of course, He could force His subjects back into line. He could throw them away like broken toys. That would prove that He had the power. But it would also prove—or seem to prove—that He hadn't really wanted subjects who could think and choose. He had wanted robots—robots who wouldn't fight. And that wouldn't be true.

Then, too, if He should throw away His people, it would appear to those looking on that there must be something harsh and cruel in His makeup. They wouldn't understand.

He could just ignore the rebellion—look the other way and pretend it hadn't happened. But if He did that, chaos would result. Rebellion would spread. His kingdom, the universe itself, would fall.

He could try to explain the wrongness of rebellion to those looking on—so they would understand why He had to throw away the people He had made. But trying to explain the dangers of rebellion to those who had never seen it would be like trying to explain trigonometry to those tin soldiers on the floor!

So what would God do? Do you see His dilemma?

Edna St. Vincent Millay died in 1950. She was an agnostic, an unbeliever. Her words were sharp and sometimes impudent. But in one of her poems, published after her death, it is evident that she understood God's problem better than most people do. Frederick B. Speakman took the poem out of its verse form and translated it into this:

"I'm not overly impressed with the job God did in creating the world. Oh, it's amazing from where I look out at it, of course. But to turn such a trick would be routine and simple if your power were such as God's must be. To manipulate matter, this heavy, obstinate stuff He used—it's stubborn to be sure—but in such hands as God's it should have been easy and great fun to bend it into shape, to toss a planet here and set off a star there, and whip up a galaxy to fit them in, and even to concentrate on our little globe and decorate its crust with life! No," she argues, "if I had the wisdom and skill and strength of the Almighty I'm certain I could turn out a world at least as beautiful and brave, and as frightened and sorrowful as ours is.

"But that other trouble God got Himself into, that's what appalls me! To fashion the human heart, then set it free, turn it loose on its own and watch it go its way and turn all botched and bawdy and profligate, then try to win us back again to what He meant us for! To read our hearts as they are by now, these layers upon layers of wrong laminated in our souls like the leaves that are pressed into coal, and then try to disentangle all that without forcing us! To understand all that without hating us! To punish our wrongs without utterly destroying us! And still to keep trying to persuade our kind of wickedness to choose His kind of goodness.

"There's real trouble," she concludes. "I can't understand why He bothered in the first place, and I don't see for a moment how anything much can ever come of it. But how I respect Him for daring to try!" *Love Is Something You Do,* pp. 35, 36.

Could a believer have said it better? Perhaps not—except that the believer knows that God will yet succeed, with enough human hearts to make it worth the trouble!

And we, too; though much may seem dark and mysterious now, will one day understand—and say it was worth it all!

The mystery of evil, even now, is not locked away from us. It is not an impenetrable secret. We can know both the origin and the outcome of rebellion against God. We can know who the opponents are and what the issues are in this conflict between good and evil. We may not understand the why of every brush with trouble. But we are not left to float like corks on an ocean, without sail or ballast or destination.

"The secret things belong to the Lord our God," said Moses, "but the things revealed belong to us and to our children forever." Deuteronomy 29:29, NIV.

And more things have been revealed than you would ever dream!

A Strange War

What kind of weapons would you expect God to use if He should be involved in a war? Certainly He would not bother with such primitive weapons as spears or guns or conventional bombs. Most certainly He who made the atom must understand all the intricacies of its possible behavior. Nuclear power would be at His instant command. For that matter, He who spoke worlds into existence (Psalm 33:6, 9) could easily speak His enemies out of existence.

But the book of Revelation tells us that there *was* a war in heaven. And there is something very strange about that war, for there is no mention whatever of weapons. And stranger still, there was not even one fatality on either side. Listen:

"And there was war in heaven. Michael and his angels fought against the dragon, and the dragon and his angels fought back. But he was not strong enough, and they lost their place in heaven. The great dragon was hurled down—that ancient serpent called the devil or Satan, who leads the whole world astray. He was hurled to the earth, and his angels with him." Revelation 12:7–9, NIV.

Not a shot was fired. Not a spear thrust. Not a bomb dropped. No death ray. And not a single fatality. Satan and his angels lost the war. They were simply thrown out, banished from heaven. No longer was heaven their home.

At this moment every participant in that war is still alive. Not one of the losers is now behind bars. All have a frightening measure of freedom, though God has placed some restrictions upon their activities.

Strange? We shall discover why!

We shall discover that this war in heaven was only the beginning of an agelong controversy that is not yet finished. But when it *is* finished, when there is not one in all the universe who will misunderstand God's dealing with rebellion, it will not be like the beginning. No issue will be left undecided. God will no longer need to place Himself on trial before His subjects. His character will never again be questioned. And in the final confrontation, here on this planet, on one side no casualties, and, on the other side, no survivors. Rebellion will be over forever—and with it all the heartache it has caused!

It may seem to us that God is slow to intervene. But remember—He is taking time to do it right. Would you want it otherwise?

But now back to this strange war in heaven. Who were the participants? Michael and His angels. The dragon and his angels. The dragon is identified as the ancient serpent, the devil, or Satan. The devil and Satan are of course one and the same. And it is appropriate also to call him the ancient serpent, for it was disguised as a serpent that he maneuvered the downfall of our first parents.

But who is Michael? Evidently Michael—or Michael the archangel (Jude 9)—is none other than the Son of God, the One we know as Christ or Jesus.

But someone says, "Wait! Jesus wasn't born until Bethlehem. And wasn't this a long time before Bethlehem?"

Yes. But the prophet Micah, in predicting the birth of Jesus in Bethlehem (Micah 5:2), tells us that the One to be born there had existed "from everlasting." And according to the apostle John (John 1:1, 14), there never was a time when the One we call Jesus did not exist along with His Father.

Jesus was not a created being. He was not an angel. He was not an angel elevated to a higher position—He was God! The apostle Paul (in Hebrews 1:3–14) makes this crystal clear. Jesus is sometimes called the archangel (compare Jude 9 with 1 Thessalonians 4:16 and John 5:28, 29) not because He was an angel, but because He was the loved Commander of the angels.

It is interesting that the name Michael in the Scriptures seems to be used primarily, if not exclusively, in speaking of the conflict between the Son of God and Satan. It seems reasonable, then, that Michael may have been the name by which Jesus was known in heaven before He was born in Bethlehem.

In that war in heaven, then, Michael and His loyal angels were arrayed against Satan and his angels—the angels who sided with him in his rebellion.

And now someone is saying, "Who are the angels? Aren't they the spirits of people who have died here in our world?"

No. That could hardly be the case, for angels were in existence long before ever this earth was created—long before any one had died. Angels are the beings created to inhabit heaven—the world where God's throne is.

But now we must identify Satan more specifically, for it is important that we understand just who the characters are in this agelong conflict. What is the background of this leader of rebellion? Who was he before he was called Satan, before he became the devil, before he rebelled? Certainly God did not create a devil. It is unthinkable that there should be a devil factory in heaven. What happened?

The prophet Isaiah identifies the author of rebellion as "Lucifer, son of the morning." See Isaiah 14:12.

Son of the morning! Only a brilliant angel would have such a title. But something happened. A change came about. The brilliant son of the morning became a devil—made of himself a devil—and fell from heaven.

The prophet gives us some details. "How art thou fallen from heaven, O Lucifer, son of the morning! . . . Thou hast said in thine heart, I will ascend into heaven, I will exalt my throne above the stars of God: . . . I will ascend above the heights of the clouds; I will be like the most High." Isaiah 14:12–14, KJV.

It all started in the heart, in the mind, where all wrong begins. This brilliant being became dissatisfied with being an angel, even the highest angel. He coveted the throne of God. He wanted to be like God—in power, but not in character.

The prophet Ezekiel has recorded for us the words spoken by God to Lucifer: "Thou art the anointed cherub that covereth; and I have set thee so: thou wast upon the holy mountain of God. . . . Thou wast perfect in thy ways from the day that thou wast created, till iniquity was found in thee. . . . Thine heart was lifted up because of thy beauty, thou hast corrupted thy wisdom by reason of thy brightness." Ezekiel 28:14–17, KJV.

Do you get the picture? This brilliant angel, so honored that he stood next to the throne of God, became proud of his beauty, proud of his brightness, and began to think that even as heaven's highest angel he was not honored enough. He was loved and adored by the other angels. But that seemed not enough. He wanted unlimited power, unlimited control. He didn't want to be an angel at all. He wanted to be God!

Evidently Lucifer didn't resist these thoughts. On the contrary, he encouraged them. And there, in the heart of the son of the morning, sin entered the universe. It had never existed before. And no one but God—because He knows all things—knew what sin was or how lethal it would be.

Sin is mysterious. It cannot be explained, for to explain it would be to excuse it. And it cannot be excused. Lucifer could not plead that he was deprived, that he was discriminated against, or that his environment was to blame. Heaven had given him everything it had to give. But he wanted more!

At first he may not have understood the strange feelings in his heart. But certainly it was explained to him. Tenderly the Son of God must have pleaded with him to turn back. Loyal angels must have urged him not to continue his fearful course. At that point he could have turned back and been forgiven. But he was too proud to repent. He began to spread his discontent among the angels until a third of them had sided with him (Revelation 12:4). Dissatisfaction turned to open revolt, to open rebellion. Lucifer, son of the morning, had become the devil. And he, along with his angels-turned-demons, was banished from heaven.

Was God in any way responsible for all this? Was this brilliant angel created with some hidden flaw? Had God, even unwittingly, created a devil? Never! God does nothing unwittingly. And God does nothing imperfectly. Lucifer, we read a few moments ago, was perfect from the day he was created. Remember?

Created perfect. But not created a robot. He was created with the power to choose. To him had been given the dangerous gift of freedom. God knew the risk He took. He knew that sometime, somewhere, someone might choose to sin, choose to rebel. And Lucifer did.

What would God do now? Destroying Lucifer and his angels would be misunderstood. It would appear to support the rebel charge that God was arbitrary and cruel—a tyrant who had no love for His subjects. The plant of sin must be allowed to grow until all the universe should see its deadly bloom. The character of Satan must be unmasked. God must place Himself on trial before His subjects and let them see who it is that cares.

It would take time—millenniums of time. But there was no other way. For if a trace of rebellion remained, if in even one mind there remained a question about God's character, it would one day rise to threaten the security of the universe again. Men and angels and watching worlds must see the horrible lengths to which sin would go. They must see demonstrated again and again the ruthless, lying, uncaring nature of sin. They must see enough of it—so much of it—in all its shameful reality—that the whole universe will turn away in settled horror—never to touch it again!

Was there no way that all this could have been prevented? Was the tragedy of sin inevitable? Did rebellion have to happen?

No. It didn't have to happen. God had a number of options. He could have filled the universe with empty worlds, with galaxies without a spark of life, with stars that spin obediently in their orbits because they cannot do otherwise. But stars could not worship. Stars could not love. Empty worlds could not heal the loneliness in the heart of a loving God. Galaxies, no matter how dazzling their brilliance, could bring no joy to worlds where not a single eye was turned their way.

How could a God of love, His heart bursting with the urge to share—how could such a God be satisfied with a vast, lifeless, untouched emptiness all about Him? How could such a God be silent when He knew that the sound of His voice could call the limitless, silent wilderness of space to life?

He could, of course, fill His kingdom with robots programmed to obey and worship and even to talk of love. But God would not be fooled by His own creation. True, there would be no risk. Rebellion would be impossible. But so would happiness and satisfaction and peace and joy. God would still be lonely.

If the Creator, knowing all things, knew who would rebel, then He could have called to life only those He knew would be loyal subjects. He could leave uncreated anyone who would ever disturb the peace of the universe. But would that be true freedom? Would such a manipulation of creation be any more excusable than manipulating the minds and choices of His subjects? Hardly! How could God be happy knowing that the universe was secure only because He squelched even the possibility of rebellion by leaving all rebels unborn?

There was one more option. God could place within every created one the power to choose, to be loyal or not to be loyal. The risk was tremendous but the possibilities were fantastic. He took the risk. He created angels, and heaven rang with song. He filled the spinning worlds with the happy sounds of life.

Worlds, did I say? Life on other worlds? Yes, I believe there is!

Tears on Other Worlds

According to a somewhat dubious legend, a distinguished astronomer, many years ago, received a message from the famed newspaper tycoon William Randolph Hearst—the father of today's publisher Randolph Hearst. The message read:

IS THERE LIFE ON MARS? CABLE THOUSAND WORDS. HEARST

The astronomer replied, as requested, in a thousand words. It was simply "NOBODY KNOWS"—repeated five hundred times!

We've come a long way since then. And we've gone a long way—230 million miles—to land *Viking* on Mars. Is there life there? That was the question in everybody's mind. Scientists watched breathlessly as the evidence seemed to teeter between "Yes, there is" and "No, there isn't."

Presumably, even if Mr. Hearst's question were extended to include the whole universe rather than simply Mars, astronomers would still answer, "NOBODY KNOWS."

But is that true? Doesn't anybody know? Can't we know?

I don't want to appear presumptuous. But on the basis of what I have read in God's Book, I can say, "Yes, Mr. Hearst, there *is* life on other worlds."

Now the Bible doesn't say in so many words that other worlds are inhabited by intelligent life. But if I were a detective looking for evidence, I'd certainly consider a number of Bible statements mighty hot clues. Listen to this:

"For thus saith the Lord that created the heavens; God himself that formed the earth and made it; he hath established it, he created it not in vain, he formed it to be inhabited." Isaiah 45:18, KJV.

God intended this planet to be the home of life. And since it *is* the home of life, its creation was not in vain. Does this not mean that if God's other worlds were uninhabited, they would have been created in vain—useless? That's the clear implication.

30

Think it through. Is it reasonable to believe that God would create billions upon billions of worlds and fit only one of them up with people?

Here is another significant scripture: "Thou, even thou, art Lord alone; thou hast made heaven, the heaven of heavens, with all their host. . . ; and the host of heaven worshippeth thee." Nehemiah 9:6, KJV.

These words suggest to me that the universe is teeming with life, intelligent life—intelligent enough to worship. And all worship God. They are loyal subjects of His kingdom. They haven't rebelled as this one unruly planet has.

But now listen to this: "God . . . hath in these last days spoken unto us by his Son, . . . by whom also he made the worlds." Hebrews 1:1, 2, KJV.

"His Son, . . . by whom he made the worlds"—plural. More than one world. Many worlds. There may be billions of worlds. And who made them? Our Lord Jesus Christ. "God, who created all things by Jesus Christ." Ephesians 3:9, KJV.

Is this a surprise? Christ—the One we know as Jesus—made the worlds? He made all things? Yes. The apostle John, in his first chapter, leaves no room for confusion on this point. He says in verse 10, concerning Jesus, "He was in the world, and the world was made by him, and the world knew him not." And in verse 3 he says, "All things were made by him; and without him was not anything made that was made."

Do you see what this means? It means not only that the One we know as Jesus existed from eternity with His Father. It means also that Jesus created the worlds, including our world. And if He made our world, He made man. He is our Creator—yours and mine.

It means, too, that Jesus created the angels—including Lucifer. Lucifer was not rebelling against the rule of a fellow angel. He was rebelling against his own Creator!

You see, in the early days of Lucifer's dissatisfaction, this planet existed only in the mind and planning of the Father and the Son. The unhappy angel knew that he was to have no part in its creation. And now we have touched the very core of his disaffection.

The Son of God had created many worlds. Lucifer had created

none. And now the Father and the Son were planning still another world, and Lucifer had not been invited into their counsel. Why? Why should he not have the same privileges as the Son? If God alone could create, if an angel could never create, then Lucifer didn't want to be an angel. He wanted to be God!

Jesus was divine. He was God. He was the Creator. An angel was none of these, nor could ever be. God explained it all carefully and tenderly to the dissenter. But it only enraged him. His jealousy knew no bounds. He wanted the place of the Son of God. He would be satisfied with nothing less. His dissatisfaction was spreading, threatening to become open revolt.

Would the Father and the Son now abandon their plan to create this earth—because of the Lucifer problem? No! They would go ahead. And there was something special about this creation. For they would create man in their own image. Evidently man was to more nearly resemble his Creator, in appearance and in character, than any of the beings previously created.

So it was that the One we call Jesus, with His Father, sped through the galaxies to this lonely spot in the universe, called a world into existence, flung it into space, and set it spinning. It was He, the One we call Jesus, who said, "Let there be light." It was He who spent nearly a week in making this planet a place of unscarred beauty, fitting it up as if for a king. See Genesis 1 and 2.

And now it was Friday afternoon. The garden He had planted pleased Him. The trees were there, casting their lacy shadows in the sunlight. The fruit was ripe and ready to eat. The animals were playing together. The birds were singing. The sound of a waterfall gave it the final touch. Everything was ready. The moment had come.

And the One we call Jesus knelt down and fashioned a body out of the unmarred soil. When it was complete and perfect, every part of it ready to function at the divine signal, He breathed life into the body. See Genesis 2:7. And Adam opened his eyes to see the face of his Creator—the first face he had ever seen.

I don't know what Jesus said to Adam. Someone has suggested that Jesus just smiled and said, "Hi, Adam!"

I like that. What a happy moment! What a happy day! What a time for singing! No wonder "the morning stars sang together, and all the sons of God shouted for joy"! Job 38:7, KJV.

It would seem that such a day could not hold any more happiness. But it did. Jesus permitted Adam to become drowsy and fall asleep. And when he opened his eyes again he saw beside him the most beautiful woman in the world. Not because she was the *only* woman in the world, but because Jesus Himself had fashioned her.

Then as the sunlight began to fade, Adam and Eve watched their first sunset together, with their Creator beside them. What a moment to remember!

At that sunset hour the sixth day of Creation week was ending, and the seventh day beginning. The work of creation was finished, and God saw that it was "very good."

What would God do now? Would He hurry back to the comfort of heaven and His throne, to enjoy the adoration of the angels? Would He turn now to other projects, giving His attention to other galaxies and other worlds—forgetting the happy couple He had made? Would He leave them to speculate about how they got here? No. He chose to spend that first Sabbath with His newest creation.

I picture Him slipping back to Adam and Eve for an evening walk as the stars came out, telling them about those lights in the sky and how He had made them too. They had so many questions—so much that they wanted to know. In the morning they must have walked and talked with Him again. How they wished that that happy day would never end! And how thrilled they were when the Creator told them that this happy, unforgettable day could be repeated—that each seventh day, as it rolled around, could be a time of special fellowship with Him.

We are told that "on the seventh day God ended his work which he had made; and he rested on the seventh day from all his work which he had made." Genesis 2:2, KJV.

I confess that there is something in that scripture that is difficult to understand. How could God rest, truly rest, no matter how successful the week had been—how could He rest when He knew that all was not well in heaven? How could He rest, knowing that the universe had been contaminated by the virus of rebellion? Especially, how could He rest knowing that the happy pair He had just created might someday rebel? It could happen. He had given them the dangerous gift of freedom to choose.

And yet God rested—the Father and the Son. Rested because in counsel together They had agreed upon a plan. Rested because in the heart of the One we call Jesus, Calvary lay hidden!

Lucifer's dissatisfaction had now become open revolt. And revolt became war. And Lucifer became Satan, the fallen angel. And Satan, with his sympathizers, was banished from heaven.

The Father and the Son must have wept together that day. For They had lost not only a brilliant and beloved angel, the highest of them all, but They had lost a great host of angels that Lucifer had led into revolt. The loyal angels must have silenced their harps and wept too. And the unfallen worlds, as they watched, must have joined in Their tears.

There was a great emptiness now in God's world. And the emptiness would remain for a very long time—until the Lord Jesus should bring home a very special company of refugees from the planet Earth to take the place of the angels He had lost. But that's getting ahead of the story.

The controversy was not over. Only its battlefield had changed. This earth had become the theater of conflict, but the target of the enemy's rage—still—was Christ, the Creator, the Son of God.

Our first parents were faithfully warned of the fallen angel's presence in the garden. But they had nothing to fear. Only disobedience could place them in any danger.

We have no record of the days that followed, of the unmarred fellowship between Adam and Eve and their Creator. We don't know how long those happy days continued. They were intended to last forever.

But one day, as Jesus watched from heaven, Eve wandered near the one tree that God had placed off bounds. And when she was near enough, a beautiful creature, sitting in the tree and leisurely eating its fruit, began talking to her. She had no idea that the voice was the voice of the fallen angel against whom she had been warned.

And the creature said something like this: "You're beautiful. You've never heard an animal speak, have you? It's this fruit that gives me the power to speak. And just think! If this fruit can make a dumb animal speak, what would it do for you who already have the gift of speech?"

Jesus watched breathlessly. If only she wouldn't listen. If only she would hurry back to Adam. If only she would not touch the fruit. And the agony of Jesus, as He saw her take the fruit and eat it, can never be described!

And then Adam, terrified at what she had done but not wanting to lose her, followed her in rebellion. The happy days were over. Now came the age of tears. Tears on this planet. Tears in heaven. And tears on other worlds!

The Strategy of Rebellion

The fall of man from his high position was the greatest tragedy this planet has ever known. The Garden of Eden was heaven in miniature—all that the wildest imagination could ever dream.

Yet the instigator of that tragedy has downplayed it, ridiculed it, painted it over, until Eden, in the minds of untold millions, is nothing but a myth, and the fall of man, a joke.

"Eden? Oh yes. Where Eve ate the apple." And then an indulgent smile. For who believes it?

Many who doubt the story have probably never read it, though it is so near the beginning of the Bible they'd have to turn at most a few pages to find it. They would be surprised to learn that "the apple" is not mentioned. And probably it has never crossed their minds that the trouble we are in today all began with an act of deliberate choice on the part of two very real people in a very real garden that could properly be called a paradise.

The instigator of rebellion doesn't want us to think of the fall of man as a fall at all. And if you doubt the success of his propaganda, consider this: Doesn't almost every university in the land teach almost as established fact that man has evolved upward from an all-the-way-down beginning in the hazy past—and never fell at all? There is no place in the reasoning of evolution for the fall of man. And of course, if man never fell, he has no need of a Saviour. He can do very nicely on his own, thank you.

The Eden experience, in some versions of the rebel angel's propaganda, is freely admitted as fact. But it is praised as man's courageous break with all restriction, his declaration of independence. A triumph, you see, rather than a tragedy.

Whatever the reasoning, the defection of our first parents is usually thought of as something very, very trivial—not worthy of the attention you would give a leaky faucet!

Listen! The game that the fallen angel is playing is certainly a lot *bigger* than we ever dreamed. The conflict between Christ and Satan involves all heaven and earth. And it absorbs the attention of the watching worlds. The stakes in the game are the souls of men. And the universe stands or falls with the outcome.

Too many of us, sincere though we may be, have skimmed too quickly over the account of the fall of man in the third chapter of Genesis. We know that our first parents had been told (Genesis 2:17) that one tree in the garden was off bounds and that death would follow disobedience. In this third chapter Eve approaches the tree, and a serpent talks her into eating the forbidden fruit. That's about all that has registered with a lot of us.

We have been like a little boy watching a parade through a knothole. And it's hard to get the big view. We need to move back to a spot where we can get an unobstructed view of the whole parade. We need to view the broad expanse of this cosmic controversy that involves us so directly. We need to know what is going on, what the issues are. We need to know something of what to expect from the enemy.

What general in active combat would not be delighted to come into possession of a document outlining the strategy of the enemy in detail? But that, I believe, is exactly what we can discover in the third chapter of Genesis. Read it carefully. Give it some time. And you may be surprised at what a find it is. For the fallen angel's strategy in that first encounter on this planet is basically what we can expect of him today. It has changed only in detail.

Notice first that Satan did not want his true identity known. He used a disguise, he used a medium, he used impersonation. And here, right at the beginning, he used the supernatural, he used a psychic phenomenon to attract the attention of his victim. The serpent, in unscarred Eden, was undoubtedly a beautiful creature. But a serpent could not speak. That is what attracted Eve—a serpent talking. We can expect the same use of the supernatural today—in infinite variation.

Satan in the garden, speaking through the serpent, making it a medium, lost no time in planting *doubt* in Eve's mind—doubts about the credibility of God's word. "Has God said you would die if you eat this fruit? Why, God knows better. He knows you won't die. He knows that if you eat this fruit you will be like a god."

Satan goes so far as to directly contradict God's word. God had said, "If you eat the fruit, you will die." And Satan says, "You will *not* die." We can expect him today not to tell the truth. For Jesus said of Satan, "He is a liar, and the father of it." John 8:44, KJV.

The fallen angel also uses half-truths. In fact, the more truth he mingles with his error, the more palatable it is to his victims—and the more dangerous. Notice his implication that God was keeping something back from our first parents—something He didn't want them to know.

That's true—very true. God *didn't* want them to know what it's like to be so haunted with guilt that you can't sleep. He *didn't* want them to know what it's like to die. He *didn't* want them to know what it's like to see a beloved son take the life of his brother. He wanted to keep that knowledge from them and from us!

But Satan called it tyranny. He said God didn't care!

"You are free to eat from any tree in the garden," God had said, "but you must not eat from the tree of the knowledge of good and evil, for when you eat of it you will surely die." Genesis 2:16, 17, NIV.

This was not an arbitrary ultimatum. It was a warning, given in love, of what the sure result of disobedience would be. Death does not follow disobedience because a threat has been made. It follows because that's just the way it works. The apostle Paul said it this way: "The wages of sin is death." Romans 6:23, KJV.

Satan, in the days when he was still the son of the morning, knew that the wages of sin is death. He had been faithfully warned of where his steps were leading. But he refused to turn back. And now, banished from heaven, past the point of no return, he knew that one day he must die. And as he saw the beautiful earth that the Son of God had made and the happy couple created to rule over it, his fury knew no bounds. He determined to destroy both *it* and *them*. He vowed that, if he must die, he would take the human race with him.

How did he propose to accomplish this? An important part of Satan's strategy would be to convince men that they *would not* and *could not* die—that God had made them with an immortal soul, making death impossible. They could live as they pleased. Nothing would happen. They could laugh at God's warnings.

But God was guilty of no such mistake. He was far too wise to build immortality into men and women before they had demonstrated that they could be trusted with never-ending life!

Another key element in the enemy's strategy surfaces in these words, "For God knows that when you eat of it your eyes will be opened, and you will be like God, knowing good and evil." Genesis 3:5, NIV.

"You will be like God." The strategy hasn't changed at all. We are bombarded with it today. Discover yourself, we are told. Know yourself. There's a spark of divinity within you—just bring it out. You're a little god yourself. The line has a thousand variations. And it all means this: Go it alone. Be independent. You don't need God.

That's the way the controversy on this planet began. At issue here, as it had been in heaven, was the authority of God—His throne, His law, and His character. The chief target of the enemy's wrath—the Son of God, His position, His creatorship. The goal of rebellion now and here—control of the minds of men. Their worship—whether by choice or by force. And their destruction.

Do you understand a little better now the tragedy of Eden? Satan had won the first round of the contest. He had persuaded our first parents to sell themselves into a slavery that, without divine intervention, could never be broken.

What would God do now?

Section Two
Play and Counterplay

Play and Counterplay
God's Desert Sandbox

Play and Counterplay

The skies were still blue over Eden. The freshly made planet had lost none of its beauty. Not a storm had touched it. No flower had yet faded, or leaf fallen.

But all was not well under those blue skies. The garden was empty. Its original tenants, evicted from the home that was meant to be theirs forever, stood weeping outside the gate, their entrance barred by angels with flaming swords.

No force or coercion had been involved in their tragic decision. They had deliberately chosen to eat the forbidden fruit. And they had felt no immediate harm. In fact, for a few moments they had felt the strange exhilaration of rebellion. Could it be that the serpent was right? Could it be that they were entering a higher state of existence—just as the serpent had promised?

But then the exhilaration faded. They knew, as Adam had known all along, that they had sinned. They knew that they must die. And they were afraid, desperately afraid. The garment of light with which they had been clothed was gone, and they were unclothed. Frantically they took fig leaves and fastened them together to cover their nakedness.

Fig leaves. It seems a symbolic act, an act so typical of what men and women have been doing through the long centuries— trying to cover their sin and cure their guilt with some man-made substitute for forgiveness.

They had waited—Adam and Eve—guilty and afraid. And then, in the cool of the day, they heard the voice of their Creator as He came looking for them. He was so kind—so wonderfully kind. But the sadness in His eyes they would never forget. They never knew how much they loved Him until they had hurt Him!

But as soon as there was sin, there was a Saviour. That very day, in the garden, the Son of God said to the serpent as they listened, "I will put enmity between you and the woman, and

between your offspring and hers; he will crush your head, and
you will strike his heel." Genesis 3:15, NIV.

The guilty pair didn't understand that first promise of a
Saviour, but somehow they sensed that in it there was hope.

Then, from the skins of animals, the Creator made them coats
to replace their fig leaves. And they shuddered as they realized
that what they had done had cost the life of innocent animals.
Death had entered this planet.

And then the Son of God, ever so reluctantly, led them out of
the garden. And now they wept alone, longing only to be back in
the home they had so carelessly lost.

The terrible day was over. And they could not retrieve it. They
had made their tragic choice. The sun was setting in the west.
And two lonely people, barred from the tree of life, had already
begun to die—just as God had said!

What would they do now? What would God do now? What
would Satan do now? It's a story of controversy, of moves and
countermoves. It's a story of tragedy—and hope. And the real-
life drama would be played out in an orbiting theater open to the
sky—open to the wondering gaze of heaven and the other worlds!

The fallen angel knew what *he* would do. His plans were laid.
He exulted that he had brought tragedy into a happy world. Hear
him boasting to Christ and the loyal angels that he would make
this planet the headquarters of his rebellion!

But Satan was not sure what God would do. Surely He would
not trouble Himself over the defection of two people on a tiny
world on the edge of the universe. With only a word He could set
it aflame. A few cinders would drift into space and never be
noticed.

But his rebel mind was troubled about the words God had
spoken to him in the garden. He pondered what they could mean.
Who was it that would one day crush his head? Whatever the
strange words meant, they seemed to bode no good for himself.
Surely the Son of God would not leave His throne and the worship of the angels and personally come to this planet to challenge
his control of men. Or would He?

Little did he know that Calvary lay hidden in the Saviour's
heart!

I picture God sitting down with Adam and explaining to him

that the wages of sin is always death. Someone must die. And then He brought a lamb and asked Adam to take its life. And Adam shrank from such an act. The little lamb had done no wrong. It was he, Adam, who deserved to die! And the Creator, the One we call Jesus, explained that God did not desire sacrifice. He would take no delight in the shedding of blood. But Adam, and every other sinner, must be reminded that his sin would one day cost the life of the innocent Lamb of God. And who would that be? The Creator Himself!

The feelings of Adam could never be described. He was over-whelmed with horror and guilt—and love. But for nine long centuries, though his sin was forgiven, he would carry the knowledge that his act of rebellion would yet cost the life of his own Creator!

Satan watched it all, and didn't understand what the sacrifice of lambs could mean. But he was a good student and soon came to the conclusion that Jesus really did intend to make a way out for the human race. But he determined to be ready to attack, to make this planet not worth the effort, to make the Saviour's life so miserable that He would turn back from His plan to save men.

It was not long until Cain, and then Abel, joined the family of Adam. Eve hoped that Cain might be the promised Saviour. Instead, he turned out to be the world's first murderer.

It happened this way. Abel brought a lamb as a sacrifice, as God had instructed. But Cain found the shedding of blood revolting and brought instead an offering of fruit. A substitute, you see. Substitute religion. Substitute worship. The kind that the fallen angel still promotes today.

When God rejected Cain's offering and accepted Abel's, Cain's anger knew no bounds, and he killed his brother. Adam and Eve had wept over the first flower that faded, the first leaf that fell. And now, as their son lay lifeless before them, their grief was beyond description.

Fifteen hundred years passed. This planet was still a paradise of beauty. The skies were still blue. Rain was unknown. The earth was watered by a gentle dew. Genesis 2:5, 6. Suddenly an old man began building a huge boat on a hillside. Why? This is what we read: "The Lord saw how great man's wickedness on the earth had become, and that every inclination of the thoughts of his heart was only evil all the time." Genesis 6:5, NIV.

For a hundred and twenty years Noah worked on that boat, building it according to God's instruction and warning men of a global flood to come. But they only scoffed. The old man and his boat were no more than a tourist attraction.

Finally the boat was finished. Noah made his last solemn appeal, gave his last invitation to join him in his boat. But they laughed.

Suddenly all was silent. They didn't laugh as they saw animals of every description, the fierce and the gentle, come from the mountains and the forests, making their way, with no visible leader, into the ship. Then, with a noise like the rush of wind, birds flocked from every direction, darkening the sky as they made their way in perfect order into Noah's boat.

Then Noah and his family went in. Not another soul was willing to brave the scoffing crowd and join them.

The mocking masses were struck with fright as they saw a flash of dazzling light in the sky. Then a cloud of glory, brighter than the lightning, descended from heaven and unseen hands closed the great door of the ship. No one could enter now. It was too late. But the skies were still blue, with no sign of the catastrophe Noah had predicted. And men returned to their scoffing. For seven days nothing happened.

But on the eighth day doom came faster than it can be told. Dark clouds—thunder—lightning—large drops of rain. Then water seemed to come from the clouds in mighty cataracts. Jets of water burst from the earth with indescribable force, throwing great rocks hundreds of feet into the air. The terror of men and animals, as they tried to reach high ground, cannot be described. But there was no place of safety except in Noah's big ship, and God had shut the door. The entire human race, except for eight people, slipped beneath the black waters, wishing for just one more invitation from the lips of Noah!

After the flood, the controversy continued. There were moves and countermoves. God won some battles. Satan won some. God seemed to be at a disadvantage, for Satan could use every sort of deception. God could not. He must wait for time to vindicate the rightness of His word and His way. It was God trying to save, and Satan trying to destroy. It was the strategy of rebellion pitted against the strategy of love!

There was the confrontation at Babel, near the site of ancient Babylon, where men determined to save themselves from another flood by building a tower that would reach high into the sky. And God came down and confused their language so that the work could not continue. See Genesis 11:1–9.

There was Egypt, where the stubborn king refused to let God's people go until the land had been ruined by the judgments of God—and until the tenth and final judgment had left one dead in every Egyptian home. Read the story beginning with the seventh chapter of Exodus.

There was Mount Sinai, where the Son of God, the One we call Jesus, came down and wrote the Ten Commandments (Exodus 20:3–17) with His own finger on slabs of stone.

Jesus? At Sinai? Yes, the apostle Paul tells us that it was Christ who led the Hebrews out of Egypt. 1 Corinthians 10:1–4. And we learn from Nehemiah (Nehemiah 9:11–13) that the One who led them out of Egypt was the One who came down on Sinai.

But Satan was ready with a countermove. And when Moses came down from the mountain with the slabs of stone in his hands, he found the people, God's people, worshiping a golden calf. You find the story in the thirty-second chapter of Exodus. Imagine how Moses felt—and how God must have felt. His people were so quick to pledge their loyalty—and so quick to forget.

But that was so often the situation in the years that followed. The heart of the Creator was often saddened as He looked down on this planet and saw smoke rising not only from altars of strange gods, though that was to be expected from those who knew Him not. But when His own people went tramping after other gods, the hurt was deep!

That was the situation in the days of Elijah. That was the background for the confrontation atop Mount Carmel, where four hundred prophets of Baal, the sun god, were arrayed against a lone prophet of God. It was time for the people to decide whom they would worship. And the call of Elijah rang out, "How long will you waver between two opinions? If the Lord is God, follow him; but if Baal is God, follow him." 1 Kings 18:21, NIV.

And the fire came down! And every soul on Carmel watching from below—even the prophets of Baal—knew who was the true God.

And so it went. Move and countermove. Play and counterplay. There was more to come. And the contest isn't finished yet. Who will win?

In September of 1977 a crowd of fifty thousand Christians assembled in Kansas City. The speaker, sensing the mood of his audience, lifted his Bible high into the air, and let his words reverberate through the auditorium: "If you sneak a peek at the back of the Book, Jesus wins!" And the great crowd roared its approval with ten minutes of cheering and applause.

Yes, Jesus will win! Rebellion is on the way out! But that day is not yet!

God's Desert Sandbox

A number of years ago I climbed to the top of Mount Sinai. Sinai—rugged, majestic, towering above the mighty plain. Windswept mountain crags that once felt the steps of Moses—and of God!

There, standing on the windswept heights of that rugged peak, I looked out across the vast plain as Moses did thirty-five hundred years ago. The plain was empty and barren as I saw it. But when Moses climbed the mountain, he looked down upon the vast, sprawling but orderly camp of the Hebrews, recently escaped from Egyptian slavery. Six hundred thousand men, besides women and children, had spread their tents in sight of majestic Sinai.

I tried to picture it as it was then. And I have tried to imagine the thoughts of a young man named Caleb as he lay awake on one of those cold desert nights, reliving the excitement of the past few months. For there really was a Caleb in one of those tents. And he was a man of great faith.

Caleb's life, until very recently, had been the hard life of a slave. The days, for his people, had been filled with suffering and boredom and despair. It seemed that deliverance would never come. Yet God had promised. And suddenly it happened—a series of judgments upon Egypt in rapid succession—and they were free!

Almost immediately after their dramatic escape came the miraculous crossing of the Red Sea and the destruction of the Egyptian army that had followed them into the sea. He would never forget their song of victory that morning—how it rose from the vast hosts of Israel and rang out over desert and sea, the mountains echoing the words of praise to God.

As they left the Red Sea they had been guided by the pillar of cloud—the cloud that was darkness to their enemies, but a great flood of light to the Hebrews as they journeyed.

49

Water was hard to find in the barren country through which they journeyed, and food supplies were dwindling. They were a month out of Egypt when they first pitched their tents. Some, in spite of God's miraculous leading, were beginning to complain. It was then that God began to send manna—their bread from heaven. And when they camped again, at Rephidim, and desperately needed water, God performed another miracle. Moses was instructed to strike a rock—and water gushed out of the rock! Yes, Caleb must have thought, it had been an exciting journey.

Leaving Rephidim, again they had followed the movement of the cloud—over barren plains, up steep ascents, through rocky gorges and sandy wastes. Sometimes they had seen before them rugged mountains, like huge bulwarks piled up directly across their path. But openings always appeared, with another plain beyond.

It was through one of these deep, gravelly passes that they were then led. And what a sight it had been! Between the rocky cliffs that rose hundreds of feet on either side, moving like a living tide as far as eye could reach, marched the hosts of Israel with their flocks and their herds. And then, bursting into view before them, lifting its massive front in solemn majesty, stood Mount Sinai. The cloud of divine presence rested on its summit, and the people pitched their tents on the plain below. This would be their home for almost a year. The pillar of fire at night was their assurance of divine protection, and while they slept, the bread fell gently upon the camp. What a wonderful God they worshiped!

The days that followed were filled with wonder. Caleb would never forget, as long as he lived, how God had come down personally to the mountain that loomed before them, and how it had smoked and quaked at His step. He would never forget how he had heard God's own voice as He spoke the Ten Commandments, His eternal law, in the hearing of this people.

I think Caleb understood what God was doing. For a people so recently out of slavery—and for the matter, for all the world and for all time to come—God was demonstrating the importance of His law and His high regard for it. He was also demonstrating, by such a display of power, that no emergency could ever arise that He could not handle.

But God must have realized that such a display of power would be very frightening. Caleb recalled that God, before speaking the first of the ten commands, had said, "I am the Lord your God, who brought you out of Egypt, out of the land of slavery." Exodus 20:2, NIV.

It was as if He were saying, "Look, you don't need to fear. I'm the same One who brought you out of Egypt and across the Red Sea. I'm the One who gives you water from the rock and bread from heaven. Now I want to give you, and all the world, My law. And I want to demonstrate My power so that you will never doubt My ability to care for you. But don't be afraid!"

Caleb recalled how God, there on Sinai, had permitted Moses to see the temple in heaven, and then instructed him to build a small, portable temple in the desert. And He told Moses just how to build it. It took a long time to construct, but now there it was, in the center of the camp, incredibly beautiful and tremendously impressive. How reassuring it was to know that God wanted to be with His people. And how comforting it was to fall asleep at night knowing that over there in that tent, perhaps only a few hundred feet away, was the place where God had chosen to reveal His presence.

Yes, what an exciting journey it was for a young man like Caleb, who loved and fully trusted his Lord!

But we must leave Caleb and his reflections and ask a few questions.

Why did God ask Moses to build this elaborate portable temple—in the Bible called a sanctuary? The answer is given right along with the request. "Let them make me a sanctuary; that I may dwell among them." Exodus 25:8, KJV.

"That I may dwell among them." God wanted to be with His people. It's as simple as that.

Why did God create the human race? Was it so that He could rule over them and enjoy their worship? No. Man was created for fellowship with his Creator. That's why He spent the first Sabbath with the newly created pair. That's why He wanted to spend every Sabbath with them. That's why it was His custom, through the week, to come and walk with them in the cool of the day.

A man named Enoch walked so closely with his Lord that he was taken to heaven without experiencing death.

Jesus, in His beautiful prayer the night before He was crucified, made this request: "Father, I will that they also, whom thou hast given me, be with me where I am." John 17:24, KJV.

The apostle Paul asks, "Do you not know that your body is a temple of the Holy Spirit, who is in you?" 1 Corinthians 6:19, NIV.

Evidently the Lord Jesus, by His Spirit, wishes to dwell not only *with* us but *in* us. And some, even in the days of Moses, understood this. They understood that what God really wanted was not simply to dwell in the camp or in the sanctuary or later in Solomon's temple. He wanted to come still closer and dwell within the human soul.

So while the controversy between Christ and Satan continued, and while Satan was desperately trying to break every tie between man and his Creator, God was patiently and quietly working at what meant most to Him—repairing broken relationships. And He would never be satisfied—He *will* never be satisfied—until the day when "the dwelling of God is with men, and he will live with them. They will be his people, and God himself will be with them and be their God." Revelation 21:3, NIV. You see, God enjoys being with His people.

God's purpose, however, His goal of being reunited with His people, can never be realized until sin is eradicated. Sin could never again be admitted to heaven. And there was the problem— His people, all of them, have been infected with sin. How could sin be destroyed without destroying them? It was a hostage situation. God couldn't go in and shoot it out with sin without harming the sinners He loved.

But God had a plan. This portable temple out there in the desert, with its system of sacrifices, was intended to demonstrate that plan, to show how God would deal with sin and sinners. It would be a continued reminder of the terrible cost of sin—that it would one day take the life of the innocent Son of God. It would be a constant and vivid reminder that "without the shedding of blood there is no forgiveness." Hebrews 9:22, NIV.

Was this portable sanctuary exactly like the sanctuary in heaven after which it was patterned? No. No structure built by human hands could possibly represent the vastness and glory of the heavenly temple, the throne room of the King of kings. Human language could never describe the wonder of that temple where "thousand thousands ministered unto him, and ten thousand times ten thousand stood before him." Daniel 7:10, KJV.

The model of an ocean liner, in the window of a travel service, hardly prepares you for what you see on a tour of the ship itself. And the tiny angels used in a kindergarten sandbox could hardly prepare a child for the brilliance and glory of real angels.

The sanctuary built by Moses was only a dim reflection of heaven's temple. It was God's desert sandbox. It was a teaching device. But it would demonstrate important truths about the work that Christ, as our High Priest, would one day do for us in heaven.

Make no mistake. That miniature model, not more than fifty-five feet long, was the most elaborate and expensive teaching device it was possible to construct. A perceptive writer described "the glory of the scene presented within the sanctuary—the gold-plated walls reflecting the light from the golden candlestick, the brilliant hues of the richly embroidered curtains with their shining angels, the table, and the altar of incense, glittering with gold; beyond the second veil the sacred ark, with its mystic cherubim, and above it the holy Shekinah, the visible manifestation of Jehovah's presence; all but a dim reflection of the glories of the temple of God in heaven, the great center of the work for man's redemption."—Ellen White, *Patriarchs and Prophets* (Mountain View, Calif.: Pacific Press Publishing Association), p. 349.

Everything about the building, everything about its service, had special significance. It's a fascinating study. You can read a brief and beautiful description of the sanctuary, its furniture, its service, and its meaning in the New Testament book of Hebrews—chapters eight, nine, and ten.

But keep in mind that God is not in the furniture business. His first concern is not with the animals, the wood and the fire, the lavishly embroidered curtains, the glitter of gold, but with people—people who without Him would have no hope. The acts and events symbolized in that desert sandbox all have to do with restoring broken relationships.

The sanctuary was not meant to make men feel good about themselves. No man could feel good about himself as he raised the knife to slay an innocent lamb—and knew that the sin he had just committed would one day take the life of Jesus, the Lamb of God. But central in the service was the Lamb of God. And the Lamb of God meant hope!

A number of years ago a lighthouse was being built on the rockbound coast of Wales. When the building was nearly completed, legend has it, one of the workmen stumbled and fell back through the scaffolding to the rocks below.

The other workmen, shocked at what had taken place, did not dare to look down for fear of being unnerved at the sight. Heavy-hearted, they backed down the ladders. But to their surprise and happy relief, they saw their fellow workman lying upon a mound of grass, shaken and shocked, bruised to be sure, but not seriously harmed. Beside him lay a dead lamb. A flock of sheep had been wandering by, and a lamb had broken his fall.

A Lamb broke your fall! A Lamb broke mine—the Lamb of God that takes away the sin of the world!

Section Three
Sometimes You Need a Prophet

Sometimes You Need a Prophet

In many living things there is some instrument of guidance. The birds travel thousands of miles and yet return to the same place. The bat, blindfolded, can fly between iron bars without touching them. And they say it is impossible to lose a homing pigeon.

Has man alone been set adrift without some inner compass? Is that why millions turn to the daily horoscope for guidance? Or to the fortune teller? To those who read the palm, the tea leaf, the crystal ball?

Is that why we are so quick to follow a leader—even if the leader cannot see where he is going?

Some of you may be familiar with the writings of Bruce Barton. But you may not be acquainted with the writings of his father, William B. Barton. Here it is just as he wrote it:

"We sojourned in Egypt, I and Keturah, and we rode on donkeys, and also on camels. Now of all the beasts that ever were made, the camel is the most ungainly and preposterous, and also the most picturesque. And he taketh himself very seriously.

"And we beheld a string of five camels that belonged in one caravan, and they were tethered every one to the camel in front of him. But the foremost of the camels had on a halter that was tied to the saddle of a donkey. And I spake unto the man of Arabia who had the camels, and inquired of him how he managed it.

"And he said, 'Each camel followeth the one in front and asketh no questions, and I come after and prod up the last camel.' And I said, 'Doth not the first camel consider that there is no other in front of him, but only [a donkey]?'

"And he answered, 'Nay, for the first camel is blind, and knoweth only that there is a pull at his halter. And every other camel followeth as he is led, and I prod up the hindermost one.' And I inquired about the donkey.

"And he said, 'The donkey is too stupid to do anything but keep straight on, and he hath been often over the road.'

"And I said unto Keturah, 'Behold a picture of human life, for on this fashion have the processions of the ages largely been formed. For there be few men who ask otherwise than how the next in front is going, and they blindly follow, each in the track of those who have gone before.'

"And Keturah said, 'But how about the leader?' And I said, 'That is the most profoundest secret of history. For often he who seemed to be the leader was really behind the whole procession.'"

Is any comment needed? It's easy to follow a magnetic personality—one who speaks smooth things and makes us feel good about ourselves. But that smooth-talking leader may be as blind as that lead camel. And the donkey may be headed straight for the ditch—or, perhaps, even for Jonestown!

What we need is a real, genuine prophet. A prophet, you know, is sometimes called a seer—one who can see. A prophet is delegated by God to be the eyes of His people. It was Solomon, the wise man, who said, "Where there is no vision, the people perish." Proverbs 29:18, KJV.

And listen to this: "Have faith in the Lord your God and you will be upheld; have faith in his prophets and you will be successful." 2 Chronicles 20:20, NIV.

Have faith in His prophets. It just isn't safe to go blindly along, following our noses, carving out a path that seems right to us. For "there is a way that seems right to a man, but in the end it leads to death." Proverbs 14:12, NIV.

Ancient Babylon didn't need a prophet—certainly not one who spoke for the God of the Hebrews. Were not the gods of Babylon superior to all other gods? Was not this great Babylon, ruler of the world, the kingdom that would endure forever? So Babylon thought and planned.

But Babylon *would* need a prophet—and soon. It would need a prophet desperately. The king would have some strange dreams—and not a one of his boasting counselors would be able to make sense out of them. A hand would one day write in letters of fire upon the palace wall. And none but a prophet of God would be able to read the fiery words.

A thousand miles away from the proud city, a teenager was growing straight and tall, never dreaming what God had in mind for him.

I wonder what he was like. I wonder if his father helped him fly kites in the March wind. And I wonder if his father taught him a truth that Will Earlton put in rhyme: "Boys flying kites haul in their white-winged birds;/ You can't do that way when you're flying words." Surely his father must have taught him that a man's destiny may depend upon his ability to say No.

His mother must have told him, more than once, the story of Joseph—the boy who was sold into slavery by his jealous brothers. She must have told him how Joseph, far from home, in a strange land where no one knew him, still refused to sin against his God.

Yes, the boy must have had wonderful parents. And he must have seen, and shared, their sadness as neighbors and friends turned from their loyalty to God and began to worship the senseless gods of the heathen.

And then, one day when he was about eighteen, suddenly it happened. He, like Joseph, was taken captive to a strange land. The king of Babylon had laid seige to Jerusalem. And to show his power and his special disdain for the God of Israel, he took some of the sacred vessels from the temple. And he took captive some of the finest youth, young men of royal line, secretly delighting in the thought that he would soon have them worshiping the gods of Babylon.

Yes, his name was Daniel. And he was being forced to march, with the Chaldean army, the thousand miles to Babylon.

But the king was to be disappointed in some of his plans. For by the time the army came in sight of the ruins of the tower of Babel Daniel and three of his friends had determined not to compromise. They would be true to their God, come what may!

And the first test was not long in coming. King Nebuchadnezzar determined to prepare the finest of the Hebrew captives to serve in his court. They were to have the very best education. And as a special favor to them, they were to have the same food that was prepared for the king's table.

Wonderful, you say. But there was a problem. Some of the food and wine prepared for the king had been offered to Babylon's idols, and eating that food would have been considered an act of communion with these false gods. Daniel and his friends couldn't do that without denying the God of heaven.

And there was another problem. These fine young men had been taught that a simple, nonstimulating diet would give them clearer minds and better health. And certainly, if they wished to stand against the temptations of this wicked city, they would need clear minds.

True, it seemed a little thing, even inconsequential. Wasn't it more important, right at the beginning, not to offend the king by refusing his favors? But Daniel and his friends recognized what was involved. Daniel, acting as spokesman, tactfully asked, and was granted, permission to eat the simple food to which they were accustomed. And they came through with flying colors. You can read the story in the first chapter of Daniel's book.

So began their education in a strange land. And while they were learning the Chaldean language and preparing for positions in Babylon's court, God was preparing Daniel to be His prophet.

Why did God need a prophet in the court of Babylon, that great center of pagan worship? What did He have in mind?

First of all, God loved Babylon, just as He loves every wicked city. He loved its proud king.

You see, God had intended for Israel to be a light to the surrounding nations. But Israel had failed miserably. Israel itself had gone tramping after forbidden gods.

God wanted Babylon to know what He was like. He wanted the pagan capital to see that He was not like the heathen gods who had to be bribed and appeased. Rather, He was a God of love. He was aware of everything that happens to His children. He was a God willing to come down personally to deliver them, or walk with them through the fire.

The book of Daniel is a fascinating book. It is full of deliverances. It tells how God delivered Daniel from hungry lions, and his friends from an overheated furnace. It tells how Jesus would come to deliver His people from their sins. And it tells of a time, still future, when God's people will be delivered from the worst time of trouble this world has ever known.

Do you begin to see why you personally need to understand the book of Daniel? Could anything better prepare you for the crisis that soon we must all face?

Tell me. Would you have the courage to stand alone as did Daniel and his friends—risking the displeasure of the king and even their lives?

And then another question. If God wanted to prepare you to stand in a crisis, how do you think He would go about it?

You say, "I suppose He would give me some little tests along the way."

And you are exactly right!

You see, it's the little tests along the way that determine how we will do in the big crisis. For if we always take the easy way out—the popular way, perhaps—in everyday decisions, we will do the same thing in a crisis. We will have formed the habit. And we are not likely to change it then.

If Daniel and his friends had failed that first test, what would have happened? We probably would never have heard of a prophet Daniel—or of his deliverance from hungry lions. Nor would we have heard of his three friends and how the Son of God personally walked with them in the flames of the fiery furnace.

This world—and Babylon—and you and I—would have lost much if they had failed that first test. We are richer—and God is richer—because four young men had the courage to say No! Sometimes there is no better way to score points for God in this controversy that involves us all!

The Confounding of the Psychics

It is reported that the Ford Motor Company asked Charles A. Jayne, author of a horoscope column in the *New York Daily News,* to chart the future of the new Mustang automobile. Jayne responded with this horoscope:

"Those born September 21 [the date the Mustang was introduced] are particularly endowed with the basic qualities of efficiency and resourcefulness. Your moon in relation to Uranus indicates you are highly innovative and highly individualistic. Essentially, your planetary pattern is so well-balanced that you should be assured of a productive and successful life."

Just a public relations gimmick? Yes. But thousands of buyers took it seriously and bought Mustangs because of it.

Who made the horoscope come true? The stars? Or the buyers?

It was in the pagan superstition of Mesopotamia, land of the twin rivers, the Euphrates and the Tigris, that astrology was born. Some think it originated in that area as early as three thousand years ago. At any rate, Babylon soon became the center for the practice of this divining art. And Nebuchadnezzar, most powerful of the Babylonian kings, made no secret of the fact that he had an assortment of astrologers and other psychics in his court.

How did God feel about these psychics and their pagan superstitions? How did He feel about their various forecasting tools? This is not hard to discover, for He specifically prohibited their use among His people. His words are a devastating condemnation of the occult. Listen: "Thou shalt not learn to do after the abominations of those nations. There shall not be found among you any one that . . . useth divination [fortune-telling], or an observer of times [astrologer], or an enchanter [magician], or a witch, or a charmer, or a consulter with familiar spirits [a medium who uses a spirit guide], or a wizard [clairvoyant, clairaudient, or psychic seer], or a necromancer [medium who consults the so-called spirits of the dead]. For all that do these things are an abomination unto the Lord." Deuteronomy 18:9–12, KJV.

Abomination. I guess you know what that word means!

Why was God so hard on the psychics? Because a practitioner of the occult was openly giving allegiance to God's enemy, the fallen angel. It's as simple as that.

Is it that God doesn't want us to know anything about the future? Is He trying to keep us in the dark? No, not at all. We read from the prophet Amos, "Surely the Lord God will do nothing, but he revealeth his secret unto his servants the prophets." Amos 3:7, KJV.

Unto His servants the psychics? No. His servants the prophets. And how does He communicate with the prophets? "If there be a prophet among you, I the Lord will make myself known unto him in a vision, and will speak unto him in a dream." Numbers 12:6, KJV.

Visions and dreams. Not through mediums. Not through spirit guides. Not through crystal balls. Not through horoscope charts. Visions and dreams!

God wants us to know about the future. But He wants us to get it straight.

But back to Babylon. God saw that mighty empire, steeped in the occult. From the king on down they worshipped other gods and turned to the psychics for counsel. Did God say, "Babylon is wicked. Babylon is without hope. Let her go!"?

No. God loved Babylon. He wouldn't let her go without doing everything He could to win her. And He determined to go right to the top of that powerful empire. He would put a prophet right into the court of that proud and arrogant king. And that prophet would be a young Hebrew captive—Daniel.

God wanted the attention of the proud king. And He was about to challenge the claims of the psychics. He began by giving Nebuchadnezzer a dream—and then causing him to forget it. The king was sure of only one thing—that the forgotten dream was something very important.

Now the psychics were in trouble—more trouble than they realized. Intepreting a dream was no problem. Anybody could do that. Anybody could concoct some sort of interpretation—if they knew what the dream was. But, in their estimation, this king was being ridiculously unreasonable: he was demanding that they tell him what he had dreamed—*or die!*

The psychics panicked. What if this was a trick? What if the king hadn't really forgotten the dream? What if he was just testing them? They didn't dare make up a dream. They complained, "It's too hard. Nobody asks anything like that of a psychic!"

But the king was unrelenting. He was determined to find out what he had dreamed. And when they couldn't tell him, he condemned them all to death. And because the king didn't know the difference between a prophet and a psychic, Daniel was rounded up with the others, to be executed.

The king didn't know the difference between a prophet and a psychic. But God proposed to show him!

Daniel now fearlessly took his life in his hands and asked to appear before the king. But first he asked for time to pray to his God, promising to give the king both the dream and its interpretation. The king was so impressed by Daniel's quiet confidence—and so anxious to know what he had dreamed—that he granted Daniel's request.

And did God fail His young servant? No. Never! In a night vision He revealed to him both the dream and its meaning.

So it was that the next morning Daniel stood before the king, who had been anxiously waiting for him. Was it possible that this unassuming young captive could do what his once-trusted psychic counselors could not? "Can you tell me the dream?" he asked.

Yes, he could, And he did. Follow along with the story, if you will, in the second chapter of Daniel's book, beginning with verse 31.

Daniel told the king that in his dream he had seen a tall, magnificent statue. That was it! The king leaned forward, unable to hide his excitement. That was exactly what he had seen. It all came back to him now. He listened breathlessly as Daniel described the statue.

Its head, said the prophet, was gold, its chest and arms were silver, its thighs bronze, its legs iron, and its feet—part iron and part clay.

The king sat there amazed. It checked perfectly with what he had seen. But something had happened to the statue. Would Daniel know that too?

Yes! A huge boulder had struck the statue on its feet. And the entire statue was ground to powder and blown away like chaff.

Daniel hadn't missed a thing. And now he continued with the meaning of the dream. "You," he said simply, "are the head of gold."

The proud king liked that! It seemed very appropriate that he should be the golden head. Evidently Daniel's God was aware of his greatness and his power!

But of course the king had been flattered before. Could it be, he wondered, that Daniel was only a clever young politician playing for royal favor? No, Daniel's next words settled that. He declared what no aspiring politician would ever say: "And after you there will arise another kingdom inferior to you." Verse 39, NASB.

The king *didn't* like that! That was enough to spoil any monarch's ambitious dreams. Daniel's God was not telling the king what he wanted to be told. Daniel's God was telling him that his kingdom would *not* last forever. It would be succeeded by another—and an inferior one at that!

Is it any wonder that at a later time, with Daniel's words still rankling in his mind, the king had a great statue constructed *all* of gold—the way he was determined it would be? He had it set up on the plain of Dura and commanded everybody to worship it or burn!

But Daniel continued: There would be a third kingdom, represented by the bronze, and then a fourth world kingdom, strong as iron.

What was God revealing to the king? Was He telling him that there would soon be an assassination in his court? Was He telling him not to get into his carriage the next day because the "stars" wouldn't be right?

No, friend! No! God was revealing to that ancient king—and to you and me—the mighty sweep of history in advance!

And did it happen that way? Yes, God's prophets have never been wrong—not even once. History has followed this prophecy of Daniel as it has followed every other Bible prophecy—like a blueprint!

Babylon was conquered by Cyrus the Persian even in Daniel's day. It happened during the feast of Belshazzar. Remember the writing on the wall?

The Medes and the Persians, represented by the two silver arms of the statue, ruled for about two hundred years. Then came Alexander the Great and the bronze kingdom, followed by the iron kingdom, the fourth, which has to be Rome. It could be no other!

Four successive kingdoms. Wouldn't you think there would be a fifth? But no. Never again would this massive land area come under the rule of one man. Rome was the last of such empires!

Daniel went on to explain that the iron kingdom would be divided. It would break up into ten kingdoms, represented by the ten toes of the statue. (See Daniel 2.) And those ten kingdoms, the modern nations of Europe, would never again be reunited permanently under the rule of one man. Listen to this: "And in that you saw the iron mixed with common clay, they will combine with one another in the seed of men; but they will not adhere to one another, even as iron does not combine with pottery." Verse 43, NASB.

What do you think of that? They will not adhere to one another. The nations of Europe will not stick together! How could God have said it better?

"They will not adhere to one another." Those seven words have collided head on with the dreams of every would-be dictator since the Caesars. They are the reason for history's uncanny repetition as one man after another, aspiring to rule the world, has gone down in defeat!

But Daniel was not through. "And in the days of those kings the God of heaven will set up a kingdom which will never be destroyed, and that kingdom will not be left for another people; it will crush and put an end to all these kingdoms, but it will itself endure forever." Verse 44, NASB.

In the days of those kings—the nations of modern Europe—as the next great event in earth's history, God will intervene. The Lord Jesus will appear in the skies. And His kingdom will never end!

Is it any wonder that Nebuchadnezzar was profoundly impressed? God had just demonstrated—for him and for us—the wide and striking contrast between the trivial fortune-telling of the psychics and the stately march of divine prediction. And the psychics were confounded! God had outlined the future as no man or woman could ever do.

Friend, I wonder if you realize what a risk Daniel took when he made this prediction—if God was not speaking through him. I wonder if you realize how unlikely every part of Daniel's prophecy was—by human standards? His was no lucky guess. Who could have guessed, when Babylon was at the height of its glory, that it was soon to fall—and to a lesser power? Who could have guessed that four world kingdoms would not be followed by a fifth, that there would be four and no more, and that the fourth would be divided into ten and never get together again?

Who can possibly explain why, with all our sophisticated weapons, with all our burst of technology, no nation of modern times has been able to form a world empire—when Nebuchadnezzar, Cyrus, Alexander and the Caesars, with their inferior weaponry, could do it? Yet one aspiring dictator after another since the last of the four empires has bumped his head against Daniel's prophecy. And it has refused to budge!

What chance was there, if Daniel spoke only in his own wisdom, that every point in his prophecy—a prophecy covering the sweep of centuries, even millenniums—would be fulfilled? Maybe one chance in seventy-five million? I don't know.

Daniel, like other Old Testament prophets, walked far, far out on a limb. But he took no risk at all. For it was God who was speaking.

How wonderful it is that God has chosen to reveal the future to His children! How reassuring it is to know what the future holds, to know that God is in control, to know that not one of His words will fail!

The books of Daniel and the Revelation, we shall discover, are closely tied together. Both were written especially for our day. Both draw back the curtain of the future.

But these books were intended to do more than give us a peek at history's last chapter. They were meant not merely to reveal the future, but to prepare us for it.

Why is it that the first half of Daniel's book consists almost entirely of stories? The first test that confronted Daniel and his friends when they arrived in Babylon—the matter of the king's food. The experience of Daniel when he was thrown into a den of hungry lions—because he prayed to his God. The experience of Daniel's three friends on the plain of Dura—when they were commanded to worship the statue that the proud king had constructed.

Entertaining? Yes, definitely. But that isn't why those experiences are there. The book of Revelation, in the thirteenth chapter, makes it clear that tests equally severe await *us*. In the near future we shall have to make some life-or-death choices. And God wants us to know that He will be with us—just as He was with Daniel and his friends. For once again, as in the days of Daniel, the music will sound, and the band will play, as on the plain of Dura. And almost everybody will bow down—to a counterfeit Christ. It will take God-given courage to stand tall and straight and wait for the real Jesus!

Decoding Bible Prophecy

The Kennedy twins—Ginny and Gracie—were a mystery. They seemed happy enough. But they baffled everyone. Their hyperspeed chatter sounded "as if a tape recorder were turned on fast forward with an occasional understandable word jumping out."

The problem was that at six years old they still couldn't speak English. For a while some thought they were retarded. But they were far too bright for mentally retarded classes. Apparently they had developed a language of their own, with a vocabulary of hundreds of exotic words along with strange half-English and half-German phrases.

Ginny and Gracie were soon among the world's most celebrated twins. Language experts tried to figure them out. Finally speech pathologists learned their private language. But when they tried to use it, the girls seemed not to understand. They just laughed.

Some feel that the books of Daniel and Revelation, the two books written especially for our day, have a secret language of their own, that they are talking to each other in completely incomprehensible phrases. Some say that we aren't supposed to understand these books—that they are sealed books. But wouldn't it be strange if God should take the two books especially targeted to our day, filled with vital information essential to our survival, and lock them away from us in a code He knew we could never break? Is that the kind of God He is? Hardly!

The truth is that a portion of the book of Daniel *was* sealed (Daniel 12:4), but only until "the time of the end." It isn't sealed anymore, for we now live in the time of the end. And the book of Revelation never was sealed (Revelation 22:10). The very word *revelation* means "something revealed." In the first chapter (Revelation 1:3) a blessing is pronounced upon those who read and act upon what is written in the book. And in the final chapter (Revelation 22:18, 19) a fearful warning is given to anyone who would presume to either add or subtract from this prophetic book. Evidently God intends for us to understand the messages He gives us.

But you say, "I've tried. But I can't make any sense out of all those animals and horns and trumpets and everything."

I know. The human mind is noted for its gullibility. And yet our capacity for belief does have limitations. It is a little difficult to believe that a single wild animal could devour the whole earth. Or that the littlest horn on the head of a goat could cast stars to the ground and stamp on them. We would have trouble believing that a modest number of twenty-four-hour days could span centuries, even millenniums.

So when we encounter such statements in Bible prediction we can only conclude that the wild animals and the horns and those particular twenty-four-hour days were never intended to be taken literally. Rather, we are dealing with prophetic symbols.

But someone says, "But how can we ever figure them out? And why doesn't God just say what He means, if He wants us to understand?"

Millions have felt that way. Pictures, of course, can say a lot. Our newspapers often use cartoons to put a point across. And if God uses animals to represent nations, don't we sometimes do the same thing? The American eagle? The Russian bear?

But you are right. Plain words are clearest of all. So why doesn't God come right out and say what He means? Is He trying to make it hard for us? Is that it?

No, not at all. God wants us to understand. It is imperative that we do. And wherever God, in the Scriptures, is telling us how men are saved—the essentials of salvation—He speaks in language we have no difficulty understanding. The gospel is not given in symbols. Illustrations, yes. Parables, yes. Jesus often put truth into a story, so that His enemies would listen all the way through before they realized the story had to do with them.

But when God through His prophets was revealing history in advance, when He was outlining the future of His children, it was often necessary to trace the future activities of nations unfriendly to Him and His people. To name names would be to invite the destruction of the Book by its enemies. So the answer is simple. God used symbols in order to protect the Book and His people from its enemies and theirs.

But how can we figure out these symbols? How can we know what they mean?

First of all, in some cases there is no figuring out to be done. In some cases the Bible tells us what they mean. You recall that when Daniel told Nebuchadnezzar what he had dreamed, he immediately interpreted its meaning.

In the seventh chapter of Daniel, the prophet is shown a vision involving four beasts and some horns. But in the latter part of the chapter he is told that the beasts are kings, or kingdoms (verse 17), and that the ten horns are ten kings (verse 24).

So we have learned one symbol. A beast represents a kingdom, a nation. The nation may be good or bad. The Bible does not use the term *beast* in a derogatory way.

Daniel is given another vision in chapter 8, and later the angel Gabriel himself comes back to explain its symbols (verse 16).

Another symbol. In prophecy a woman is used to represent a church—a lovely and beautiful woman represents God's true church (Jeremiah 6:2 and Revelation 12:1–5) and a corrupt woman represents a false church, a fallen church (Revelation 17:3–5).

Notice that the symbols are not random, meaning one thing on one occasion and later something else. The symbols are consistent, whether we are studying Daniel or the Revelation, the Old Testament or the New.

We are not left to concoct our own meaning of the symbols. They are defined for us in Scripture—so far as we need to know them. It may take a little searching. It may take much searching. But they are there.

The trouble is that some people do not bother to search. They seem to enjoy dreaming up answers out of whole cloth, with little or no Bible support for their speculations. At the present time, there is terrific interest in Bible prophecy—even among those who know very little of Scripture. Everybody wants to know what is going to happen, and sometimes it seems as if everybody has his own interpretation of what he reads. But Bible prophecy is not a toy for speculators, to be manipulated to suit one's liking.

It is the expression of the infallible wisdom of God. And when last-day prophecy happens, when Bible prediction is fulfilled, it will happen only one way, not a thousand ways. It will happen as God predicted it will happen—without any reference whatever to how "it seems to me."

One of the greatest pitfalls we face in interpreting Bible prophecy is trying to make a scripture passage symbolic when it is really literal.

But how can we tell which is which? The best rule is to consider everything in Scripture as literal unless there is good reason to believe it is symbolic. Read the context carefully. Many interpretations today are nothing more than personal preferences. "This is the way I would like it to be," as one person put it.

It's so easy to label as symbolic anything we do not like. But when the Bible speaks of the worst earthquake this planet has ever known (Revelation 16:18), it means exactly what it says. And when it predicts hailstones the weight of a talent (Revelation 16:21), it isn't talking about frosted balloons.

I am not talking here about something trivial. We are really in trouble when we begin writing off as symbol or myth or legend whatever we don't like in the Word of God.

Here's what can happen. Millions of people, reading the first chapters of Genesis, have written them off as myth or legend. Then they read a little farther and find it hard to believe that a global flood ever happened. After all, they've never seen one. So they write that off too. Then, at some point, they encounter the books of Daniel and Revelation. And along with the good news those books contain, there are serious warnings about God's final judgments, His final accounting with men. But if they have symbolized away the beginning of this planet, they will likely do the same with its end. They will file away the coming judgment by fire along with the judgment by water in Noah's day, and forget them both. God says they are "willingly ignorant." See 2 Peter 3:5-7, KJV. And that ignorance can be fatal.

In other words, it is a *mistake* to call things literal when they are only symbolic. But it is *absolutely fatal* to call something symbolic, such as the judgment, and find out too late that it is very, very real!

We might call this way of thinking the "symbolic escape." But the attempt to escape reality by symbolizing it, by juggling Scripture, reinterpreting it, twisting it, misapplying it, maneuvering it, shoving it out of where it belongs and wedging it into where it doesn't—this refuge of wishful thinking, this house constructed of self-made symbols, will collapse like water in the final crisis!

Another caution. It is wise to tread softly with unfulfilled prophecy, wise not to read into a prophecy details which are not there. Many a sincere expositor of divine prediction has embarrassed himself by being too dogmatic about *exactly how* a prophecy is going to be fulfilled. There is always the temptation to go farther than the prophecy goes, to explain what the prophet has not explained.

Jesus once said to His disciples, "I have told you now before it happens, so that when it does happen you will believe." John 14:29, NIV.

It is usually *fulfilled* prophecy that makes believers. It was *after* His crucifixion that the disciples of Jesus boldly pointed out how He had fulfilled Old Testament prophecy. It was *after* His crucifixion, after His resurrection, that Jesus, walking with two of His followers on the way to Emmaus, "beginning at Moses and all the prophets . . . expounded unto them in all the scriptures the things concerning himself." Luke 24:27, KJV.

Bible prophecy holds a special fascination for this generation—probably because nearly everyone senses that we are approaching some kind of crisis. Time prophecies are especially intriguing. And frequently there is someone who can't resist the temptation to set a time for the end of the world—supposedly backed up by Scripture.

This is unfortunate, for predictions that fail lead to embarrassment and discouragement. For those looking on, seeing one prediction after another fail, and not knowing that such predictions have had no foundation in Scripture, may decide that they want nothing to do with any Bible prophecies. And that, of course, delights the fallen angel.

Actually there is no need to take seriously any prediction that sets a definite time for our Lord's return and for the end of this world as we know it. Jesus said plainly, "No one knows, however, when that day and hour will come—neither the angels in heaven, nor the Son; the Father alone knows." Matthew 24:36, TEV.

There are, however, time prophecies in the Bible. They do not reach to the end of the world, but they are extremely important. Much depends on them, and it is urgent that we understand prophetic calculation.

Both Daniel and Revelation foretell a time of persecution of God's people. So important is this time period that it is mentioned seven times. In Daniel 7:25, KJV, it is expressed as lasting for "a time and times and the dividing of time." In Daniel 12:7, KJV, we read that "it shall be for a time, times, and an half." In Revelation 12:6, KJV, the same time period is said to be "a thousand two hundred and threescore days." In verse 14 it is "a time, and times, and half a time." And in chapter 13, verse 5, it is said to continue for "forty and two months." See also Revelation 11:2, 3.

Is this confusing? That is understandable. But the confusion lifts when we discover that in Bible prophecy a day is often used to represent a literal year. This is a principle recognized by most Bible expositors.

Using this principle, the "thousand two hundred and threescore days" become 1260 years. Forty-two months of thirty days each are also 1260 days, or literal years. The Aramaic word translated "time" or "times" is used several times in the fourth chapter of Daniel, where "seven times" obviously means "seven years." Scholars generally agree that in Daniel 7:25 the translation should be "two times" rather than simply a plural. And the word translated "dividing" may also be translated "half." So the Revised Standard Version, which reads "a time, two times, and half a time," is clearer and in this case more correct that some other translations. A year, two years, and half a year equal once again 1260 prophetic days, or literal years.

But you say, "All months are not thirty days in length, and our year contains 365 days, not 360."

True. Actually our year is 365.2422 days in length, and we adjust with leap years. But God kept time prophecies simple and thus easy to understand. In prophetic calculation a month has thirty days, a year 360 days.

In other words, a prophetic day stands for a *solar* year. And a prophetic year, or "time" (made up of 360 prophetic days), stands for 360 literal, natural, solar years.

This year-day principle was not new, even in Daniel's day. You recall that Jacob served his uncle seven years for Rachel, whom he loved, only to be tricked into marrying Leah. He then agreed to "fulfil her week" (Genesis 29:27, KJV) and served seven more years for Rachel. A week—seven years.

When the Hebrews, on their way from Egypt, came up to the Jordan River, they spent forty days spying out the land on the other side and concluded they couldn't handle its giants. Because of their lack of faith in God they were sentenced to wander in the wilderness forty years (Numbers 14:34)—a year for each day spent in spying out the land.

Ezekiel was instructed to illustrate his prophecy by lying on his side for forty days (Ezekiel 4:6)—each day for a year.

Our problem, in interpreting a Bible prediction involving time, is to discover whether the time period is literal or prophetic. Some contend that the 1260 days are literal days, not years. But a prophecy definitely set in the Christian era, such as Revelation 12:6, cannot be pushed back into Old Testament times. Was Jesus, who was the real Author of the Revelation (see chapter 1, verse 1), unaware that this prophecy had already been fulfilled?

If taking a time period to be literal doesn't make sense, when it leads us to absurd conclusions, we can know we are on the wrong track. For when we get it right, it will fit into history with a precision that leaves no room for doubt. Prophecy, said the apostle Peter, is like a light that shines along the course of history, illuminating the future before it happens. 2 Peter 1:19.

So much for the mechanics of decoding prophetic time. We will deal later with the fulfillment of the 1260-year prediction. And at the appropriate time we will probe Daniel's prophecy of 2300 years (Daniel 8:14), which includes mathematical proof that Jesus was who He claimed to be. It is the longest period of prophetic time in the Bible, reaching farther toward our day than any other time prophecy—to the year 1844. Divine prophecy yields no specific date beyond it. And what really happened in 1844 has staggering significance for every rider of this planet, including you and me!

But first, what was happening behind the scenes during these long, dull years of the prophets? Why didn't Jesus come to earth sooner? And what of the fallen angel? Were his malignant attacks against Jesus in a period of remission?

Countdown to Bethlehem

Time passed slowly in the days of the Old Testament prophets. They were popular only if they prophesied what kings wanted to hear. Jeremiah spent many days and nights in a damp, dark, smelly dungeon—because he dared to give God's message straight. Israel just was not noted for being kind to its prophets. Jesus would one day cry out, "O Jerusalem, Jerusalem, you who kill the prophets and stone those sent to you, how often I have longed to gather your children together, as a hen gathers her chicks under her wings, but you were not willing." Matthew 23:37, NIV.

It would seem that Daniel's situation was different. He had been promoted to high office in the court of Babylon. He was loved and trusted by Nebuchadnezzar, and lived to see the proud and arrogant king become a humble and devoted worshiper of the true God. Daniel even survived the fall of Babylon and served, still loved and trusted, under Darius the Mede.

It might seem at times that his was an easy life. But always he carried on his heart the burden of his people. Babylon was not their home. They were captives in a strange land—captives because they had been less than loyal to their God. Daniel, homesick for his native land, prayed three times a day with his window open toward Jerusalem. That's what got him thrown into the lions' den.

The fallen angel was not sleeping. Nor was he idle. He did everything he could to make life hard for the prophets, everything he could to keep God's messages from getting through. He was determined to divert the minds of the people from God, determined to distort the character of God at every opportunity, until they should think of Him as a cruel and uncaring tyrant.

Through the long centuries God had showered His people with favors. He had tried to show them what He was like. But they were so slow to understand, so quick to be deceived. Only one option remained. He Himself would come to earth and let them see how much He cared. For little did that chief of fallen angels know—nor could he have understood—that beating in the heart of Jesus was a love so deep and strong that only Calvary could express it!

Why did Jesus wait? He waited because the earth had not yet reached its darkest hour. The time was fast approaching. But it was not yet. The proud keepers of the law were becoming more and more absorbed with theological debate. Rites and ceremonies and sacrifices held their attention, while they scarcely thought of the Lamb of God to whom the sacrifices pointed. They were making life harder and harder for the people, while they made it easier and easier for themselves. Sin was becoming a science, and vice a consecrated part of religion. Jesus would step into the world at a time when it was so depraved, and so violent, that His message of love would seem like lunacy. But the time was not yet.

Jesus, through Isaiah the gospel prophet, had predicted much concerning His ordeal in the hands of men—even some of His thoughts upon the cross. Micah had predicted the place of His birth. But Daniel had predicted the very year that He would begin His public ministry. "From the going forth of the commandment to restore and to build Jerusalem unto the Messiah the Prince shall be seven weeks, and threescore and two weeks." Daniel 9:25, KJV.

Sixty-nine weeks—483 years—to the Messiah. Beginning with the decree of Artaxerxes, which went into effect in the fall of 457 B.C. Ending with the baptism of Jesus in the fall of A.D. 27. The religious leaders had studied the prophecies. They should have known that the time was near. But they were absorbed with trivia. And besides, they had their own ideas about how the Messiah should appear and what He should be like—ideas incompatible with God's.

So while the world was getting darker, while Jesus waited, history was moving steadily toward Bethlehem, counting down according to a prophetic clock. And then, "when the time had fully come, God sent his Son, born of a woman . . . to redeem [man]." Galatians 4:4, 5, NIV.

Three wise men, in a far country, had been studying the prophecies. They knew that the time was near. They prayed earnestly to be led—and then followed the star. They expected all Jerusalem to be astir. But only the wicked Herod seemed interested—and he only because he was not one to let a possible rival to his throne live a moment longer than necessary.

Angels sped earthward with their happy song, their incredible news. But no one seemed to be waiting for the Promised One. Would they have to return to heaven without singing their song and sharing their news? Finally, on the hills near Bethlehem, they found some shepherds watching with their sheep. They had been talking of the prophecies, longing for the day when the promised Messiah would bring light to this dark world. To them the angels sang.

The fallen angel saw the light above Bethlehem—and trembled!

Section Four
A Piece of the Sidewalk

A Piece of the Sidewalk

You've seen them—standing on the corner, holding out a piece of paper to bystanders. Or in the middle of the sidewalk—so that it's difficult to avoid an encounter. They have something to say, and they are desperately anxious for somebody to listen. So anxious that it matters not how the wind blows or how hard it rains or how far the thermometer plunges. They keep their sidewalk vigil with a smile, hoping that this time you will stop and listen.

John was one of those sidewalk enthusiasts. Always on the job—no matter how rough the weather. A friend of mine, Jim Meadows, had encountered him once before on a windy street. But today he was standing in front of the main post office. He looked so terribly cold that Jim invited him into his car for a while. He let him talk. And that made John happy.

They met a third time in a cafeteria, and Jim determined to ask him some questions. "John," he said, "you're always talking about how humanity should become reunited with God. How is humanity going to do this?"

John answered quickly, "Man must submit himself to the will of God. He must learn about the way God wants him to act, as well as about the things God wants him to do."

"But what about Jesus Christ? Doesn't He have anything to do with it?"

"Jesus Christ. Oh, yes," he said politely. "He was a good man."

"Was He the Son of God?"

John thought a minute. "He may very well have been."

My friend was surprised. "John," he said, "the Bible *says* that Jesus Christ was the Son of God and that He's the only way we can get back to God. You do believe in the Bible, don't you? You read it, I hope."

And John said, "Certainly. But I don't happen to have my Bible with me just now. I left it in Kansas City."

81

"You left it in Kansas City?"

"I was at a rally in Kansas City and forgot to bring it back with me."

My friend Jim said that the bottom dropped out of his stomach at that point. He could hardly believe what John had said. Here was a young man almost fanatically involved in trying to get God and man back together. But he didn't seem to need Jesus Christ. And he had left his Bible in Kansas City! Accidents happen, of course. People do forget—even their Bibles. But the point is, John didn't seem to mind. His Bible, like Jesus Christ, seemed to him an unimportant accessory!

John, you see, had become enamored with a contemporary evangelist who has managed to collect a few million followers. This man—not God or Christ or the Bible—was the real focus of John's dedication. For a man—a mere man—he was willing to stand on the sidewalk and shout in the wind and cold to an unresponsive humanity!

My friend asked him one more question. If the Bible and the writings of the man he followed should turn out to be in conflict, which would he choose?

And John answered without hesitation. Knowledge is progressive, he said. He would choose the later and more modern message—the writings of the man he was following!

It's hard to forget John—and hundreds of others like him. Dedicated. Involved. Willing to stand long hours in the biting cold. Willing to be ignored and snubbed and ridiculed. Shaming us all with the measure of their devotion—all for a man, a mere man!

John, if you're listening, let me have a piece of your sidewalk, because I want to tell you about Jesus of Nazareth. One who is not a mere man. One who is worthy of a devotion like yours. Because He claimed to be, and is, the Son of the living God!

Yes, whoever you are, wherever you are, whether you believe or don't believe; whether you are religious or not; whether you are searching for truth or think you have found it—please let me have a piece of your day. Because I want to talk to you, and to John, about Jesus. I want to tell you what He can do for you that no one else can. I want to tell you why He is worthy of your unstinted service—and your love—and your worship!

John, can the man you serve answer your prayers? Do you

have access to him at any time, day or night? Do you have a direct line, a private line, into his presence? If you write him, does he read your letter? Does he reply? Does his reply solve all your problems? And tell me, if access to him is restricted, if he is not with you at all times, how can he heal your loneliness?

Listen. The God I worship says, "Before they call, I will answer; and while they are yet speaking, I will hear." Isaiah 65:24, KJV.

He's done it for me a thousand times. And the Lord Jesus says, "Surely I will be with you always, to the very end of the age." Matthew 28:20, NIV.

And I know it's true. I've experienced it again and again.

Jesus of Nazareth can say, "Take heart, son; your sins are forgiven." Matthew 9:2, NIV. And the guilt is gone.

A mere man can say the same words. But the guilt remains. The load is still there. And guilt is the heaviest load there is. I don't want to worship a god who can't take it away!

Can any man-made god create a world? Or hold the stars in orbit? My God can. And He can use that same creative power to give me a new heart and make me a new person. The apostle Paul said, "If anyone is in Christ, he is a new creation." 2 Corinthians 5:17, NIV.

I need a God who can give me personal victory, who can keep me from falling. See Jude 24. I need a God who can guarantee that sin will not have dominion over me. See Romans 6:14.

John, has the man you are following conquered death? Isn't he just as subject to death as you are—just as vulnerable? If death should bring your life to a close, is he able to raise you from the dead? Can he give you back the loved ones that you have lost?

Jesus met death head on and conquered it. Death couldn't hold Him. Mountains upon mountains piled over His tomb couldn't have held Him there. He walked out of the tomb that Sunday morning and left it empty. No other man has done that. No other man can. Death is too much for any other man. But Jesus says, "I am the resurrection, and the life." John 11:25, KJV. "I have authority over death and the world of the dead." Revelation 1:18, TEV.

Wouldn't you rather worship a God like that?

Tell me, when those bad conditions you talk about get much

worse than they are now, when this earth has been so plundered and polluted that it is no longer a desirable place to live—can the one you follow rescue you from this planet? Is he, at this moment, preparing a home for you in another world? Is he able to take you there—up through the corridors of space to the City of God? Jesus is! He says, "There are many dwelling-places in my Father's house. . . . I am going there on purpose to prepare a place for you. And if I go and prepare a place for you, I shall come again and receive you to myself, so that where I am you may be also." John 14:2, 3, NEB.

Don't you like that? No more windy corners and hard sidewalks and bitter cold. No more heartache. No more pain. No more tears. No more death!

What we need is a way to get rid of sin on this planet. Can any self-appointed saviour of the world do that? Does any aspiring messiah have the power to destroy the fallen angel with whom sin originated—and all his cohorts? Can any human leader set this world aflame and recreate it—new and clean and beautiful as it was at the beginning? God can. And He will. He says, "Behold, I create new heavens and a new earth." Isaiah 65:17, KJV.

Can anything less solve our problems?

Listen. A man may have charisma. He may have influence in high places. He may have millions of followers. He may have unlimited funds. He may be able to initiate legislation—or even set forces in motion. But the morning news may report that he died of a heart attack during the night. So frail is boasting humanity!

Friend, wherever you are placing your faith, whether you worship gods of the East or gods of the West, whether you worship gods of wood and stone or those of chrome and steel and neon, whether your gods are ancient or contemporary, all must answer No to the vital questions we've been asking. A god that cannot conquer death, that cannot rescue you from this planet, that cannot give you a new heart is not big enough to meet your need or mine!

But there is one more question, more vital than any other. If you are worshiping any other god than the Lord Jesus Christ, it's a question that needs to be asked. You may not think of the object of your faith as being a god at all. You may say, "I'm not a religious person." It may be some theory, some philosophy, some system that you are depending on to take you through life and into the future. In that sense it is a god. Of all of you I must ask, "Did your god die for you? Did your god love you enough to leave the throne of the universe and come down to this rebel planet to die in your place, on a cross that should have been yours? Did your god love you personally so much that he would have made that sacrifice even if you were the only one he could hope to save?"

Jesus did. That's what He did for you—and for me. Not just for Christians. Not just for religious people. Even if you have never given Him a thought until this moment, that's how much He loves you personally. That's the price He paid to be able to offer you forgiveness—and life. Isn't it unthinkable to reject a gift that cost so much?

Friend, in place of all the gods that cannot save, in place of all the theories and philosophies that cannot heal the soul's deep hurt, in place of all the answers that leave you searching still, and guilty still, and lonely still—I offer you the Lord Jesus Christ!

Handbook for Messiahs

If you should land your plane in a hayfield—and another plane should land beside you—and the pilot of that other plane should tell you that he is a messiah who has quit his job—what would you think? And what would you do?

Would you believe him? Ask to see his pilot's license? Look for something supernatural about him or his plane? Ask him some tough questions? Or get out of there fast?

Richard Bach, after breaking all sales records with a fable he called *Jonathan Livingston Seagull,* came out with another book—*Illusions*. He didn't want to write it, he says, but decided he had something more to say.

What he has to say is strictly his imagination, he admits. And the most profound truth in the book is probably stated in the words with which it ends: "Everything in this book may be wrong."

But in between the disclaimers at front and back the message comes through like a fire alarm—equally clear and equally frightening.

Bach is definitely preparing his readers for the possibility that they personally, any day now, might meet a messiah. A messiah from out of this world, yet curiously in it. A messiah who gives substance to his claims by flying a plane day after day without fuel. Without bugs on the propeller or on the windshield. A messiah who can land his plane in a hayfield repeatedly without getting hay on the floor of the cockpit. A messiah who can vaporize clouds at will. Who can make water solid and walk on it, or make the ground liquid and swim in it.

The message is clear that, according to Bach, all a messiah has to do to prove his claims is work a few miracles. If there is anything supernatural about him or his plane, he must be genuine.

Time magazine, in its issue of November 13, 1972, says that

Richard Bach feels he did not really write *Seagull*. He says he was walking near the beach one evening when he heard a voice say, "Jonathan Livingston Seagull." He turned. There was no one there. He went home, sat on the bed, and said, "Look, voice. If you think I know what this means, you're absolutely out of your mind. If it means something, tell me."

And what happened? "The voice comes through to Bach like a three-dimensional movie, and as Bach writes it all down with a green ballpoint pen, it shows-and-tells the story of Jonathan Livingston Seagull."

One problem. The voice stopped without ending the story, and Bach couldn't finish it until eight years later when he awoke from a dream about seagulls. Another vision was in progress, he says. He jumped out of bed and recorded it. And the book was complete.

You understand now why Bach feels he didn't really write the book. And are you beginning to get an idea who did? Could anyone be blamed for suspecting that *Illusions*, with its reluctant messiah, came from the same source as *Seagull*—an occult source?

Both books carry the same message: there is no death. That people do not die but simply change consciousness. That great powers reside within a person if he or she will only tap them. That is is possible to triumph over matter by thought control. That nothing is real, that everything is an illusion. That every man is free to do as he pleases. That it is possible to be anything you want to be.

Are these the earmarks of a legitimate messiah? No. They are the philosophy of a fallen angel. They bear the telltale marks of his now-familiar strategy. Remember?

Unquestionably, by Richard Bach's *Illusions* and a host of other books we are being conditioned for something. And it isn't too hard to figure out what it is. Because Jesus said that "false Christs and false prophets will appear and perform great signs and miracles to deceive even the elect—if that were possible." Matthew 24:24, NIV.

False christs. False messiahs. And notice that they will work miracles. The supernatural will be prominent. No bugs on the propeller, no straw on the cockpit floor—these may seem impressive to the uninformed. But they are no trick at all for the fallen angel. And they are just the sort of trivia we can expect from a counterfeit messiah.

Richard Bach talks about a handbook for messiahs. The suggestion is that you can even be a messiah yourself, if you just follow the instructions. And don't miss the subtle implication that messiahs are of human origin—and that Jesus, too, was only human, not divine.

But did you know that there really is a handbook for messiahs—a handbook that clearly outlines what a messiah would have to do if he wants to prove his claims? It's the Old Testament—specifically its prophecies about the One to come.

It's true that the life of Jesus, His words, His teaching, His miracles, all stamp His mission as divine. But for irrefutable proof that Jesus was who He said He was, it is still to the scores of Old Testament predictions that we must turn—to the Handbook, if you please, the Handbook to which anyone claiming to be the true Messiah must measure up. If Jesus didn't measure up to those predictions, then it doesn't matter how many miracles He worked!

It is absolutely fascinating to compare the Old Testament predictions with the way Jesus fulfilled them in the New. For who ever heard of a man's life story being recorded centuries before he was born? But that's exactly what we discover.

For instance, the prophet Micah predicted (Micah 5:2) that Jesus would be born in Bethlehem. Taking quite a chance, wasn't it—to pinpoint the place of His birth? What if it didn't work out that way? But it did—thanks to a decree that got Joseph and Mary to Bethlehem just in the nick of time.

The prophet Isaiah said that Jesus would be born of a virgin (Isaiah 7:14). And Matthew, in the New Testament (Matthew 1:22, 23), tells us that prophecy was fulfilled.

We have already talked about the prophecy of Daniel which gives us mathematical proof that Jesus was who He said He was. You recall that sixty-nine weeks, or 483 years, beginning in the fall of 457 B.C. and reaching to the fall of A.D. 27, would extend to Messiah the Prince. And Jesus was exactly on time. For it was in the fall of A.D. 27 that Jesus was baptized and began His ministry as the Messiah.

(By the way, if you have trouble getting your calculation to agree with ours, remember that it is necessary to cross the line between B.C. and A.D., and that you must count backward before the line and forward this side of it. Actually, since we are calculating from autumn to autumn, there are approximately 456-and-a-third years before the line and 26-and-two-thirds years this side of it. Adding those two figures will give you the 483 years.)

But there is *more* in Daniel's prophecy. The sixty-nine weeks, you see, are a part of seventy weeks (Daniel 9:24, 25) allotted to the Jewish nation. At the end of that seventieth week, in A.D. 34, when the rejection of Jesus was sealed by the stoning of Stephen, the gospel went to the Gentiles.

But now listen. *After* the sixty-nine prophetic weeks were ended (verse 26) the Messiah would be "cut off." And the prophecy is still more precise. "In the midst" of the seventieth week (verse 27) He would cause the sacrifices to cease. That is, the sacrifices offered through the long centuries would now cease to have meaning, because Jesus, the Lamb of God, to whom all the sacrifices pointed, had come and given His life.

Was this accurately fulfilled? Yes. Again, Jesus was right on time. For it was in the midst of the week, halfway through that seventieth week, in the spring of A.D. 31, that Jesus was crucified!

There are those who try to lift that seventieth week out of its place and bring it down into the future, building a mountain of speculation around it. But the tragedy is that by tampering with that divine prediction thay have lost the cross of Calvary, the heart of it all!

I say again, Bible prophecy is not a toy. It is not a set of blocks that we can pick up and put down wherever we choose. When God says seventy prophetic weeks He means seventy consecutive prophetic weeks—not sixty-nine and then one more whenever we get ready for it, wherever it suits our fancy.

Do you see? Jesus *came* at exactly the right time. Anyone coming at any other time and claiming to be the Messiah could only be an impostor.

And Jesus *died* at the right time. He died in the right year, at the right time of the year. If you examine carefully the Old Testament system of sacrifices that pointed forward to Christ, that typified His unique sacrifice for us, you can only conclude that He died on the very day and at the time of day to fit the types!

But now to another remarkable prediction written five hundred years before the time of Christ: "And I said unto them, If ye think good, give me my price; and if not, forbear. So they weighed for my price thirty pieces of silver. And the Lord said unto me, Cast it unto the potter: a goodly price that I was prised at of them. And I took the thirty pieces of silver, and cast them to the potter in the house of the Lord." Zechariah 11:12, 13, KJV.

Now Judas comes into the picture. And here we have three striking predictions. *One*—the exact amount of money for which Jesus would be sold. *Two*—where it would be thrown down. *Three*—what would be purchased with the money.

Judas, who wanted to make a name for himself—and did! But what a name it has been! He was not a victim of prophecy. He didn't have to do what he did. Jesus had done everything possible to save him from his terrible deed.

Judas thought Jesus would free Himself from the crowd by a miracle. The people would then make Him king. And he, Judas, would get the credit!

He was delighted when the mob, in the presence of Jesus, fell to the ground as if they were dead. See John 18:6. His plan was working. But then Jesus let the mob take Him! He made no protest! Jesus was going to let Himself be crucified! And Judas couldn't endure the terrible guilt. He rushed into the hall of judgment, crying in a hoarse voice, "He is innocent! Spare Him, Caiaphas!"

Pale and haggard, he pressed through the startled mob and threw down before the plotting priests the thirty pieces of silver—the price of his Lord! He grasped the robe of the high priest, pleading with him to release Jesus. "I have sinned!" he cried. But Caiaphas only shook him off.

I picture him then turning to Jesus. Casting himself at His feet, he pleads with Him to deliver Himself from the mob. But neither Caiaphas nor Jesus Himself could reverse his act of betrayal. He could not bear to see Jesus crucified. He rushed from the hall exclaiming, "It is too late! It is too late!"

The story of Judas ended under a tree beside the road that led from Pilate's hall to Calvary.

And the prophets had told it all before—even what would be done with the thirty pieces of silver. The priests, perplexed because they couldn't put the price of blood back into the treasury, bought a field to bury strangers in—and called it "the potter's field." Just as the prophet had said.

Strangely wonderful, isn't it, to see the minute details of Old Testament prophecy as they unfold in New Testament fulfillment.

Did you know that David, a thousand years before the crucifixion, had described where the nails would be driven into the flesh of our Lord? Listen: "They pierced my hands and my feet." Psalm 22:16, KJV.

This statement is all the more remarkable when we remember that death by crucifixion was not the accepted method of capital punishment in the time of David, when these words were written. And even after crucifixion did come into use, rope, not nails, was often if not usually used to fasten victims to the rough beams.

Then you recall that the clothing of Jesus was given to the soldiers, and they divided the pieces among them. But when they came to His robe, they decided to cast lots for it rather than damage the singly-woven piece. Again it was just as Jesus, speaking through the prophet, had foretold: "They part my garments among them, and cast lots upon my vesture." Psalm 22:18, KJV.

Friend, if those soldiers had divided that piece of fabric equally among them, or if Jesus had been bound to the cross rather than nailed, or if He had been sold for forty pieces of silver rather than thirty, or if the priests had made some other use of the money that was the price of blood—then you might have reason to question the true identity of Jesus of Nazareth, to wonder if He was really who He said He was. But the precisely accurate fulfillment of the words of the Old Testament prophets leaves no doubt.

Evidently we can be very certain that Jesus was who He said He was!

But wait! In spite of His faultless life, in spite of His incomparable teaching, in spite of all His miracles, in spite of all the prophecies fulfilled—it all narrows down to this. It all stands or falls with one question: Did this Man Jesus have power over death? Did He walk out of that tomb?

If He didn't, He was the greatest impostor this world has ever known. If He claimed to be God but couldn't conquer death, then it is all a heartless hoax. And all this mountain of evidence only adds to the enormity of the deception!

Jesus said, "I am the living one; for I was dead and now I am alive for evermore, and I hold the keys of Death and Death's domain." Revelation 1:18, NEB.

Did He tell the truth? I believe He did!

But there are still some who say that Jesus' resurrection was all a hoax. The story bribed into the mouths of the Roman soldiers (Matthew 28:11–15) is still circulated. There are some who refuse to believe even when they are sunburned by the evidence!

I ask you, *Was it a hoax* dreamed up by the disciples of Jesus when they themselves, holed up in a locked room, scared to death, didn't believe it?

Was it a hoax when Roman soldiers saw it all and were too excited to tell anything but the truth to the priests—or to those they had already met along the way?

Was it a hoax when the Jewish leaders didn't even visit the tomb to verify the resurrection claim? Why didn't they launch a massive investigation and produce the body? That would have put an end to Christianity before it was born!

No. It was not a hoax. It remains the most fantastic fact of history. As we probe the story of the empty tomb, it is the frustrated silence of the enemies of Christ, their utter inability to explain it away, that speaks loudest of all. That silence is absolutely deafening!

God knew that all else would hinge upon the resurrection. He knew the attacks that would be aimed against it. He has tightly closed every loophole, every niche that might give entrance to uncertainty. He wanted us to be sure!

But friend, being convinced is not enough. Acknowledging the evidence is not enough. Conviction and commitment are not the same thing!

Pilate heard that Christ had risen. And it troubled him till the moment of his death. But it did not save him.

The religious leaders knew it was true. But they only tried to control the news. Knowledge didn't change their hearts!

Thomas heard it—and *didn't* believe it. But when he saw the evidence in the Saviour's hands, he knelt at His feet in an ecstacy of joy!

A small band of followers examined the evidence and not only believed but acted upon it. And the resurrection stamped their faith with a certainty that was willing to face death!

That same certainty can be yours!

Shortcuts

The fallen angel was restless, apprehensive, troubled. Not everything was going according to plan. It had been so easy bringing about the ruin of the first inhabitants of this planet. Just one little sales pitch—and it was all over. In fact, since that day, almost every member of the human race had been an easy mark. It was the exceptions that troubled him.

The rebel angel had been so sure that God wouldn't bother with this one tiny world on the edge of His universe—and only two people on it. This planet would be his, now that Adam had sold out to him. And Eden would be the headquarters of rebellion. But it hadn't worked out that way. Flaming swords of light had barred him from Eden. And he was perplexed about the words God had spoken to him there in the garden. Who was it who would crush his head? See Genesis 3:15.

He couldn't believe that the Son of God Himself would leave His throne and come to this earth to challenge his control and make a way out for fallen men. That kind of love was far beyond his understanding. Yet through the long centuries, as he studied the words of the prophets, he was convinced that such indeed was Heaven's plan.

The fallen angel trembled as he saw the light over Bethlehem and heard the angels' song. Was this Child, born in Bethlehem, the One who would challenge his control, limit his power, and finally crush his head? He would take no chances. He had influence with King Herod. Herod would dispose of the Child. But Heaven intervened.

The boy Jesus, at the age of twelve, traveled with His parents to Jerusalem. For the first time He saw the magnificent Temple of which He had heard so much. He was fascinated as He watched the white-robed priests performing their duties, offering innocent lambs as a sacrifice for sin. He understood well the meaning of it

94

all, for even at twelve He was a keen student of the Scriptures. But now as He watched intently, oblivious to the passing of time, thoughts were churning in His young mind. What He was watching seemed to have something to do with Him personally. And then He knew. He knew why He had come to this earth. He, He Himself, was to be the Lamb! He Himself was to be the Sacrifice to which the sacrifice of lambs, through the long centuries, had pointed. His mission now was clear. And every step He took would lead Him closer to the place of sacrifice. For He would be the Lamb!

Jesus returned with His parents to Nazareth and continued to be an obedient Son, though He now knew that Joseph was not his father. He worked at Joseph's side in his carpenter shop and learned the trade well. He made no move to go public with His mission.

The fallen angel watched intently. He thought that Jesus might well be the Son of God, but he was not completely sure. He tried all his temptations, but without a single success. It annoyed him greatly that he who had brought about the ruin of kings could not bring this Teenager, this unassuming Youth, this quiet Carpenter of Nazareth, to yield an inch!

In the meantime, John the Baptist, the desert prophet, was baptizing in the Jordan. It was he who had been designated by the prophet Isaiah as a voice crying in the wilderness (Isaiah 40:3), preparing the way for the Messiah. His was to be the high privilege of introducing the Messiah to the world.

John believed Jesus to be the Messiah, though he had no positive proof. The two had had no communication with each other. And John wondered, as time passed, why Jesus, if He was the Messiah, remained still in the carpenter shop, making no move to present Himself to the people.

But John continued His preaching of repentance, speaking always of One to come whose shoes he was not worthy to unlace. And his preaching was so powerful, his denunciation of sin so unvarnished that people flocked to the Jordan to be baptized.

News of the wilderness prophet was told in the carpenter shop at Nazareth. And the young Carpenter recognized the call. The time had come. He put away His tools for the last time, bade farewell to His mother, and made His way to the Jordan. He, too, would be baptized—not because of any guilt of His own, for He had none, but as an example to those He had come to save. See Matthew 3:13–17.

He felt so unworthy. John was reluctant to baptize Jesus. But Jesus insisted. And then, with dripping clothes, the Saviour of the world knelt upon the bank of the Jordan and prayed.

What Jesus said to His Father is not recorded, but it must have been no ordinary prayer. He was entering upon a mission never before attempted. On the success or failure of that mission hung the destiny of the world and everyone in it. He needed special strength. He needed an assurance that would sustain Him in His confrontations with the fallen angel. For He alone knew how fierce the enemy attacks would be.

The angels had never heard such a prayer. They must have longed to answer it, to bring their loved Commander the assurance He longed for. But no. The Father would give that assurance Himself. Suddenly, as the people gazed silently upon the kneeling Saviour, His form was bathed in light from the throne of God. And from the open heavens was heard a voice, declaring, "This is my beloved Son, in whom I am well pleased." John 1:29, KJV.

John had been deeply moved as he saw Jesus pleading with tears for the approval of His Father. And now, as he heard the voice, he knew, and knew for sure, that he had just baptized the Messiah. Urged by the Spirit of God, he stretched out his arm toward Jesus and cried, "Behold the Lamb of God, which taketh away the sin of the world!"

The fallen angel, unseen by human eyes, was present, watching it all. And now he, too, as he heard the voice, knew that Jesus was indeed the Son of God, come to rescue man from his control, come to make heaven—the home that he, Satan, had lost—available to the human race. And the rebel chief determined that He should fail!

Jesus had gone public. John had announced Him to be the Lamb of God—as the Messiah so long promised. Jesus had placed His feet in a blood-stained path. And He had made Himself a target, the Number One target, of Satan and all his host of angels-turned-demons. He was on collision course with the great rebel!

What would Jesus do now? Gather men about Him to share and help to expedite His mission? No. Not yet.

What follows next is usually passed over rather lightly, as if it were a sort of parenthesis between Jesus' baptism and the calling of His disciples. But believe me, it is far more than that. It is outranked in critical importance only by His struggle in Gethsemane and by the cross itself—if it is outranked at all!

The inspired account begins with these words: "Then was Jesus led up of the spirit into the wilderness to be tempted of the devil." Matthew 4:1, KJV.

Led by the Spirit. Moved by the Spirit. Urged by the Spirit. The search for disciples can wait. He has headed for the wilderness—alone. He wants to spend long hours with His Father as He begins His public mission. He knows that all hell will soon be breaking over His head, and He will need the full measure of strength. And that strength will be found not only in prayer but by meeting head on the strongest temptations the fallen angel can devise. Everything depends upon who it is who walks out of that wilderness the victor!

Picture it with me. Catch the high drama of this all-important encounter. As Jesus enters the lonely, desolate wilderness, His face is still illuminated by the light from the throne. His step is strong and steady, for His is a physique fresh from the carpenter's bench. But soon the light in His countenance is gone. We are told that for forty days He eats no food. He becomes pale and emaciated. Think of it! He who has flung worlds into space is hungry. He is weak. He is alone!

The fallen angel has been watching. Now is his chance. The Son of God, so powerful in their first encounter, has laid aside His divinity and taken upon Himself the weakness of humanity. He has taken humanity not as it was in the days of Adam, when men still retained much of the vital force imparted in Eden's innocence. No. He has entered the human race after sin and depravity for thousands of years have left their terrible marks. The Son of God is now inferior in strength to the fallen angel. This is the hour for which Satan has waited.

Does the rebel chief reveal his true identity? No. True to his strategy he appears as an angel of light (2 Corinthians 11:14) and flatters himself, that in his disguise, Jesus will not recognize him. He claims to be an angel fresh from the throne of God. He has prepared well for this encounter. And it must have proceeded something like this:

Pretending sympathy for Jesus in His plight, he says the Father has sent him to say that it will not be necessary, after all, to travel the bloodstained path. He has set His feet in the path of sacrifice; He has shown His willingness. And that is enough. The Father was only proving Him.

It's like it was with Abraham, he says. And then the lying angel claims that he is the one sent to stay the hand of Abraham when he had raised the knife to slay his son Isaac. Now, on a similar mission of mercy, he has come to save Jesus from starving. That's the line.

Adam and Eve, though not even hungry, placed in a perfect environment with all their needs supplied, had fallen so easily on the point of appetite. And through the centuries the tempter had repeatedly appealed to man's love affair with food, with horrible success. With Jesus in His weakened condition, desperately hungry and alone, He should be a pushover. But He isn't!

When the wily enemy sees that his arguments have failed to have any effect on Jesus, he turns to another line. He begins to taunt Jesus about His pale, emaciated appearance, and contrasts it with his own brilliance and power. He suggests that surely God would not permit His Son to suffer like this, hungry and alone. Is He really sure that He is the Son of God?

Precious to Jesus, sustaining Him in this crisis, are the words spoken from heaven at His baptism. But the deceiver is determined to shake the confidence of Jesus in that assurance of the Father's approval. He now confides to Jesus that one of heaven's most honored angels has rebelled and been banished from heaven. "Really," he says, "if You could just see Yourself! You look like You might be that fallen angel. If You really are the Son of God, I don't think I'm out of line in demanding some proof. If You are indeed God's Son, why don't You use some of Your power and turn these stones into bread? You don't have to suffer like this!" See Matthew 4:3.

A shortcut, you see. An easier way to get on with His mission.

Work some miracles. Use His divine power to make it easier for Himself.

But Jesus will not use any power not available to those He has come to save. And He answers firmly, "Man shall not live by bread alone, but by every word that proceedeth out of the mouth of God." Matthew 4:4, KJV.

The enemy, his frustration mounting, now takes Jesus to Jerusalem and places His feet on a pinnacle of the Temple. And this time, the tempter will quote Scripture too. "Why don't You jump? Doesn't it say in the Psalms that the angels will bear You up? If You are the Son of God, He won't let You get hurt. And that will be all the proof I need."

"Besides," he goes on, "people love magic. That's what they expect of the Messiah. Work a few miracles. You'll have them eating out of Your hand. Isn't there a legend that says the Messiah, when He comes, will descend on the temple in a cloud? Do something spectacular. *Your* way to power is too slow. Go ahead and jump!"

But Jesus answers, "Thou shalt not tempt the Lord thy God." Verse 7.

The Saviour knows that there is a thin line between faith and presumption. Of course His Father would protect Him in a real emergency. But He will not *create* that emergency. He will not force His Father to work a miracle just for show.

Another shortcut has been suggested—an easier way to complete His mission. But Jesus knows that there is no shortcut. There is no easy way. There is no road that will bypass Calvary. He will not swerve from the path He has chosen.

The enemy now is desperate. He is getting nowhere with Jesus. He throws off his disguise and determines to negotiate a compromise, to settle the conflict here and now. He is ready to settle out of court. It will be in his own favor, of course. But he will make an offer so attractive that Jesus won't be able to resist.

This time he takes the Saviour to a high mountain. He shows Him the kingdoms of this world at their very best, in all their glory. And he makes this proposal: "All these things will I give thee, if thou wilt fall down and worship me." Verse 9.

The mask now is gone. Satan makes no attempt to hide his

motives. What he wants is worship. And he wants it from the Son of God. "Look," he says, "You don't have to go through so much trouble to get this world back. It's mine. Adam sold out to me. But You can have it all right now, without waiting, if You'll just bow down and worship me. Worship me just once. Worship me just a little. And it will all be yours!"

A shortcut for sure! And Jesus glances at the spectacular panorama for a moment and then turns away. He will run no risk of being swayed by the sight.

Jesus has known all along who His visitor is. He has recognized him not by his appearance, but by his words—his suggestions of doubt. "*If* You are the Son of God." That was the key to his identity.

Up to this point Jesus had let Satan talk, let him present his most alluring arguments. But now the Saviour is rightly indignant. Such an insult to the Creator, the cruel daring that demanded for himself worship *from* divinity, cannot go unrebuked. "Get thee hence, Satan," He says with finality, "for it is written, Thou shalt worship the Lord thy God, and him only shalt thou serve." Verse 10.

Writhing in defeat, Satan retires from the scene. The chief of rebels has no power to resist the divine command. Without another word the encounter is ended.

After the tempter has departed, Jesus must have fallen to the ground as one dying, exhausted from the terrible conflict. Angels had watched it all, and now they came to bring Him food and strength. Perhaps, without their ministry in the wilderness as in Gethsemane, Jesus could have died right there.

Exhausted? Near death? Yes. But He walked out of that wilderness untainted, the clear Victor in a conflict that decided more than you think!

I say again, this wilderness conflict, so little spoken of, so seldom in our thoughts, ranks along with Gethsemane in critical importance. For do you realize that without the victory gained in the wilderness, Gethsemane and the cross would never have happened?

Don't misunderstand me. Jesus, on the cross, made a perfect sacrifice. It was complete in every way. He paid the penalty for our sins. He purchased, at infinite cost, the right to forgive us.

But forgiveness alone is not enough. There must be also *the power to stop sinning*. And that's what the wilderness experience was all about. Sin was cast out of heaven once. It can never be readmitted. *Forgiven* sinners, because of the blood of Jesus, will be freely welcomed there. But those who are *still sinning* must be excluded.

Early in the controversy the fallen angel had charged that it is impossible for man to keep God's law. And Adam's easy defeat seemed to support the charge. Satan felt sure that even Jesus, once he had taken on the weakness of humanity, could not keep His Father's law.

It is perfectly true that we, in our own strength, cannot keep from sinning. The power to stop sinning must come from *outside* ourselves. If Jesus had failed, where would be our hope?

That's why it was necessary for Jesus, right at the beginning of His ministry, to shatter Satan's charges by demonstrating that even as a Man, even at His weakest, even alone and hungry, without food for forty days, it was still possible to obey God.

Adam and Eve failed on the point of appetite under the most favorable conditions. Theirs was a relatively easy test. Jesus was Victor on the point of appetite under the worst possible conditions. His was a test far more severe than any man will ever be called to meet.

And that wilderness victory, by the way, has to do not only with hunger, with food and water, but with *everything* that we are ever tempted to put into our bodies—to eat or drink or breathe or inject into the bloodstream. It has to do with every urge of the appetite or of the natural passions, of the mind as well as the senses. All are linked. All are included. For Jesus "was in all points tempted like as we are, yet without sin." Hebrews 4:15, KJV.

In all points, friend. Not only appetite, but also pride and selfishness and presumption. That's the kind of victory that Jesus won for us in the wilderness. That's the kind of life He lived—so that He could live it again in us, at our request.

I think you can see now that if Jesus had failed in the wilderness, there would not have been any point in going on to Gethsemane and the cross. For what a tragedy it would be to buy us back from the enemy, to pay the ransom with His own blood, and then leave us sinners still—still captive, still under enemy control, as helpless and hopeless and unfit for heaven as before!

I keep remembering a story that comes from those dark days of American history when men and women were bought and sold. A slave was about to be sold on the auction block.

This huge specimen of a man stood in chains cursing those who were bidding for his life. At the far corner of the crowd a little white-haired gentleman outbid the others. The sale was completed. The purchase price was paid, and the slave was led to his new master.

In angry tones the slave cursed the white-haired man. He swore that he would never work. He taunted his new master for spending so much money on him.

Then, with quiet patience, the buyer took the papers and handed them to the slave. "I bought you," he said, "so I could set you free."

It took a long moment for the truth to dawn on the slave's darkened mind. And then that huge frame dropped to the feet of his benefactor. He sobbed out his heart, "Sir, I will serve you till my dying day!"

That's the way it's been with some of us. We've rejected Jesus, taunted Him, laughed at Him, even cursed Him. And then, when finally we realized that He paid for us with His own blood, we fell at His feet and promised to love and serve Him forever. And we meant it.

But something has gone wrong. We've failed again and again. Somehow we've been unable to keep our high resolve. And some decide that the Saviour who bought us *isn't able to set us free*.

But thank God it isn't true! He is able to keep us from falling. See Jude 24. He is able to save to the uttermost. See Hebrews 7:25. And when the Son sets us free, we are free indeed! See John 8:36.

Jesus paid it all at Calvary. But He carried with Him from the wilderness the papers that set us free!

The Ragtag and Bobtail

In the early days of Christianity the pagan critic Celsus jeered at Jesus. Scornfully he called Him the strangest of teachers. Why? Because "while all the others cry, 'Come to me, you who are clean and worthy,' this singular Master calls, 'Come to me, you who are down and beaten by life'; and so, being taken at his word by these impossible people, he is followed about by the ragtag and bobtail of humanity trailing behind him."

To this the Christian scholar Origen gave a devastating reply. "Yes," he said, "but he does not leave them the ragtag and bobtail of humanity; but out of material you would have thrown away as useless, he fashions men, giving them back their self-respect, enabling them to stand up on their feet and look God in the eyes. They were cowed, cringing, broken things. But the Son has made them free."

Have you ever noticed—and of course you have—that sometimes the people hardest to have around are those who have never sinned? At least they have never acknowledged any imperfection. The Bible says that "all have sinned" (Romans 3:23). But there are those who consider themselves exceptions to the rule.

People are supposed to be good. Right? Then how is it that some saints are so hard to live with? How is it that so many obviously good people seem to have been washed—but certainly not ironed? Have you ever been guilty of thinking you would rather have some terrorist as a neighbor in heaven than your Aunt Kate?

How is it that Jesus—though He was perfect, though He was divine—was so comfortable to be around, so easy to live with? How is it that the worst of sinners found in Him an understanding Friend? Yet the religious leaders of His day, with their rigid and picky man-made requirements, with their frowns of disapproval, made the people tense and fearful.

The answer is that Jesus loved sinners, even those whom

others considered the ragtag and bobtail—the riffraff, the rabble. He ate with them, comforted them, healed them, lifted them up. The one class that He could not tolerate were those who considered themselves to be without sin. They were the ones He could never reach. He loved them, but they did not want to be loved. He wanted to save them. But they were offended by any suggestion that they needed saving.

Jesus had "not come to call the righteous, but sinners to repentance." Matthew 9:13, KJV. He had come "into the world to save sinners." 1 Timothy 1:15, KJV. And only sinners need apply!

Does all this mean that Jesus was slightly soft on sin? No. Never. It means, rather, that He had the remarkable and priceless ability to hate sin and love the sinner—at the same time. He managed to be on the side of the sinner without ever once condoning his sin.

A woman was dragged unceremoniously into His presence one day as He was teaching. She had been caught in the act of adultery, her accusers said. Should she be stoned as specified in the law of Moses? They pretended to want His counsel. But under the pretense was a carefully laid plot. If He said she *should not* be stoned, they would accuse Him of forsaking the law of Moses. And if He said she *should* be stoned, they would report Him to the Roman authorities. For the Romans, you see, didn't want the Jews playing around with capital punishment.

Jesus saw through the trap they had set. He appeared to ignore their question. He stooped down and began to write with His finger in the dust at His feet—as if He had not heard them. And this angered them. They didn't like to be ignored.

They moved closer, pressing Him for an answer. And then, looking down, they read what He was writing. And they were stunned. Could it be? Could it be that there, traced before them in the dust, were the guilty secrets of their own lives?

"All right," He challenged, "hurl the stones. But only he who has never sinned should throw the first stone!" And He went on writing.

Did Jesus know that her accusers were the very ones who had led her into sin? I believe He did. No wonder they disappeared. Fearful that the curious crowd would look over their shoulders and read what was written in the dust, they just slipped silently away, leaving the woman alone with Jesus.

Paralyzed with shame and fear, expecting that first stone to strike at any moment, she had been afraid to look up. But now she heard the gentle voice of Jesus. "Where are your accusers? Didn't even one of them condemn you?"

"No, sir," she replied.

And then came the most beautiful words she had ever heard. "Neither do I condemn you. Go and sin no more."

Jesus had the perfect opportunity to indulge in a cross examination and lecture that she would never forget. But He didn't. Rather, He sought to cover her embarrassment and her shame. He said only, "Go and sin no more." And that was enough. She knew He wasn't soft on sin. But she knew, too, that she had found an understanding Friend. Is it any wonder that she would love Him forever?

Yes, it was the hypocritical accusers, not the victim, that went away from that encounter embarrassed and licking their wounds.

Jesus had come "to heal the brokenhearted" (Luke 4:18, KJV), not to create new hurts. He was always sensitive to the feelings of others. He never needlessly embarrassed anyone or exposed a guilty one publicly. Not even Judas. Again and again He could have exposed the evil intentions of the one who would betray him. Instead He tried to love him away from his terrible deed.

Barbara Walters was interviewing Patty Hearst for television. Patty Hearst. Kidnapped at the age of nineteen. A girl who "had never had anything bad happen" to her. Locked in a closet, blindfolded, for fifty-seven days. Tortured, interrogated, raped. Repeatedly threatened with death. Forced to rob a bank. Now a criminal wanted by the FBI. Convinced that her parents had abandoned her, that they would never have anything to do with her, that she could never go home again. Convinced that this was the end, that she was finished, that she might as well give up and join her captors. Convinced that the FBI would shoot her on sight—or if they didn't her SLA companions would. So convinced, so desperately convinced, that when she had opportunity after opportunity to escape, the thought never entered her mind to try!

Barbara Walters, relentless reporter that she is, pressed the questions closer and closer—at times almost mercilessly, it seemed. "Why did you give up?" "Why didn't you say, 'I don't want to make that tape'?" "Why did you behave that way?" "You had many opportunities to escape. . . . Why didn't you?" "You were alone for several days. . . . You could have picked up the phone and called your folks. Why didn't you do that?"

"It never crossed my mind."

And we can't understand. We can't understand why someone does not do what we think we would have done. We are so sure that in similar circumstances we would have grabbed a phone in seconds, or let out a bloodcurdling scream that could be heard for blocks, or raced to the nearest police officer. And we are certain that once we were free, in the friendly hands of police, we wouldn't have clenched our fists in a gesture of loyalty to the revolution and given our occupation as "urban guerrilla." It wouldn't have taken us a week to realize that we "didn't have to say those things anymore" in order to survive. We are so good at asking questions—and measuring the answers by our own "un-kidnapped" thinking.

But Jesus understands. He understands the kidnap victim. He understands the sinner. He understands you and me.

Think for a moment of the embarrassing questions that Jesus could ask *us*—if He were a reporter! But He doesn't. He isn't like that!

Come with me back to the day when Jesus sat beside a well at noon—tired and thirsty. A woman came with her waterpot to draw water. And Jesus asked her for a drink.

A Jew? Asking a Samaritan for a drink? She was shocked that a Jew would even speak to her!

But Jesus knew that she was far thirstier than He. He knew that she had been drinking from polluted wells, disappointing wells. And He said to her, in a voice filled with a sympathy and tenderness she had never known, "If you knew the gift of God and who it is that asks you for a drink, you would have asked him and he would have given you living water." John 4:10, NIV.

She wanted that living water. And Jesus told her to go and call her husband and come back.

"I have no husband," she replied. And Jesus told her that she had had five husbands, and that the man with whom she was now living was not her husband.

Startled, she tried to change the subject. And who wouldn't? For she realized that she was in the presence of One who knew everything about her. Yet He still wanted to give her living water. Could He possibly be the promised Messiah? And Jesus told her, "I who speak to you am he." Verse 26, NIV.

She was so excited that she forgot her waterpot, forgot to give Jesus a drink, and rushed back to the city, telling everyone she met, "Come, see a man who told me everything I ever did. Could this be the Christ?" Verse 29, NIV.

Jesus had told her to call her husband, but she called everybody she knew. The Saviour looked out across the fields and there they came! The plumber. The ditchdigger. The banker. The landlord. The tenant. The doctor. The neighbor. The friend. The uncle. The brother-in-law. The fields were white with the robes of Samaritans coming to see a Man. And Jesus was glad. Because He knew how much they needed living water!

What a lecture Jesus could have given to a woman with a past like hers! What scathing denunciations could have fallen from His lips! He could have pressed the embarrassing questions mercilessly. But no one would have come back across the fields to see the Man!

Friend, I want to echo the words of that Samaritan woman, "Come, see a Man! Leave your disappointing wells that never satisfy. Stop trying to dig your own wells. Digging is thirsty work. Come and meet Jesus. Come and drink. And you need never thirst again!"

San Francisco and the East Bay were in the grip of a heat wave. And it was camp meeting time. In those days everyone lived and cooked and slept in tents at camp meeting. And tents were stifling in the heat. Even so, the campers had crowded into the big pavilion to hear one of their favorite speakers—Pastor Luther Warren. Among them was a mother with two small children. And of course they were restless.

Finally the charming little two-year-old fell asleep in her mother's arms. The older child was blue-eyed with slightly curling blond hair. The mother was eager to hear the message and tried patiently to help the child at her side sit quietly. But it was so hot, and the folding chair was so hard. Soon came the inevitable request—a drink of water.

The mother waited, reluctant to disturb the sleeping child. Then suddenly the little girl pointed vaguely in some direction. "There's a man over there who has a drink of water!"

In those days it was not dangerous for a child to ask a stranger for a drink—especially at camp meeting. The mother gave her permission, telling the little girl to be sure to come back right away. Then she settled back and relaxed. Maybe now she could listen to the message.

Suddenly, with unbelieving eyes, she saw her small daughter walk right up on the platform and ask the speaker for a drink! She sat transfixed as she saw Pastor Warren stop and pour a glass of cold water from the pitcher that had been placed on the desk. And the child expressed her thanks by lifting her blue eyes to gaze into his.

If you ever knew Luther Warren, you would know that he didn't mind the interruption a bit. Instead, it gave him the perfect opportunity to talk about cool, invigorating, living water—on a hot, thirsty day.

Look, friend! There's a Man over there on that cross who has a drink of water! Living water! And you can walk right up to Him and ask Him for a drink. He won't mind being interrupted!

Jesus was dying that Friday afternoon. The guilt of the world's sin was crushing out His life. In all history there had never been a more important moment. And the thief on the cross beside Him interrupted His dying with a request.

What happened? The whole plan of salvation stopped and waited while Jesus answered the prayer of the repentant thief!

He will stop to answer *you*—any time! You can walk right up and ask Him for a drink—and never thirst again! You can ask Him now!

The Thunder and the Smoke

A friend of mine, Donald John, tells of a rather violent hail-storm that bombarded his neighborhood one day. It sounded, he said, as if thousands of good-sized ball bearings were being pelted against a metal roof. When the storm had passed he looked out to see what damage had been done. Leaves and small branches had been ripped off the trees, and the delightful autumn-colored foliage on the bushes by the door now lay strewn on the ground.

At that point his little four-year-old daughter slipped up beside him and asked timidly, "Who delivered this to us?"

He didn't know what she meant. Was it the hail that she didn't understand? But she repeated her question and this time amplified it a bit. "Who delivered that stuff? Jesus or God?"

When asked to explain, she answered without hesitation, "I mean, Jesus is too nice to do things like that. It was probably God!"

There, in the mind of a four-year-old, was the question that has puzzled millions. How is it that Jesus seems to be so much nicer than God?

Jesus, the Friend of sinners. Jesus, who went about healing the people. Jesus, who gave children free access to Him. Jesus, who couldn't bear to see people hurting and not do anything about it.

James and John, two of His closest friends, wanted to call down fire from heaven to punish some Samaritans who refused to welcome Jesus to their village. But Jesus said, "The Son of man is not come to destroy men's lives, but to save them." Luke 9:56, KJV.

But the God of the Old Testament seems far different. We see Him destroying almost the entire human race in a global flood. We see Him raining fire and brimstone on the cities of Sodom and Gomorrah. We see Him sending terrible judgments on Egypt when its stubborn king refused to let God's people go. We see Him coming down on Mount Sinai—setting it smoking, speaking in a voice like thunder that frightened the people out of their wits. Repeatedly we read of war and bloodshed—apparently at God's command.

The picture becomes still more puzzling when we realize that one of the main reasons Jesus came to this planet was to correct its impression of what God was like. He came at a time when the world was dark with misapprehension of the character of God. Satan had horribly succeeded in marketing his picture of God as a harsh and cruel tyrant—One who stood with a big stick, just waiting for people to do something a little bit wrong so He could dump a big bag of calamities on their heads.

Jesus came to correct that impression, to show us what His Father is really like. He said to Philip, one of His men, "Anyone who has seen me has seen the Father." John 14:9, NIV.

We picture Jesus seated in a garden, with children crowded around Him, one or two on His lap, apparently all happy and content in His presence. Would the Father be like that? Evidently.

From childhood we are taught to repeat the words, "God so loved the world, that he gave his only begotten Son." Somehow we grasp, or try to grasp, the fact that Jesus was willing to come and die in our place. But those familiar words of John 3:16 say that it was *God* who loved us enough to let Him do it!

Evidently the Father loved us too. Evidently He, too, carried Calvary in His heart through the long centuries before Bethlehem. Evidently, though silent and unseen, hidden by the darkness of that terrible Friday—evidently the Father suffered all the agony of the cross along with His Son!

Why, then, do we see such a difference between the God of the Old Testament and the Jesus of the New?

The gentle Jesus, Or the God of the thunder and the smoke. Which is the real God? Have you ever felt like asking, "Will the real God please stand up"? If you haven't, then you're an exception!

We try to soften the picture with our children. We tell them about the baby Jesus, Jesus with the children, Jesus rocking in a boat on Galilee, Jesus who wants us to be a sunbeam. In the Old Testament we tell them about the baby Moses hidden in a basket in the river and discovered by a princess. We tell them about Joseph being sold by his brothers. We tell them about the boy Samuel hearing the voice of God speaking to him in the night and thinking it was Eli calling him.

But our children grow up and read the Bible itself—not just stories *about* the Bible. They discover that the baby Moses grew up and killed a man. And the boy Samuel—that's a real shocker. For they discover that Samuel not only killed a man but cut him in pieces. See 1 Samuel 15:33.

How will our children handle these problems? How will we handle them? How will we explain what we read in the Old Testament—the violence, the wars, the swords dripping with blood?

First of all, the Bible, even with its heroes, does not gloss over the facts. Moses sinned in killing the Egyptian and was forced to flee for his life because of his act. It is to the credit of the Bible writers, and adds to the reliability of their accounts, that they made no attempt to hide, to cover up the sins of those whose lives they recorded.

In the case of Samuel, the context of the entire chapter (1 Samuel 15) will put the matter in a different light. It was God, not Samuel, who had ordered the destruction of the wicked king.

You see, in Old Testament times the people of Israel were a theocracy, a nation ruled directly by God. It was God who made the decisions, not some politician or group of politicians. And God makes no mistakes. When God ordered the destruction of a nation it was because that nation had filled up its cup of evil. It was only after God had done everything possible to save it from such an end.

But add this to your thinking about wars in Old Testament times. It was the people, not God, who thought they had to have weapons to drive out the nations that occupied the promised land. God's plan, believe it or not, was to drive them out with hornets! See Exodus 23:28. And I happen to believe that God's plan would have been very effective!

Now I don't like hornets any better than you do. I've had an encounter or two with them. But what a load of fear and apprehension would be lifted from this world today if it were only the threat of hornets hanging over our heads—instead of splitting atoms!

Remember, it was God who made the atom. But it was man who split it. Man, not God, has put terror into the winds that circle this planet!

And now we come to something else that will help us understand why the God of the Old Testament sometimes comes through to us as harsh, almost cruel. It's the same God. The love was there all the time. But the circumstances were far different from those familiar to you and me. Love prefers to speak softly. True. But, when children are playing in the streets, or reaching for razor blades, love must shout. There are times when love must be firm. And this was one of those times.

You see, the people that God led out of Egypt and through the Red Sea were a people who for generations had been oppressed by slavery. God cared for them tenderly, supplied their every need, protected them from their enemies and from illness, and worked spectacular miracles, time after time, to show them that they could trust Him. You would expect their hearts to be indelibly impressed by His incredible love. You would expect them to be fiercely and forever loyal to the One who had done so much for them.

Instead they were quick to complain, quick to blame both God and Moses for any hardship, quick to turn to the worship of other gods, ready at the drop of a hat to return to Egypt and hopeless slavery.

The lash of the whip and the slavemaster's curse had effectively choked out the language of love. How could God communicate at all with this unruly band of ex-slaves? The thunder and the smoke were necessary—and sometimes the sword. For these were the only language they understood. The thunders of Sinai may have drowned out the tears in His voice. But down in the valley, there on the plain below Sinai, was a preview of Calvary to be repeated daily—while God patiently waited for the day when, on a rough, splintery cross, He could demonstrate His incredible love in a way that even slaves could understand!

God, through the centuries, has had to deal with people where He found them. He has had to communicate with people as they were, not as He wished they were. He could not wait for perfect people, or perfect circumstances, before calling men to His side. He called men out of cultures where multiple wives were the order of the day. This does not mean that God condoned polygamy. Abraham lied. He said his wife was his sister. Isaac did the same thing. Jacob obtained the coveted birthright by claiming to be his brother Esau. This does not mean that God condones lying. He takes men where He finds them—and leads them as far as He can toward the ideal.

Slavery was common in Bible times. Yet, the Bible makes no tirade against it. Nor did Jesus. He had not come to make political or social reforms. He had come to change the hearts of men. The Bible principles, if followed, would certainly bring an end to slavery. But in the meantime slaves are encouraged to obey their masters, and masters are urged to be kind to their servants. See Ephesians 6:5–9. It is interesting that the apostle Paul sent a runaway slave back to his master—and wrote to the master, urging that he receive him kindly and treat him as a Christian brother.

Through all this, as we seek to understand the rather puzzling picture of God that we find in the Old Testament, in contrast to the New, it may come as a surprise to you, as it did to me, that Satan is seldom mentioned by name in the Old Testament. This seems strange. In the third chapter of Genesis he is simply called a serpent—the disguise which he assumed in his encounter with Eve. It is in the New Testament, in the book of Revelation, that we are told that the serpent and Satan are one and the same being. In the New Testament Satan is frequently mentioned by name.

In the experience of the ancient Job, however—the devoted worshiper of God who suddenly, without explanation, lost all his possessions and all his family except for his wife, and then was afflicted with boils all over his body—in that experience, Satan is repeatedly mentioned by name. Read the story again, even if you have read it before, in the first two chapters of Job. It will do you good.

There, in the story of Job, we are taken behind the scenes and shown one particular encounter in the ongoing controversy between Christ and Satan. Though we see clearly that it was Satan, not God, who brought all the calamities, Job did not have this insight. The book of Job had not been written! He never was taken behind the scenes. He didn't know what was going on. He thought that God was his tormentor. But, to his credit, he said of God, "Though he slay me, yet will I trust in him," Job 13:15, KJV.

Why didn't God explain to Job what was going on behind the scenes—at least after the test was over? Why is it that all through the Old Testament we run across statements that make it appear that God is the author of trouble, that He sends evil to men? It is true that nothing can touch us without God's permission. But it is more than that. God, in the Old Testament, seems to be deliberately accepting responsibility for evil, rather than placing the blame where it belongs. In the New Testament it is clear enough. Why not in the Old? Why didn't God step out on a cloud and say, "Look! I didn't do this to you! Satan did it"?

Alden Thompson, who has carefully studied this problem, suggests a possible reason. The Old Testament world was riddled with the worship of other gods. Strange gods. Heathen gods. Counterfeit gods. Gods everywhere. Gods that were good and gods that were evil. Gods that had to be kept happy or they would surely shower trouble on the heads of the people.

If God had identified Satan as the troublemaker, even God's own people, in their ignorance, might have been tempted to worship Satan as another god that must be reckoned with if they wanted to escape his calamities. And God didn't want that to happen. Rather than take that risk, I believe He chose to temporarily accept the responsibility for that which was far from the intent of His heart of love.

And if this seems strange, remember that Jesus, the Lamb of God, in the most incredible act of all eternity, would carry the sins of the whole world on Calvary as if they were His own. He would let the weight of them, the guilt of them, crush out His life. He would take the blame for them all—when not a single one was His own. That's the way Jesus is!

And that's the way God is. The love may not seem so obvious in the Old Testament. But it is there. You will find it if you look.

And now, as we move in to focus more closely on the cross, remember that Calvary was the act, the free choice, of both the Father and the Son. There is no way to separate the love of One from the love of the Other. Jesus, the ultimate demonstration of love, is called "the Lamb slain from the foundation of the world" (Revelation 13:8, KJV). But, the plan to save man was made with the Father's full consent and deepest involvement. Calvary was His act, His choice, His love, and His sacrifice—too!

The God of Sinai, of thunder and smoke, is the God of Golgotha!

Section Five
The Foolishness of Golgotha

The Foolishness of Golgotha
Identity Crisis

The Foolishness of Golgotha

God has some strange ways of doing things. His ways of fighting wars, of resolving conflicts, seem peculiar, even bizarre. There isn't an army general alive who would approve His strategy.

Imagine, if you can, that you are a watchman atop the wall of the ancient city of Jericho. And one day an army of six hundred thousand ex-slaves approaches. You smile at the idea of Jericho ever falling into *their* hands. This is going to be interesting!

So what happens? A strange procession begins to circle the city. First a company of selected warriors. Then seven priests with trumpets. Next priests in their sacred dress, bearing on their shoulders a golden chest. Then the entire army of Israel. See Joshua 6.

There is no sound except the mighty tread of marching feet— and the solemn peal of the trumpets, echoing among the hills and sounding through the streets of Jericho. Once around the city, and the army returns silently to their tents. What is going on?

The same thing happens the next day, and the next. There is something mysterious about this, something even terrifying. What can it mean? You remember that the Red Sea parted before these people and that a passage has just been made for them through the Jordan River at flood stage. And the Jordan is too close for comfort. What might the God of the Hebrews do next?

For six days a single circuit of the city is made once each day. Nothing more. On the morning of the seventh day of the siege something happens that is strange and foreboding. The army does not withdraw after a single circuit of the city. It continues a second time around, and a third, and a fourth. Six times around. What will happen now? What mighty event is impending?

You have not long to wait. As the seventh circuit of the city is completed, the army pauses. The trumpets have been silent for a time, but now they break forth in a blast that shakes the very earth. The walls, with their massive towers, teeter and heave, and crash to the earth. And you can be glad that you were atop that wall only in imagination!

What a way to take a city! What a seemingly ridiculous way! Just march around it and blow trumpets! But it worked!

In the days of Jehoshaphat, king of Judah, something equally strange happened. His country was invaded by an army that would make anyone tremble. But the king, with God's encouragement, put a band of singers at the head of his army, and sent them out praising God for victory!

Who ever heard of sending a choir out at the head of the army? Isn't that a little too much? But again, it worked! When the invaders heard the singers claiming victory, they were so frightened and confused that they simply turned on each other, destroying themselves!

Then there was Gideon. He had an army of 32,000 men. God told him that was too many. So Gideon kept sending men home till he had only three hundred left. These three hundred, at God's direction, were divided into three companies. Each man was given a trumpet and also a torch which was concealed in an earthen pitcher. The three companies approached the enemy camp from different directions. In the dead of night, on signal from Gideon's war horn, every trumpet was sounded. And then, breaking their pitchers so that the blazing torches were displayed, they rushed upon the enemy with the cry, "The sword of the Lord, and of Gideon!"

Suddenly roused from sleep, the enemy soldiers saw flaming torches on every side. From every direction came the sound of the trumpets and the cry of Gideon's men. Thinking they were being attacked by an overwhelming force, the Midianites became panic-stricken. Fleeing for their lives, they mistook their own countrymen for enemies and destroyed one another!

What strange ways of fighting! Blowing trumpets! Breaking pitchers! Shouting!

Why such unconventional methods? We find the answer in the directions God gave to Gideon. Listen: "And the Lord said to Gideon, 'The people who are with you are too many for Me to give Midian into their hands, lest Israel become boastful, saying, "My own power has delivered me." ' " Judges 7:2, NASB.

Do you see? God works in ways so simple, so seemingly ridiculous, so lacking in potential, so unlikely to produce results—He does this so that we can never say, We did it ourselves!

Yes, again and again it has happened. Time after time, by doing that which appeared not very smart, God has made it plain that there is no way man could have done it. He Himself has been at work!

So, when God, back in eternity, was confronted with the greatest crisis of all—the entrance of sin into His perfect universe—it is no wonder that He did not meet it in the way we might expect.

Here was a conflict involving not a single world, but the entire universe. God's character had been called in question. God Himself was on trial. His government had been challenged. The fate of all God's creation was at stake!

How would God respond? With massive force? With His superior power? Would He extinguish rebellion with one great mushroom cloud? No. God made His decision. *He would fight rebellion with a cross!*

A strange plan? Yes. And some have called it foolish!

This Jesus, from the day He arrived on this planet, seemed to violate all the rules of getting ahead. Born in a manger. Brought up in poverty. He never wrote a book. He never led an army or a protest march or a revolt or a revolution. He never enrolled in the schools considered best. He was forever at odds with the doctors of religion. He bypassed the students of Plato and Aristotle and selected uneducated fishermen as His helpers, choosing "the foolish things of the world to confound the wise; and . . . the weak things of the world to confound the things which are mighty." 1 Corinthians 1:27, KJV.

Jesus could have led a revolt against Rome. Such a move would have meant instant popularity with those who instead became His enemies. With His power to work miracles Rome wouldn't have had a chance. And think of the advantage to an army led by One who could feed all His soldiers with a little boy's lunch!

He could easily have taken the throne of David—if He had played it right. But He seemed to miss all the cues. He appeared to have no sense of timing. When the tide of public opinion had turned His way and the people were ready to make Him king, He sent the crowd home and went off into the mountain to pray. Judas was not the only one who thought He would have to get His cues better than that!

The hopes of His followers reached a peak once more on the Sunday He rode triumphantly into Jerusalem, accompanied by the waving of palm branches and the shouting of His praise. Surely He was about to assume power!

But only days later He let His enemies lead Him out of the city to a place called Golgotha. He let them put Him on a rough, splintery cross without a word of protest—and prayed for those who drove the spikes into His hands.

Not one in that crowd knew what was happening that day. Not His enemies. Not His friends—especially His friends. They knew He could deliver Himself from His enemies. They had seen Him do it before. They knew He could come down from the cross at any moment, if He chose. Why didn't He? Why was He letting Himself die? They couldn't understand.

Little did they know that what was happening was no accident. Little did they know that Jesus, according to plan, was dying in man's place. He was dying the death that sinners who reject His sacrifice must finally die. And that is not the ordinary death we all must die. It is not the death of one surrounded by friends and loved ones in his final hours. It is not the death of one attended by nurses who hold a glass of cold water to his parched lips. It is not the death of a martyr who looks into heaven as Stephen did and sees the Saviour standing over him in sympathy and love. It is not the death of the Christian who is sustained by the hope of the resurrection. In the death we are talking about there is total, complete, and final separation from God!

Jesus, there on the cross, His agony mercifully veiled by darkness, was dying the death that sinners must die. He was experiencing a rendezvous with the terrors of hell itself!

What do I mean? Simply this. Hell, when it happens, will be very, very real. The flames will be hot. But the flames will not be the worst of it. Hell's worst terror will be in the hours that precede the fire. It is knowing that the decisions of this life have been final, that it is too late to reverse them. It is seeing the glory of the City of God—and being forever shut out. It is the awful realization of what might have been, but now can never be. It is the terror of separation from God, separation from the Source of life. It is a death that will have no morning. The flames will be a quick and merciful end to the terrors of hell.

But did Jesus experience all this? Didn't He know all the time that He would be resurrected?

No. Not all the time. It is true that on several occasions He had said He would rise again. He knew it then. But that was while He was sustained by His Father's presence. As He hung there in the darkness that Friday, His Father's presence had been completely withdrawn. Not because the Father didn't care. The Father, unseen, was suffering along with His Son. But Jesus was bearing the crushing, stifling guilt of all the world. He who had no sin of His own had identified Himself with our sins, with everybody's sins, as if they were His. And there must be a gulf between God and sin. The sinner, dying his final death, will not be sustained by the Father's presence. Nor could Jesus, dying in our place. He must die alone.

The sinner must die without hope of living again. So must Jesus. He must experience that too. And He did. For as His Father's presence was completely withdrawn, He was seized by the fear that sin, the sin He was bearing for others, might be so offensive to His Father that the separation would be eternal. In those awful moments He could see no light beyond the tomb!

All the while Satan was whispering his vicious temptations with hypocritical sympathy. "You'll never see Your Father again! No one will be saved. You've wasted all these years. Even Your friends have forsaken You. Why don't You let men pay for their own sins?"

Every labored breath was drawing the Saviour nearer to what He thought might be eternal death. But He never wavered in His decision. He was willing to stay in the tomb forever—if only one, if only *you*, could be saved. That's how much He cared!

So fierce was the battle that Jesus was hardly aware of what was going on below the cross. His tormentors were looking on in compassionless scorn, and saying, "He saved others; himself he cannot save." Matthew 27:42. And Roman soldiers were playing their games of dice, unaware that the contest of the ages was going on above them.

That contest was decided not in the light of His Father's presence and approval, but in the long shadow of death—a shadow His eye could not penetrate, until the very last. It was only in His final moments that His faith broke through the darkness and He knew that He had won. Studdert-Kennedy said it so well!

> And sitting down they watched Him there,
> The soldiers did.
> There, while they played with dice,
> He made His sacrifice,
> And died upon the cross to rid
> God's world of sin.
>
> He was a gambler, too, my Christ.
> He took His life and threw
> It for a world redeemed.
> And ere His agony was done,
> Before the westering sun went down,
> Crowning that day with crimson crown,
> He knew that He had won!

Yes, what happened that day at Golgotha looked like foolishness to ambitious men. The apostle Paul would say, "We preach Christ crucified, unto the Jews a stumblingblock, and unto the Greeks foolishness." 1 Corinthians 1:23.

The foolishness of Golgotha. Sheer nonsense to those who do not understand. But God knew what He was doing. What appeared to be a terrible mistake was the most brilliant move Love could make. And what looked like ignominious defeat turned out to be Love's finest hour!

Identity Crisis

The story is told of an airline pilot assigned to international flights. Since he had five days off between work assignments, he had time for other interests and purchased a small service station.

One day, in need of some small item, he dropped in at the hardware store up the street. His purchase made, he stopped to chat about something of interest on his last flight overseas.

When he had gone, another customer asked, "Who is that man?"

And the owner replied, "Oh, he has a service station down the street here." And then with a smile, "He thinks he's an airline pilot!"

Most of us have only indulgent smiles and little compassion for the man who is confused about his own identity. We put him in what we consider to be an appropriate pigeonhole, along with the man who thinks he's Napoleon, and go on our way. But sometimes we are the ones confused, and we make some embarrassing mistakes.

It was no different in the days of Jesus. Some thought *He* was confused. Others wrote Him off as an impostor, even a blasphemer—for Jesus did claim to be God. But the matter of His true identity refused to be put to rest. For what if He was telling the truth? What if He really was God? Even His enemies could not quiet the conviction that it was they who were wrong. And it haunted them.

They asked Him right out one day, "Who are you, anyway?"

And Jesus said, "When you have lifted up the Son of Man, then you will know who I am." John 8:28, NIV.

"When you have lifted Me up. When you have crucified Me. When you have scorned Me and mocked Me and laughed at Me. When you have driven spikes into My hands. When you have hung Me between heaven and earth on a despised Roman cross and dared Me to come down if I could. When you have left Me to die without even a drink of cold water. *Then* you will know who I am!"

There He was—alone—dying. Once—yes, twice—a Voice from heaven had acknowledged Him as His Son. But now there was no voice. All was silent—except for the taunts of the mob and the angry sounds of an offended creation. Who was this Man, this compassionate Healer, this beloved Teacher? What had He done that Heaven now refused to defend Him? What crime was His that even nature was punishing Him with its fiery darts? Who was He, anyway?

Was this a man—just a good man—the best man who ever lived—dying as a passive victim in the hands of wicked men? Or was it incarnate God paying the price for a lost race being weighed in the balance?

Never forget it! If He were only a man, we are describing murder. If He was God, we are describing an Offering. If He was only a man, we are witnessing a martyr. If He was God, we are witnessing a Sacrifice!

The thief on the cross beside Him knew who He was. He knew that his own moments of grace were fast slipping away. And he broke the awesome silence with the prayer, "Lord, remember me when You come into Your kingdom!"

Jesus was busy dying. Would He have any word for a thief who was dying too? Time seemed to stand still as heaven and earth waited for the Saviour's reply. "I say unto you today—today when all have forsaken Me, today when it looks as if I shall never have a kingdom—I say unto you today, You will be with Me in paradise."

The Roman centurion knew who He was. He sensed that this was no ordinary crucifixion. And when Jesus had breathed His last tortured breath, he said with conviction, caring not for the scoffing crowd, "Surely this was the Son of God!"

The enemies of Jesus knew more than they wished they knew. They had prodded Him to tell them who He was—not because they wanted to know, but because they wanted to trap Him. They desired only to be rid of Him. They couldn't bear the presence of One so pure, so untainted that their own hypocritical characters looked blacker than black. Jesus must go!

But when they had killed Him, when they had accomplished

their foul deed, satisfaction escaped them. Their crime brought no sweetness at the end of the day. They feared the dead Christ more than the living Christ!

The haughty Caiaphas knew who He was. He had demanded of Jesus, "Tell us if you are the Christ, the Son of God." And Jesus had told him plainly, "Yes, it is as you say." No wonder the wily ruler would turn pale as death when he learned from the Roman guard that Jesus had walked out of the tomb!

And Pilate knew. He found no fault in Jesus. He longed to save Him from His conspiring enemies. He tried to wash the guilt from his hands. But he couldn't. To the day of his death he would live in fear of the One he ordered scourged and sent off to be crucified. Even in the supposed security of the palace, how could he be sure that the risen Jesus would not suddenly confront him and demand a reckoning?

Yes, they had prodded Him—"Who are You, anyway?" And Jesus had told them, "When you have lifted Me up, then you will know who I am."

Among those who watched Him die that dark Friday were some who never slept till they had determined from the Scriptures who He was. And many a conscience was tortured with guilt—the guilt of having joined in the cruel cry of the crowd, "Crucify Him! Crucify Him!"

Picture it if you can—a man caught up in the crowd, a man who has watched about the cross, a man who has seen and heard strange things that day—frightening things.

The crowd has dispersed now, and he makes his way home alone. His accusing conscience is haunting him. Why has he done what he did? Why did he allow himself to join the crazed mob in calling for the death of a Man who has done him no wrong—a Man whom Pilate declared to be innocent? He hopes to find peace, relief from his guilt, within the walls of home. But what happens when he steps across his own threshold? The poet tells it:

> His son—the idol of his heart—lies ill.
>   They weep beside his bed.
> One hope is left—the Man of Nazareth will heal.
>   They know not He is dead!

His son's parched lips—he sees them moving now,
"Please take me right away."
How can he tell him—cold and guilty words—
"I crucified Him, son, today!"

Fifty long days passed. Truth and rumor, side by side, passed through the land—adding to, or detracting from the turmoil in the hearts of men. One question, above every other, demanded to be settled—*the identity of Jesus of Nazareth, Jesus the Crucified.*

Then came Pentecost. And Peter stood up to speak. Peter, the disciple who had run away. Peter who swore he didn't know Jesus. Peter who cursed rather than be identified with Him.

But something has happened to Peter. Boldly, without fear, and with the enemies of Jesus listening, He says, "Therefore let all Israel be assured of this: God has made this Jesus, whom you crucified, both Lord and Christ." Acts 2:36, NIV.

Think of it! What fearlessness! "This Jesus, whom you crucified! The One you crucified is the Son of God!"

And what happened? How did the crowd respond? Did they turn upon Peter? No. "When the people heard this, they were cut to the heart and said to Peter and the other apostles, 'Brothers, what shall we do?' "

Three thousand were converted that day. Three thousand fell at the feet of the Crucified One and found healing for their guilt!

"This Jesus, whom you crucified." This was the message of the early church. This was its power!

We say, We didn't do it. We didn't crucify Him. It was Pilate who did it. It was Judas. It was the Roman soldiers. We weren't there. We are not to blame!

But Jesus didn't die from nail wounds. It wasn't the pain of the spikes that killed Him. He died of a broken heart—from the weight of the sins that He carried with Him to the cross.

And listen! If our sins—yours and mine—weren't included, if it was not our sins, too, that crushed out His life, then how can we say that Jesus paid the penalty for our sins? And if they *were* included, then you and I are guilty, too, of crucifying Jesus. Our fingerprints are on the nails!"

Cyril J. Davey tells the story of Sundar Singh, a boy of India. He was almost fourteen when his mother died and his world collapsed. He was desolate. No one could comfort him. He knew he could not live without God. But it seemed to him that God had taken away the only person who could ever make Him real.

Sundar attended a Christian mission school—because the government school was too far away. He had always been a quiet and courteous student. But now everything changed. Now, in his grief, he became a violent young ruffian. The kindness of the teachers only infuriated him. He hated them. He hated their school. He hated their Book. And he hated their Jesus!

One day he approached one of his teachers and politely asked to buy a New Testament. Little did anyone suspect why he wanted it.

Soon he was saying to his young friends, "Come with me. You are surprised that I should buy this Book. But come home and see what I do with it! How long I shall live I cannot tell you. Not long, certainly. But before I die I will show you what I think of Jesus and His Book!"

He led the way to the courtyard of his home, brought a bundle of sticks and a tin of kerosene, and set the wood burning. Then, slowly and methodically, he tore the pages from the Book one at a time and threw them on the fire. He wanted it to be his last gesture of contempt for the Christians' Book!

Suddenly his father walked out of the house and thundered, "Are you mad, child? Are you beside yourself to burn the Christians' Book? It is a good Book—your mother has said so. And I will not have this evildoing in my house. Stop it! Do you hear? *Stop it!*"

Sundar bent down, stamped the rest of the New Testament into the flames with his foot, and went to his room without a word. He stayed there for three days and nights.

Then came the night that was to decide it all. He knew what he would do. Not far away he heard the sound of a train as it rushed toward Lahore and was gone. The next express would pass a short time later at five o'clock in the morning. And if God had not spoken to him before then, he would go out and lay his head on the rails and wait for the train from Ludhiana to Lahore to end his miserable existence.

His mind must be clear this night. He went to the bathhouse and bathed in cold water for an hour before returning to his room. It was seven hours till the express would come through.

He prayed, "Oh God—if there be a God—reveal Thyself to me before I die!"

The hours passed.

At fifteen minutes to five he rushed into his father's room and grabbed the sleeping man by the shoulder. He burst out, "I have seen Jesus!"

"You're dreaming, child," his father said. "Go back to bed."

But Sundar was not dreaming. He told how he had planned to end his life—and rushed on with his story.

"A few minutes ago," he said, "Jesus came into my room. . . . And He spoke to me. . . . He said, 'How long will you persecute Me? I have come to save you. You were praying to know the right way. Why do you not take it? I am the Way.' "

Sundar went on. "He spoke in Hindustani, and He spoke to *me*. I fell at His feet. How long I knelt I cannot say. But when I rose the vision faded. It *was* a vision. It was no thought of mine that called Him there. . . . Had it been Krishna, or one of my own gods, I might have expected it. But not Jesus!"

He paused a moment, and spoke again. "I am a Christian. I can serve no one else but Jesus!"

His father spoke sharply, "You *must* be mad. You come in the middle of the night and say you are a Christian. And yet it is not three days past that you burned the Christians' Book!"

Sundar stood rigid, looking at his hands. And then he said with deep feeling, *"These hands did it. I can never cleanse them of that sin until the day I die!"*

No wonder he loved Jesus! No wonder he preached Jesus till the day of his death! No wonder he made his way, almost every summer, into the forbidden land of Tibet, enduring the cruelest persecution. But the more he was persecuted, the happier he was that he could suffer for his Lord. From his last trip into Tibet, he never returned!

Friend, look at your hands, as I look at mine. These are the hands that crucified Jesus! And nothing but the red blood of Calvary can ever make them clean!

Here is an identity crisis that must he settled by every one of us. We need to stay with it until we know who we are—and who we are not. Are we innocent bystanders, safely separated from Calvary's guilt by two thousand years? Or are we, too, the ones who crucified our Lord? When we have looked long and honestly at the cross, we will know!

But there is hope! For when Jesus prayed, "Father, forgive them," I know He meant me! I know He meant you!

Section Six
Truth and Propaganda

What Really Happened at Calvary
The Repainting of Golgotha

What Really Happened at Calvary

We are a generation obsessed with investigations. An airliner crashes. And even before the survivors are rescued or the fatalities counted, we launch an investigation of all available facts concerning the accident. Before a highrise fire is out, we are searching for the cause.

When a public figure is assassinated or dies under mysterious circumstances, our probing of the facts is long and thorough. Many years later some are still investigating the assassination of John F. Kennedy. Millions are not satisfied yet that we know the truth. Questions are still raised about the death of Robert Kennedy in a Los Angeles hotel just at the height of his popularity. And the full extent of responsibility for the slaying of Martin Luther King is, in many minds, a matter not completely settled.

And it is good to have an inquiring mind. It is not always wise to accept the first answer that surfaces. But have you ever really investigated the death of Jesus of Nazareth? Without question it was the most mysterious death of all time. Yet it remains a mystery only casually probed. Why? Would you like to know the inside story?

Millions of pages have been written about the death of Jesus of Nazareth, and uncounted assumptions have been made. But many of us haven't the foggiest notion of what really happened that Friday in A. D. 31 on a hill outside Jerusalem. Why has not some credible investigation ever been launched—and the facts made known? Why has so much been assumed—and so little known for sure?

Was the death of Jesus an accident? Or was it planned? And if so, by whom? Why did He die? Was His death the greatest tragedy ever to involve this planet? Or was it a victory so tremendous, so complete, that it set angels singing—and spelled doom for death itself?

Could it be that the death of Jesus has startling implications for you personally—implications of which you have never dreamed?

Calvary was like a giant billboard proclaiming to all who passed by that Jesus had failed. Whatever His mission—whatever He had hoped to accomplish—it had misfired. Jesus lay dead in Joseph's new tomb. And His enemies, visible and invisible, were determined to keep Him there forever!

The disciples of Jesus, till the last, had not believed He would die. He was the Messiah. And the Messiah would not die, could not die. They had expected Him to work some miracle to save Himself from His enemies. But there had been no miracle. Jesus was dead. And as they carried His lifeless body into Joseph's tomb and left it there, their spirits plummeted into deep depression.

Hear them reasoning, "We trusted that it had been he which should have redeemed Israel." Luke 24:21, KJV. But now it seemed they had made a terrible mistake. Jesus must not be the long-awaited Saviour after all. Life seemed empty and pointless. And as the sun dipped low in the western sky, reminding them that the Sabbath was about to begin, they went into hiding, fearing that they themselves might now be on the hit list of the enemies of Jesus.

Twenty-four hours later, as the sun again dropped low in the west, signaling now the end of the Sabbath, Joseph's tomb was secured by the Roman seal, with a guard of one hundred soldiers stationed close by. Jesus was locked in His rock prison as securely as if He were to remain there till the end of time.

The long night passed slowly as the soldiers kept their careful watch. A great company of angels, unseen, waited to welcome Jesus. Satan was there, for his only hope was to keep Jesus forever in the tomb. And the host of his evil angels was there too, instructed not to give ground whatever might happen.

Suddenly the angel Gabriel, the powerful angel who took Lucifer's place, flew swiftly toward the earth. The planet trembled at his approach, and the evil angels scattered in terror. The Roman soldiers, petrified with fear, saw Gabriel remove the huge stone at the door of the tomb as if it were a pebble. They heard him cry, "Son of God, come forth! Your Father calls You!"

They saw Jesus walk out of the broken tomb and proclaim over it, "I am the resurrection and the life!" And they saw the angels bow low in adoration, welcoming their loved Commander with songs of praise. The soldiers heard and saw it all. And, no bribe could keep them from telling it! Not now!

Yes, the cross of Calvary, that dark Friday, had stood like a giant billboard of defeat. But not for long! Now Jesus of Nazareth had walked out of the tomb with the tread of a Conqueror. He had conquered death!

Jesus had not failed at all! He had accomplished His mission in every detail. But not even His own disciples understood what His mission was. He had not come to challenge Rome. He had not come to take the throne of David. He was a Man born to be crucified. He was the Lamb of God who had come to take away the sin of the world. He had come to take our sins upon Himself and die in our place, so that we could be forgiven, so that we could live. His death was not a defeat. The moment of His death marked a victory so great that it must have set the angels of heaven singing. Jesus had won!

You see, Calvary was a battlefield. It was the scene of the most crucial, the most critical, the most decisive showdown in the controversy between Christ and Satan—a controversy that began in heaven and today is moving toward its final windup. It is only in the setting of that controversy that we can begin to comprehend what really happened at Calvary. In fact, to understand that controversy is to understand the Bible. For the Bible is the story of that ongoing conflict—the story of God's plan to save men, and Satan's attempt to thwart it.

We stand in wonder at the incredible love displayed on that old rugged cross. The God-Man dying in our place. How could we live without forgiveness? We thank God that we have a risen Saviour. We rejoice that He has conquered death, that we can look forward to a resurrection morning when loved ones will be reunited, never to part again.

All this we see in that memorable weekend. *But there is more. So much more!*

What did Jesus mean when, in the last moment before He bowed His head and died—what did He mean when He cried out, "It is finished!"? Here was not the feeble groan of a sufferer. It was the cry of a Conqueror. The words were spoken in clear, trumpetlike tones that seemed to resound through creation. What did He mean? What was finished? Why had Jesus come to this planet? What was involved in His mission? Why did He have to die to save men? Was there no other way? Did His mission, and His death, involve only fallen men? Or other worlds too?

Jesus had come to earth, and He had died, to silence the charges of Satan concerning the character of God. The rebel chief had charged that God was a harsh, tyrannical Ruler who had no real love for His subjects. He claimed that he, Satan, was the only one who cared!

But you have only to look at Calvary to see who it is that cared! That cross is the ultimate demonstration of caring. And it is a demonstration that has not been lost on the watching worlds!

Jesus had come to unmask Satan before all the universe, to let the angels and the unfallen worlds see how deadly, how lethal, how ruthless sin is—to let them see how far sin would go. When the rebellion began, it had seemed incredible that something called sin could be as dangerous as God said it was.

But as they watched through the centuries, as they saw the fallen angel spreading war and destruction everywhere, leaving a trail of heartache and pain and death, they began to understand. And when they saw Satan placing his own Creator on that despised cross, there was not a trace of sympathy left for him anywhere in the universe—except on this planet.

Jesus had come to honor His Father's law, even at the cost of His own lifeblood. From the very beginning of the controversy between Christ and Satan, God's law had been the key issue. It was the issue that divided heaven. It was the issue in Eden. His first encounter on this planet was a shameless, brazen invitation to disobey God.

In the final crisis, just ahead of us, the issue will still be the law of God and its authority. For in the book of Revelation we see Satan, in these last days, angry, making war with those who keep the commands of God. "Then the dragon was enraged at the woman [the church] and went off to make war against the rest of her offspring—those who obey God's commandments and hold to the testimony of Jesus." Revelation 12:17, NIV.

Why did Jesus have to die to save men? Was there no other way? No. God's law had been broken, and the penalty was death. Someone must die.

My friend Lew Walton, a practicing attorney, has said it so well:

"The Creator was between the horns of a terrible dilemma, between His love for man and His love for truth.

"The entire universe depended upon a law He Himself had written, by which everything from worlds to atoms moved in order—a perfect law—and how does one change perfection? If He bent the divine law to accommodate even one small human challenge, He would be saying that perfection can be altered— and He would be following Lucifer straight into the valley of doom where there are no absolutes except one's own shifting wants."

Well said, wouldn't you say?

Could not the law be set aside, disregarded—just once? No. The law is the foundation of God's government. To play games with divine law is to invite chaos. Without law, the universe itself would fall.

Could not the law be altered just a little—to save Jesus? No. The law is a perfect transcript of the perfect character of God. He could not change His law without changing His character. He is a God of love. His law is a law of love. If defines how love will act.

The fact that Jesus did die on Golgotha's cross, in spite of its terrible cost, in spite of the incredible horror of the ordeal through which He personally must pass—here is mighty evidence, unanswerable evidence, that the law could not be changed—even to spare God's own Son. If the law could have been changed or altered or disregarded or set aside or ignored or bypassed, then the death of Jesus was unnecessary—and Calvary was only a meaningless drama!

Jesus came to demonstrate that it was possible for men to keep God's law. Satan had charged otherwise. Wasn't Adam's fall the proof? But Jesus took humanity, not in the strength of Adam, not in the perfect environment of Eden—He took humanity after it had been weakened by thousands of years of rebellion. For thirty-three years He lived just as we have to live, using no power that is not available to us—and never once sinned. And this in spite of every hellish scheme Satan could think of to trip Him up!

Jesus died to make the universe, all of it, forever secure. Rebellion *must not* happen again. And the prophet says it *will not.* "Affliction shall not rise up the second time." Nahum 1:9, KJV.

Thank God, the dreadful demonstration of sin's lethal nature will never need to be repeated! Why? Will God take away our power to choose and make us robots after all, so that we cannot sin? No. We will have seen enough of sin—at Calvary. And we shall never want to touch it again!

Jesus died to make the whole universe safe. Calvary is for other worlds too—not just for us. The unfallen worlds will be safe from rebellion through unending ages. And heaven will be safe. Not because of law. Not because of fear. But because what happened that day on a cross outside Jerusalem, as they watched in breathless horror, has made them safe!

A little boy—just a toddler—was restless one evening. He wanted to play. He wandered into his parents' bedroom and pulled open the drawer in the nightstand. He found there a shiny black pistol. It looked just like his own—the one he played with.

He carried it out to the living room, pointed it at his father, and said, "Bang, bang, Daddy! You're dead!" And his father fell to the floor. Then he pointed it at his mother and said, "Bang, bang, Mommie! You're dead." And she fell to the floor. Just the way they had always played.

But they didn't get up, and he didn't know what to make of it. Something must be wrong. He threw the pistol away—as far as he could throw it—and knelt beside his father. "Get up, Daddy! Get up! I don't want to play anymore!"

Oh friend! Do you see what sin has done to the Saviour? Do you see what it has done to this once-beautiful world? Do you see what it has done to those you love? Do you see what it has done to you?

What else can you do but throw sin as far as you can throw it and kneel at the Saviour's feet? What can you do but let the tears roll down your cheeks unchecked and tell Him you don't want to play with sin anymore?

That's what He's been waiting for—all these years! And that's what you've been waiting for! Isn't it?

The Repainting of Golgotha

The Battle of Kadesh was reported by Ramses II, of Egypt, as only a skirmish in which he, of course, was victorious. But Ramses was a vain fellow. The Battle of Kadesh turned out to be not a skirmish at all, but one of the significant battles of history. And Ramses, rather than being the victor, barely escaped with his life.

On the massive pillars and palace walls of mighty Karnak, Ramses described again and again his conflicts with the king of Hatti. The Assyrians also frequently mentioned the land of Hatti. But historians did not guess the truth. It was assumed that the Hatti were only some unimportant tribe. No one thought to ask how an unimportant tribe could skirmish with two great powers— and for so long a time. The Hatti turned out to be not a tribe at all, but a third giant empire of that day—the Hittites, with their borders stretching from the Black Sea to Damascus!

But no matter. Ramses felt quite capable of handling the Hittites. At least he must be given credit for putting on a bold front.

One of the Egyptian inscriptions concerning the Battle of Kadesh described Ramses as the "fearless one" who "put an end to the boastfulness of the land of Hatti." He was "the son of Re who trampled the land of Hatti underfoot. . . . He was like a bull with sharp horns . . . the mighty lion . . . the jackal who in a moment traverses the circuit of the earth . . . the divine, splendid falcon." There was also a long poem describing the tremendous victory of Ramses.

Today it is known that these claims were a shameless piece of propaganda. Yet it was believed for more than three thousand years!

The truth is that Ramses allowed himself to be taken in by the story of two Bedouin spies sent into his camp by the Hittite king. These men, claiming to be deserters from the Hittite army, told

Ramses that the Hittite king had already retreated from him in fear. And susceptible as he was to flattery, he allowed his army to fall into the trap, escaping only with his life.

A neat trick, isn't it? Lose the battle, but convince the world you won it. And succeed for three thousand years. I'm not sure who thought of such a strategy first. But there's a parallel here that I can't escape. The Battle of Kadesh was fought about 1300 B.C. But about A.D. 31 the chief of the fallen angels—we call him Satan—set out to try the same strategy. He had lost a battle infinitely more important than Kadesh. And it could be said of him, too, that he barely escaped with his life. But his record of horrible success is today approaching the 2000-year mark, and comparatively few suspect the truth!

The story, which is terribly true, began at Golgotha, known as the place of the skull—probably because a rock formation in the hillside resembled a human skull. Most often we call it Calvary, which is an English word derived from the same meaning—skull.

Jesus of Nazareth, crucified there, had just died. And I picture Satan, the rebel chief, sitting in the shadows not far away—absolutely dejected. He had lost the battle. He knew it. He knew that his doom was sealed!

You would expect him to be happy, wouldn't you? After all, it was he who was the chief instigator of the crucifixion.

Yes, he wanted Him crucified, but I'm not sure he wanted Him to die. He probably wanted to push Jesus to the limit, short of death, hoping that He would call it quits—not worth it—and return to heaven.

You see, Satan's purpose was to defeat the plan for man's salvation. All the way from Bethlehem to Golgotha the evil angel had hounded the steps of Jesus, trying to discourage Him, trying to trip Him up, trying to get Him to sin if only by a word, trying to get Him to quit.

In the first place, he had thought that God would certainly never bother with the fallen race. The cry of a lost and lonely planet would stir no lasting sympathy in the heart of the Almighty. It was incomprehensible to the rebel's selfish mind that the Son of God would be concerned enough to come down here and die in man's place so that he could live. Selfishness has trouble understanding love. And Satan seemed to think that if he just made things miserable enough, Jesus would surely turn back and abandon His plan to save men. The human race would then be left to certain destruction. And nothing delights the rebel chief more than mass destruction.

Satan knew that Jesus could easily work a miracle to deliver Himself from His enemies. He knew that Jesus, if He chose, could easily come down from the cross and let ten thousand angels sweep Him heavenward in the sight of His tormentors.

But Jesus didn't quit. He didn't come down from the cross. He stayed there to the last and let the world's sins crush out His life. And Satan wasn't stupid. He knew that his mask had been torn completely away. In the eyes of all the universe he had now been exposed as a murderer—the murderer of his own Creator. He could expect no sympathy now, ever again, from the unfallen worlds.

Satan hated the cross. He hated it with an intensity that cannot be described. But there, in the shadow of the instrument of death that had sealed his doom, he hit upon the same idea that Ramses had used to feed his pride. He had lost the battle. But he would make it appear that he had won. He would concoct his own story of what happened at Golgotha. He would repaint the cross. He would misinterpret it, distort its meaning, and promote worldwide misunderstanding by means of massive propaganda. *He would make the cross he hated a weapon against God!*

You see, Satan's rebellion from the beginning has been an attack upon God's authority, His government, and His law. In his encounter with our first parents, in Eden, it was a direct command of God that was so brazenly questioned. And in these last days, according to the book of Revelation, it will still be the authority of God that is at issue. It will still be the people who accept God's authority and keep His commands—it is these who will be the target of the rebel angel's greatest wrath. See Revelation 12:17.

Lucifer, when first he rebelled, campaigned for the repeal of God's law. But how could God repeal a law that is a transcript of His own character, a law that is the foundation of His government? How could God alter in any way a law so important, so vital, so perfect, so unchangeable, so sacred that its violation could not be overlooked to save His own Son from Calvary?

Tell me. Isn't it strange to contend that the cross cancels out the law or in any way weakens it? Can you believe that God would let His own Son die because the law could not be changed—and then turn around and change it as soon as His Son was dead? Hardly!

Ask the apostle Paul, and he will tell you that God's law is "holy, and the commandment holy, and just, and good." Romans 7:12, KJV. Ask David, and he will tell you that "the law of the Lord is perfect, converting the soul." Psalm 19:7, KJV. Another psalm will tell you that all of God's commandments "stand fast for ever and ever." Psalm 111:8, KJV. And God Himself says, "My covenant will I not break, nor alter the thing that is gone out of my lips." Psalm 89:34, KJV. He tells us this about Himself: "I am the Lord, I change not." Malachi 3:6, KJV.

There is no way to separate the integrity of God's law from the integrity of God Himself. They stand or fall together!

Satan well knew that God's law would not, and could not, be set aside. He had just witnessed, in the death of Jesus, the mightiest argument of all for the unchangeable nature of the divine law. For if the law could have been set aside, Jesus need not have died!

In the light of all this knowledge, and much more, the once-brilliant angel conceived his bold and reprehensible scheme there at Golgotha. He would tell the world that the cross he hated, the cross that had sealed his doom, the cross that had upheld the law at the cost of the Creator's lifeblood, had in reality given him everything he wanted. He would tell the world that the purpose of Calvary had been to remove God's law, that God had decided, after all, to free men from its restrictions and give them liberty to do as they pleased!

Satan knew that the cross he hated would be honored by all Christians, that the story of God's dying in man's place would be told and retold through every generation, that men through all time would preach and pray and sing about it. But the rebel chief cared not. He would gladly join in their praise of Calvary's sacrifice—so long as it was misunderstood, so long as its meaning was distorted, so long as it could be turned to the advantage of his rebellion.

Satan would picture Sinai, with its thunder and smoke, as the work of a harsh and tyrannical God, and Calvary as the work of a loving Saviour. He would pit one against the other—as if Sinai were a mistake that had to be corrected at Calvary. He would contend that Sinai was law and Calvary was grace. And he would be delighted as he saw men making of grace an excuse to sin. He would remind men repeatedly of what the apostle Paul said about Christians being "not under the law, but under grace," hoping they would never notice Paul's very next words: "What then? Shall we sin, because we are not under the law, but under grace? God forbid." Romans 6:14, 15, KJV.

Yes, the fallen angel would actually pirate the grace of God that enables us to keep the law, and market it as a license to sin!

The rebel chief would stop at nothing. He would foist upon the world the notion that God has actually abolished His constitution, thrown away His moral standard, and left men to follow their own inclinations.

But it is precisely that notion—that we are subject only to our own inclinations, our own feelings—it is that notion, eagerly accepted and passed on from one generation to another, that has made our streets unsafe and our homes armed fortresses. And in our rush to permissiveness we have rejected the only answer to the epidemic of crime that surrounds us!

But obedience is not popular today. It is not sophisticated enough for this permissive society. We prefer to talk about love. We have not escaped the infection of easy religion that makes of us no demands. The shocking thing is that the cross of Calvary has been so manipulated as to help create this situation!

Isn't it a tragedy that the cross which cost the lifeblood of Jesus, the cross that stands as the ultimate in obedience to the Father's will, should be so misunderstood? Isn't it frightening to realize that the very sacrifice which has forever established the authority and unchanging character of God's law should be represented as destroying it? How is it that millions can be so blinded? But here will come the last great deception. Here will be the issue in the last great conflict that will separate the loyal from the disloyal.

Yes, Satan will fight the cross while pretending to love it. He will gladly join in praise of what happened that dark day on Golgotha's hill. But all the while he is going for the jugular—using the cross that sealed his doom as an unsuspected weapon in his desperate and insane attempt to dethrone God!

From old England comes an account of a young boy named Bron who went to church for the first time with his governess.

The minister climbed high into the pulpit and then told a piece of terrible news. He told how an innocent Man had been nailed to a cross and left to die.

How terrible, the lad thought! How wrong! Surely the people would do something about it. But he looked about him and no one seemed concerned. They must be waiting for church to be over, he decided. Then surely they would do something to right this horrible deed.

He walked out of church trembling with emotion, waiting to see what the crowd would do. And his governess said, "Bron, don't take it to heart. Someone will think you are strange!"

Strange—to be upset, disturbed by injustice? Strange—to be stirred by so tragic a recital? Strange—to care, and want desperately to do something about it?

Shame on us for our casual, superficial commitments—left at the door of the church and forgotten! There is something to be done about what happened at Calvary. Jesus said, "If ye love me, keep my commandments!" John 14:15, KJV.

Love is more than just something you say. Love is something you do!

Section Seven
Love Is Something You Do

The Jericho Road

If you should set out to walk from Jerusalem to Jericho, you would be vividly aware of just one direction—*down*. The two cities are only twenty miles apart. But Jerusalem is high on a mountain ridge, 2500 feet above sea level. Jericho is 770 feet *below* sea level in the Jordan Valley.

The Jericho Road isn't one you'd want to travel every day even today. Nor was it in the time of Christ. To make it easier to travel, whether going down or going up, the road was constructed with switchback after switchback. And these tortuous turns, along with the hills and gullies beside the road, made it easy for robbers to hide.

Jesus told a story one day—a story about a certain man who was going *down* from Jerusalem to Jericho. And now you know what Jesus meant by *down*. You will find the story in the tenth chapter of Luke.

As the traveler made his way down the treacherous road, it was necessary to pass through a portion of the wilderness of Judea. The road led through a wild and rocky ravine which was infested by robbers. It was here that he was attacked, stripped of everything valuable, beaten, and left beside the road to die.

Now what would happen? Who would show concern for this poor man, beaten and bleeding? All heaven watched to see.

First a priest came along, but he merely glanced at the wounded man. Then came a Levite. He was curious, and stopped to see what had happened. He knew what he should do, but he didn't want to do it. He wished he hadn't come that way. He persuaded himself that the poor man's plight was no concern of his. And besides, what if he were a Samaritan?

But now along the road comes one of those hated Samaritans. He didn't stop to question whether the wounded man was Jew or Gentile. He didn't stop to think that he himself might be in danger in this deserted place. Someone was in trouble, and that was enough.

He took off his own cloak to cover the victim. He gave first aid as best he could and refreshed him with provisions intended for his own journey. He lifted him onto his own animal and proceeded slowly so as not to cause him more pain. He took him to an inn and cared for him tenderly through the night.

In the morning, seeing that the injured man was much improved, he left him in the care of the innkeeper, paid for his lodging, and promised to take care of any additional expense when next he should stop at the inn.

That was the story. What would you have done if you had passed that way?

Love is not just something to talk about. Love is something we do. We measure *God's love for us* by looking at Calvary. And God measures *our love for Him* by looking at the Jericho Road!

He looks at the Jericho Road. And if neither He nor His angel watchers can find the mildest evidence that we have been there, a single life that we have touched, one lone tear that we have dried, even one hurt that we have healed—if instead of the Jericho Road we have chosen the high-speed turnpike that bypasses the world's need, then how can either God or man say that we have loved at all?

Love is something we do. The Christian life is not a dreamlike drift toward heaven. You and I, whether we want to be or not, are involved in the great controversy between good and evil. And there's no such thing as sitting back in some neutral corner and letting God and Satan fight it out!

Who of us cares enough to listen to the heartbeat of despair? Who of us stops to feel the dwindling pulse of hope? The heartbreak of the world is the heartbreak of Jesus. And it ought to be ours!

Are we allowing the corruption around us to drive all the compassion from our hearts? To be sure, it's revolting. But can the violence in our streets ever excuse us for letting compassion die a violent death in our hearts?

The late Moshe Dayan, soldier par excellence that he was, had a great deal of compassion for the Arab people. He invited to his wedding an Arab who had once tried to kill him. On another occasion some Arabs came up to a checkpoint with a cart of fruit all carefully arranged for market. The inspectors dug into it, looking for weapons, and left it in disarray. It was Moshe Dayan who severly reprimanded them for their insensitiveness.

Love, if it is love at all, will be seen on the Jericho Road. It will be seen in the marketplace. It will be seen in the church. It was the apostle James who said, "What good is it, my brothers, if a man claims to have faith but has no deeds? Can such faith save him? Suppose a brother or sister is without clothes and daily food. If one of you says to him, 'Go, I wish you well; keep warm and well fed,' but does nothing about his physical needs, what good is it? In the same way, faith by itself, if it is not accompanied by action, is dead." James 2:14–17, NIV.

It's a strange faith that sits by and does nothing. True, we are not saved by anything we can do. But what we do is an indicator of what we are. Our actions either authenticate the genuineness of our commitment to Christ—or they betray our hypocrisy. One or the other.

Jesus was repeatedly puzzled and disappointed by the inconsistency of those who claimed to love Him. And it is no different today. He says to us as He said long ago, "If you love me, you will obey what I command." John 14:15, NIV.

Another time He said it this way: "You are my friends if you do what I command." John 15:14, NIV.

And catch the hurt in these words of Jesus: "Why do you call me, 'Lord, Lord,' and do not do what I say?" Luke 6:46, NIV.

You've seen these bumper stickers that say, "Honk if you love Jesus." But one was different. It said, "If you love Jesus, pay tithe. Anybody can honk!"

Yes, anybody can honk. Anybody can hold up a placard that says, "I believe in Jesus." But the Saviour is waiting for something more than that. And He has a right to expect it.

Seven men worked side by side in the blazing sun, hoeing long rows across a huge plot of land. The boss would return at evening to inspect their work. C. V. Garnett, writing in *Insight* magazine, tells the story.

At noon the men exchanged their hoes for lunch pails and

found a refuge of shade. As the others began eating, a gray-haired man—they called him Old Lew—dropped to one knee and bowed his head. They were used to this ritual and paid no attention.

All too soon the half hour allotted for lunch was over, and Old Lew rose to go.

"Sit down, Lew. It's too hot to be hurrying out there," said Dan. "The boss'll never know the difference if we take an extra fifteen minutes."

"You men do what you want," Old Lew replied as he stepped out into the sun.

When he had gone, Dan shook his head. "I don't get it. What difference would a few extra minutes make anyhow?"

"To him, plenty. An honest day's work is part of his religion, part of him." It was Young Lew who had spoken up. They called him Young Lew to distinguish him from the older man.

And now it was Dan again. "Look, you don't have to stick up for him just because you're courting his daughter. The way I look at it, we work because we got to. So if you can go easy on yourself, who's it hurt?"

"It would hurt him," Young Lew tried to explain. "The agreement was for a half-hour lunch."

"I don't trust him and that crazy religion of his," countered Dan.

Bill disagreed. "He's OK. He don't bother nobody."

And now Rube spoke up. "I admire him. If only he didn't have that funny religion."

And Young Lew said, "Wait a minute. What makes him the man you admire *is* his religion. You can't have it both ways."

Maybe it was to ease the tension that Tom Wilson came up with a joke he'd heard the night before. That reminded Bill of one, and Rube told his favorite. The time was forgotten.

Suddenly Rube shouted, "Hey! Look at the time!"

The men leaped to their feet and began running toward the field. "That old man will be across the field and back," Dan shouted.

"The boss will know we've been goofing off," called another.

"The old man will probably tell him." That from Dan.

But Young Lew panted, "He won't have to tell him. Our rows will tell the story."

They raced on together. In the distance they could see Old Lew, bent over his hoe. Then, as they neared the field, suddenly they stopped. There, just as they had expected, Old Lew's row was a long way ahead of where it was before lunch. *But the other six rows were all even with his!*

They couldn't believe what they saw. But when they saw the old man step from one row to the next, they knew it was true. He had been stepping from one row to another, keeping each man's row even with his own!

What a sermon! A sermon preached by a man with a hoe! Here was love in action!

Friend, what if the love of God for us had been all talk and no action? What if Jesus had not bothered to come and die for us? What if He had cast us off like broken toys—and created new men and women in our place?

What if He had wept divine tears over our plight—and sent us messages filled with pathos, eloquent in their sympathy for our fallen condition. But nothing more.

What if He had stepped out on a cloud and punctuated His pledge of love with celestial fireworks—and never followed up? What if He had come as far as Calvary—and decided it was more important to save Himself than to save us?

We sing about the love of God—and how it would take a great scroll and an ocean filled with ink to tell it. But have you ever thought how dark this world would be if Calvary had never happened? Just the scroll—stretched from sky to sky?

This Is How It Works

The story is told of a soldier in a foxhole. He was young—and scared—and his body hugged the earth like a glove. Even so, he felt all too visible. In his hand was a rosary that someone had given him. He didn't quite know what it was all about. Just then a priest slid into the hole beside him. The boy looked into his face and asked the one question that seemed to matter: "How do you make this thing work?"

All over this world frightened men and women, trapped in the path of a future they can neither understand nor escape, are turning their eyes toward heaven. In their hands is something called Christianity. They're not quite sure what it is all about. They aren't ready to accept it. But they hesitate to reject something that in a day like this might be their only hope. Holding it up to the light they have been turning it, studying it, admiring it, puzzling over it, philosophizing about it, arguing its merits and its mysteries. And they hope God is listening as they ask what may be life's most important question: "How does it work?"

Teenage youth are just as bewildered as the rest. Some of them have tried the Christian way and it hasn't worked—for them. But they'd be willing to try it again—if only they could get the hang of it. If you listen closely enough to get past the casual teenage jargon, you might hear their real question: "Mother, Dad, Teacher, Preacher, how do you make this work?" And they don't want a theological treatise for an answer!

The question is not new. A jailer asked it one night when he was in bad trouble. Two very important prisoners had been placed in his custody the day before. But later, around midnight, there had been a severe earthquake, and certainly the prisoners had all escaped. But the apostle Paul—for he and Silas were the two important prisoners—the apostle Paul anticipated the jailer's fears and called out to let him know that no one had fled. The jailer—happy but still trembling—"fell down before Paul and Silas, and brought them out, and said, Sirs, what must I do to be saved?" Acts 16:29–31, KJV.

It had been the same on the Day of Pentecost. The people reacted to Peter's landmark sermon with the question, "Men and brethren, what shall we do?" Acts 2:37, KJV.

What shall we do? What *must* we do? What *can* we do to be saved?

Millions believe that we must somehow make ourselves better before we come to Jesus. Clean ourselves up. Stop smoking. Get rid of all our bad habits. Do something to atone for all our bad deeds. Make a big contribution, maybe.

Some think God will accept them if they walk through fire with bare feet. The flagellantes of the Philippines lacerate their backs with paddles set with broken glass—and then flail their bleeding backs into intense pain. And Martin Luther was laboriously climbing a staircase on his knees when he discovered he had the wrong idea.

This notion that you must work a miracle on yourself before you can ask God to work a miracle on you—it is a little strange, isn't it? Like saying you must get yourself perfectly clean before you reach for the soap!

The trouble with all these efforts at self-improvement is that God says they are useless. We are trying to do the impossible. He says, "Can the Ethiopian change his skin or the leopard its spots? Neither can you do good who are accustomed to doing evil." Jeremiah 13:23, NIV.

And evidently God doesn't rate our brand of goodness very high, for He says that "all our righteous acts are like filthy rags." Isaiah 64:6, NIV.

Those are our good deeds, the best we can do. What must He think of our bad deeds? There's simply no way we can straighten ourselves out. We need a miracle!

The Christian way, however, is a road that has soft shoulders on both sides. And millions have been caught up in a completely opposite extreme—an error just as dangerous. Realizing that we can't save ourselves, they say that Jesus does everything—and all we have to do is believe. Just believe!

Is this really all that is involved?

It is true that Paul and Silas said to the jailer, "Believe in the Lord Jesus, and you will be saved." Acts 16:31, NIV. And it's true that Peter answered the question "What shall we do?" by saying "Repent and be baptized, every one of you, in the name of Jesus Christ." Acts 2:38, NIV.

But Jesus did not speak very highly of a belief that includes no *doing*. He said, "Why do you call me 'Lord, Lord,' and do not *do* what I say?" Luke 6:46, NIV.

So just what *must we do* to be saved? How do we take the first step toward the Saviour? A story illustrates it so well:

It happened in the early part of the seventeenth century. The Duke of Osuna, who was viceroy of Sicily, and later of Naples, came aboard a galley ship one day as it lay at anchor in the harbor of Barcelona.

Below deck were criminals who for one crime or another had been sentenced to row at the oars of the galley ship. Some of them would row at the oars until the day of their death.

The duke sat down on the deck of the ship and ordered that these men, one at a time, be brought before him. Of each man he asked the same question, "For what crime are you here?"

They were serving their sentences for various crimes—some for robbery, some for murder, some for treason. But through their answers ran a common thread. Each man protested his innocence. Each had some excuse. And each blamed somebody else.

Finally a young man only twenty years old was brought on deck. He was so ashamed to be appearing before the duke that he hung his head. "For what crime are you here?" the duke asked.

And the young prisoner replied, "Sir, I wanted some money, and I stole to get it. I was justly tried and convicted. I deserve this punishment."

The duke was so surprised to hear this honest admission of guilt, so happily amazed, that he granted the prisoner a full and complete pardon. He said to him, with a twinkle in his eye, "Young man, you are far too bad to be among all these good and innocent men."

And he set him free!

That young man may not have known it, but he had just taken the first step, often the hardest step, in becoming a Christian. He had admitted his guilt.

The hardest thing in the world, for a proud heart, is to admit its guilt. A proud man wants to be independent. He is horrified at the thought of needing a Saviour.

Two men were praying one day. One of them, a Pharisee, had done a lot of good things, and he told the Lord, and anyone else listening, all about them. The other, a despised tax collector, had done a lot of bad things, and he just said, "God be merciful to me a sinner." Luke 18:13, KJV.

Jesus was listening. And He said the tax collector had the right idea.

Jesus found the Pharisees, as a group, the most nearly hopeless. To admit their need was too great a hurdle. And so long as they felt no need, He could not help them. He had come to save sinners. And they weren't willing to come through that door.

Notice how simple the tax collector's prayer was. Nothing complicated about it. No prescribed terminology. Right to the point. Jesus said it was the heathen who thought they would be heard because of their "much speaking," Matthew 6:7.

The first step, then, is to *admit our need of a Saviour*. And we need not make ourselves better before we approach Him. We do not change our lives so that we can come to Him. We come to Him so that He can change our lives.

And there are other necessary steps, though the sequence in which they are taken may not always be the same.

Certainly we must *believe in the Lord Jesus*. Believe that He exists. Believe that He is the Son of God. Believe that He died in our place. But belief must be more than information, more than a theory. Belief must include *commitment*. It involves a personal *acceptance* of the sacrifice He made for us.

Do you find it *hard* to believe, but you *want* to believe?

Jesus said to one man, "All things are possible to him who believes." And the man responded, "I believe; help my unbelief!" Mark 9:23, 24, RSV.

You will never perish while you pray that prayer!

Repent. All through the Scriptures we find the call to repent. Don't we first have to repent before we come to Christ? How can He accept us if we have not repented?

No. True repentance—genuine sorrow for sin, a desire to turn away from our life of sin—is something the Saviour gives us. See

Acts 5:31. We can no more repent without the Spirit of Christ than we can be pardoned without Christ.

But suppose you aren't sorry. You want to be, but you aren't. You want desperately to be forgiven. But at the same time you'd like to go right back and do it again. What should you do? You can't be sorry if you aren't. But you can place yourself in an environment where repentance can happen. Keep looking at Jesus. Keep looking at the cross. And, if you keep looking, sooner or later, it will break your heart!

Now comes *confession*. Does this mean parading our sins publicly as if they were something to be proud of? No. Only if a group has been wronged should confession be made to a group.

But confession, if it is genuine, must come from a heart that God has touched. It is meaningless if it is loaded down with excuses and explanations and qualifications that cancel it out. It must spring from the deep and true repentance that only God can give. And that kind of confession will be something more than just, "I guess I goofed!"

Making things right. A new Christian will almost surely have some things to make right with others. The Spirit of God will tell us what those things are and show us how to make them right. Zacchaeus knew immediately what he must do. See Luke 19:8.

Forgiveness. We all desperately need it. Guilt is the heaviest load we carry. It poisons the springs of life. But it can be healed. And it can be healed only at the foot of an old rugged cross.

Forgiveness is never merited. It is never deserved. We cannot earn it by the length or the detail or the beauty of our confession—or by anything we can do. It is a gift beyond our ability to understand. It is the costliest gift in the universe, for it cost the lifeblood of the Son of God.

Forgiveness hurts. Sin is not a light thing. Someone must pay. Jesus doesn't say, "Forget it—there's nothing to forgive," as we sometimes say to each other. He doesn't overlook our sins. He doesn't say they don't matter. He doesn't say there isn't any hurt. He says, "I'll bear the hurt Myself." And that's what He did at Calvary!

But you say, "There's no hope for me. I've made such a mess of my life that God wouldn't want me now. I've gone a bridge too far."

No, friend, you haven't. Not if you want to come back. Even the worst sinner is not beyond the reach of forgiveness. "If we confess our sins," says the apostle John, "he is faithful and just to forgive us our sins, and to cleanse us from all unrighteousness." 1 John 1:9, KJV.

And God says through the prophet Isaiah, "Though your sins be as scarlet, they shall be as white as snow; though they be red like crimson, they shall be as wool." Isaiah 1:18, KJV.

Do you still say, He will not forgive you—that you've gone too far? Is this God making you feel this way? No! It isn't the Spirit of God who tells you that. It's another spirit.

Tell me. If Jesus was willing to give His own lifeblood for the privilege of forgiving you—if that's how much He loved you and *wanted* to forgive you—then when you come to Him and ask to be forgiven, would He turn you away? Never!

Whoever you are, wherever you are, whatever you have done, your guilt can be healed. No matter how long it has haunted you, tortured you, crushed you, you can take it to the Saviour—just now—and come away without it. You can come away clean!

I picture a large group who in the final day will come up to the City of God and say, "Open the door." And a voice asks, "What right have you to enter?" And they say, "*We* have a *right* to enter. *We* have worked miracles. *We* have cast out devils. *We* have done many wonderful works. *We* are all right." See Matthew 7:21-23.

But *we* doesn't count in that day. And the voice of Jesus says, "Depart from Me. I never knew you!"

And then I picture another group. They too come to the city gate. And if anyone should ask, "What right have you? What have you done to deserve to enter?" I hear them say something like this:

"I have not done anything at all to deserve it. I am completely dependent upon the grace of Christ. I was a sinner—a helpless captive to sin. I was in such bondage that no one but the Lord could set me free. I was so blind that no one but the Lord could make me see. I was so naked that no one but the Lord could clothe me. All the claim I have is what Jesus has done for me!

"When I cried out in my desperation, He delivered me. When in my blindness I asked Him to show me the way, He led me—

and made me see. When I was so naked that no one could clothe me, He gave me this garment that I have on.

"So all that I can present, the only claim I have, is what He has done for me. If that is not enough, then I am left out. And that would be perfectly just. I could have no complaint. But won't what He has done entitle me to enter?"

And a voice says, "Yes, we are perfectly satisfied. Your deliverance is what the Lord did for you. The garment you have on—the Lord gave it to you. And it is all divine. It is all Christ. You can come in!"

And angel voices break into a song of welcome that echoes from star to star!

For the past few moments I have been paraphrasing the words of A. T. Jones as he spoke to a vast audience in the year 1893. As he finished, someone in that great congregation broke out in song spontaneously,

> Jesus paid it all;
>   All to Him I owe;
> Sin had left a crimson stain;
>   He washed it white as snow.

The Pardon and the Power

Dr. Paul Tournier, the famed Swiss psychiatrist, in his college days had become quite attached to a Greek professor who took an interest in him. Though the professor was not religious, he was a kind man.

Many years later Dr. Tournier, long after becoming a Christian, completed his first book manuscript about the Christian life. He wanted someone to read it critically. He thought of his old Greek professor.

The professor asked him to read the first chapter aloud, for his eyesight was no longer the best. When the chapter was completed, Dr. Tournier looked up for some reaction. The professor said, "Paul, continue." He read another chapter. "Paul, continue." He read the third chapter. Then the aging teacher said, "Paul, we must pray together."

They prayed. And then, still amazed, Dr. Tournier exclaimed, "I didn't know you were a Christian!"

"Oh yes!"

"When did you become a Christian?"

"Just now."

Just now. That's how long it takes to become a Christian. That's how long it takes to make a decision. And that decision can mark the beginning of a new life—a life that is happy and satisfying and productive beyond the wildest expectation.

That decision can make a kind and attentive husband out of the town drunk. It can make a devoted follower of Christ out of an avowed atheist. It can make an apostle Peter out of a rough and bungling fisherman. It can make an apostle Paul out of a persecutor of Jesus.

But unfortunately it doesn't always work out that way. A man may become a minister of the gospel. He may preach eloquent

161

sermons. He may make the most beautiful appeals for commitment to the Saviour. He may win thousands. But he himself could finally lose out. The apostle Paul knew that such a thing is possible, for he said, "I keep under my body, and bring it into subjection: lest that by any means, when I have preached to others, I myself should be a castaway." 1 Corinthians 9:27, KJV.

A decision for Christ does not take away a man's power to choose. His decision can be reversed. It is not a matter of once-saved-always-saved. Judas decided to join up with Christ. He was the most brilliant of the disciples, and his companions were proud that he was one of them. But he ended up betraying his Lord.

There are other reasons why a decision for Christ may not turn out well. It may have been only a shallow commitment, made for shallow and superficial reasons. It may have involved only the emotions. There may have been no real surrender of the life to the Saviour. Such ones may say they have been born again. But there is no real transformation. The old life-style, and the old sins, have not even been disturbed. There is a superficial witness, for a time. And then it fades out.

What does it mean to be born again?

Nicodemus was a good man, a Pharisee of excellent reputation, and a member of the ruling council of the Jews. He had been attracted by the teaching of Jesus—what he had heard of it. He was convinced that there was something different about Him. The simple, uncomplicated truths that He taught were like a breath of fresh air. The desire to talk with this Teacher from Nazareth refused to be quieted.

But Jesus was not popular with the religious leaders. And Nicodemus knew that his own popularity would suffer if he approached Jesus openly. So it was that he came to Jesus secretly, at night—ready for a stimulating discussion. But in that respect he was to be disappointed. For Jesus cut through the formalities to the real need of this proud ruler who stood before Him. He said simply, "I tell you the truth, unless a man is born again, he cannot see the kingdom of God." John 3:3, NIV.

Nicodemus was flustered, taken by surprise. He had expected a deep theological discussion. But this? He tried to take the

Saviour's words literally. How could a man back up thirty or forty years and be born all over again? How could this be?

Jesus didn't answer his question directly. It's a question that can't be answered directly. The work of the Spirit of God cannot be explained. Jesus said it is like the wind. We hear the sound of it, but we cannot see it. We can only see what it has done—and wonder at its power. So it is with the Spirit of God. We cannot see Him work, or tell how He works. But we see the results in the life He has touched—and marvel!

An inspired pen, writing many years ago, said it so well:

"No one sees the hand that lifts the burden, or beholds the light descend from the courts above. The blessing comes when by faith the soul surrenders itself to God. Then that power which no human eye can see creates a new being in the image of God."—*The Desire of Ages,* p. 173.

No man sees the hand. No man can see the creative power at work—or take it apart and analyze it. The miracle cannot be explained. But thousands can see the results of the Spirit's work.

Many today, unfortunately, have misunderstood. They have it backward. They want to see the wind, and hear the wind. They are not concerned with the results. They are not concerned with whether or not the life has been changed, so long as there has been a rushing, mighty wind.

But there is more than one spirit in the world (1 John 4:1), and more than one wind (Ephesians 4:14). Ecstasy may well be present. But ecstasy is not the sole evidence of the Spirit of God at work. When the Spirit of God takes possession of a man He will change more than the way a person talks. The Spirit will change his life. Emotion will be balanced with responsibility. The Spirit of God will never lead a man to bypass the written Word of God or to place an emotional experience above the requirements of God. The Spirit of God will never tell you or me anything contrary to what He has told the Bible writers!

But the presence of counterfeit conversions in our world today, the activity of lying spirits, the blowing of deceptive winds— these are evidence that the genuine does exist. A counterfeiter does not bother to counterfeit that which has no genuine. Neither does the fallen angel!

True conversion, the new birth—whatever you choose to call it—does happen. It is a miracle—a miracle that cannot be explained. It is something only God can bring about. See John 1:12, 13. Peter says it is accomplished by the Word of God. See 1 Peter 1:23. And Jesus says it is absolutely essential. See John 3:3. Without it the Christian life can be drudgery!

Yet thousands of Christians—very sincere Christians—are living just such humdrum lives. Somehow they have managed to miss the miracle. They have kept the commandments—just as Nicodemus had. They have faithfully performed every known duty. They know their Bibles. They know truth from error. They consider themselves converted. They work hard for their Lord. But they have *no living, breathing, personal relationship with Him.*

And sooner or later they discover that their commandment keeping, their duties performed, their knowledge of truth, have not given them joy in the life and victory over sin. They are often defeated, helpless before the attacks of the enemy. There is no power in their lives. And they are bewildered. They are stunned. Doesn't Christianity work, after all?

Thousands have made a sincere commitment to Christ. They have experienced the new birth. They are elated by the assurance that their sins are pardoned. They are exhilarated by the new life. They live for months on miracle clouds. And then they fall off. What is wrong? Does God work a miracle at the beginning of the new life—and then leave us to struggle and blunder on our own, and fail in the end? Something is wrong!

This may shock you. But forgiveness, costly as it is, wonderful as it is—*forgiveness is not enough.* And even *the new birth,* miracle that it is, *is not enough.* If the gospel of Christ offers nothing more than forgiveness, it is a defective gospel. And if Jesus can give us a miracle boost at the beginning of the way, but is unable to make any *continuing* provision to free us from the power of sin, He might just as well not have come to earth at all!

I ask you, Did Jesus make such a mistake? Did He intend only to forgive us and get us started right—and then leave us on our own, still the slaves of sin, still powerless to break its hold upon us? No, He didn't!

We desperately need pardon. We need to be born again. But just as desperately we need the power to stop sinning. *The pardon and the power.* Could Jesus provide one but not the other? Did He forget about the power? Is He able to forgive our past, but unable to change us, to fit us for the future life?

No, says the apostle Paul, "I am not ashamed of the gospel, because it is the power of God for the salvation of everyone who believes." Romans 1:16, NIV.

No, says the apostle Jude. "Now unto him that is able to keep you from falling, and to present you faultless before the presence of his glory with exceeding joy." Jude 24, KJV.

And No, says the apostle John. "But as many as received him, to them gave he power to become the sons of God, even to them that believe on his name." John 1:12, KJV.

The power is there. But it is the power of God. Not our power. Not will power. Not self-discipline. The source of power is outside ourselves. It is something that God does for us. The Christian life all the way through—*not just at the beginning*—is a miracle of God's power.

We should have known that we would fail—struggling along on our own, trying to polish up the outside while we were mocked by what we knew about the inside. We should have known. For Jesus has told us plainly, "Apart from me you can do nothing." John 15:5, NIV.

But sometimes the words don't register until we need them desperately. *Then* they shine like neon. *Then* we see that we have been trying to do what only God can do!

Yet strangely enough, this rock-bottom experience, this discouragement and despair over our repeated defeat—this seems to be a part of the process, a part of the way God saves us.

God's plan for us is not complicated. The secret of a happy Christian life is so very simple—if we are willing to accept it. Many years ago Ellen White, a writer with deep spiritual insight, defined it in these words: "It is the work of God in laying the glory of man in the dust, and doing for man that which it is not in his power to do for himself."—*Testimonies to Ministers,* page 456.

I have never heard it defined better—or even so well!

The experience we so desperately need comes in two parts. In the first part, the glory of man is laid in the dust. In the second part, God does for us what we cannot do for ourselves. And the first must precede the second!

We are not ready for the wonder of what God can do until we are convinced of the utter futility of what *we* can do. It is only when we have tried and failed, when we have reached the end of our resources and the end of our hope—only then are we ready for the miracle of the life of faith. Only then will we experience what we have been denied so long—the peace and joy and victory that comes with trusting Christ alone to save us.

Why have we been so slow to let God work His wonders in us? We have struggled along with our little five-watt power when we could have been connected with the power that made the worlds! We have taken the slow train when God's planes were flying. We have pushed our trolley cars when power lines were within reach. As if God had a power shortage and we had to help Him out!

No wonder it sets us singing when we discover the simple secret that can change it all!

Color Choice

A lady stopped her car for a red light. When the light turned green, she stayed right where she was. The light changed several times, and still she waited. Finally a traffic officer walked over to her car and politely inquired, "Madam, haven't we any colors you like?"

The world is looking for some colors it likes. Some look for it at the end of a rainbow—in the color of gold. Some look for it in a continual round of night life, punctuated by the hypnotic beat of rock. Some look for it in great accomplishment, in fame, in the applause of the crowd. Some look for it in the depths of the inner self, and meditate the hours away. And some, with good reason, having tried all these, say, "None of the above."

Lonely people with aching hearts and heavy burdens and inner longings and a guilt that never leaves them day or night—these have found the pot of gold, and danced the nights through, and accepted the trophies, and turned aside to probe the mysteries of the East. But they have come back unsatisfied—still with their aching hearts. Their burdens are no lighter, their inner longings are keener than before. And their guilt, still unhealed, is poisoning all their artificial joy.

They have tried the colors of the world and found them an empty sham. They are tired of the glitter and dash of Broadway, the flashing neon of Hollywood, the painted shadows of their night spots. Their hurt will never be healed by offering them more of the same. They are looking for something different. They are looking for colors worth living for, worth dying for.

But unfortunately some professed Christians have made the better life seem harsh and gray and gloomy. They have lingered at the outer fringes of the Christian way. They have been caught up in its rituals and supposed restrictions. They have never discovered its springs of pure joy. And those looking on say, "I'm miserable enough already. I don't need this!"

167

Five-year-old Missy and her little neighbor Joey were playing artist. For a few minutes they were busy with their crayons, and then Missy looked over at Joey's work. "That's a dumb picture!"

And of course Joey shouted, "It is not dumb!" Then he turned down the volume and asked, "Why is it dumb?"

"Is that supposed to be a church with people praying?"

"Yeah."

"Well why'd you put smiles on all the people?"

"I don't know."

And then she explained. "Joey, everybody knows people are sad in church."

"They are?"

"Sure. I laughed at Tommy in church once and I got yelled at. I don't think God likes people to laugh in His house. And when you talk to Him you're supposed to put your head down and be real sad."

Evidently a lot of people have picked up the same idea—that God doesn't want you to smile, that happiness is strictly forbidden, and that being a Christian means being sentenced to a life of hard gloom.

God suffers much from the misrepresentation of those who claim to know Him but don't.

On the other hand, not all Christians are misrepresenting their Lord. Professor Josh McDowell, who has led so many youth to an unshakable faith in Christ, tells how in his own youth he resisted the claims of his Lord for years, determined to remain an unbeliever. But one thing kept troubling him. The Christians he met were so disgustingly happy!

Such happiness, of course, is never discovered by halfway Christians. It is never dreamed of by the man who keeps one hand on a parachute, ready to jump the moment things get rough.

Our Lord asks of us a complete surrender. Nothing less will do. But we shrink from making an unreserved commitment. Somehow we can't seem to get rid of the idea that if we gave God a free hand, if we gave Him a chance, if we turned over the management of our lives to Him without any reservation—well, who knows what would happen? Surely God would push open one of heaven's windows and dump on our heads, with perfect aim, a bag of calamities that would leave us bruised and limping until He could find another bag with worse troubles.

Is that what we think God is like?

I say again, it's the halfway Christian who is miserable, and who finds the way hard and restrictive. It's the halfway Christian who mutes his colors, hazes up his commitments, and blurs his loyalties—hoping no one will know which side he is on.

A young man had just returned from a summer camp where he was the only Christian in attendance. A friend asked him how he got along. "Fine," he said. "No one ever guessed that I was a Christian."

But is that the kind of follower God is looking for? Is He looking for underground Christians? Will He be satisfied with neutrality? No. There are no neutral colors in the battle of life. And God employs no secret agents. Not once has he ever commissioned a man to wear the uniform of the enemy while he secretly serves the God of heaven.

A true conversion will change a man. It involves more than doing commercials for a different sponsor. It means more than simply saying "I believe in Jesus" instead of "I believe in Campbell's soup."

True conversion will change the way a man lives. It cannot be otherwise. Not only will it make a difference in his appearance. See 1 Peter 3:3, 4. It will make a difference in what he reads, in his choice of recreation. See Philippians 4:8. It will make a difference in the way he turns the dials. The fingers that turn them now have been touched by a new commitment. He will no longer choose the same music or frequent the same places of entertainment as before.

And it will make a difference what he eats. See 1 Corinthians 10:31. No longer will he want to put into his body that which would destroy it. See 1 Corinthians 6:19, 20. No longer will he want to cloud his mind with chemicals that render his conscience inoperative. He will guard carefully his heart—his mind. See Proverbs 4:23.

Yes, a true conversion will lead to some changes.

"Sounds hard," you say. "Sounds restrictive."

But it isn't restrictive at all to one who loves his Lord. These are just things that he *wants* to do for One who has done so much for him. Love is something you do. And that which springs from love is not a burden.

We need not be afraid of a complete commitment. God will ask us to do nothing that would harm us. He will ask us to give up nothing that would do us good. After all, He is the Creator of the good and beautiful. You need not fear that He will ask you to wear some outlandish thing that will make you a laughingstock. He will not ask you to design your clothes from unbleached muslin—or shoddy material out of some musty attic. Remember that as a Christian you are a son or daughter of the heavenly King. And He wants you to dress in a way that will represent Him.

We worship a God who is lavish in His use of color and design. Look at the sunsets—an original every evening. Look at the red-winged blackbird in flight, its color flashing in the sunlight. Look at the aspen tree, its leaves quaking and shimmering, scattering light in a thousand directions. Look through the microscope at the wing of a butterfly. Evidently our Creator loves color and shimmer, texture and design. We have nothing to fear.

It is He who brings all creation to life in the spring. It is He who paints the skies in photographer's blue, and flowers in delicate pastels, and the sunsets in never-ending uniqueness. And then, for a few exciting weeks in autumn, He empties His paintpots over the North and splashes color with a happy abandon that takes your breath away!

This is the God we worship. Doesn't He have any colors you like? Will you wait at the intersection for something better? Could anything He ever asks of you be too much?

He asks you to return to Him a small portion of the wealth that He has placed at your disposal. But read the third chapter of Malachi, especially verses ten to twelve, to see what really does happen when God opens heaven's windows. It isn't calamity that He dumps on our heads!

He will ask you, when you have chosen His colors to be your colors—He will ask you to profess your loyalty publicly by stepping into the water and being baptized as Jesus was baptized. But would you want it otherwise? Would you want to neglect the privilege of being publicly united to the One you love?

I think of the apostle John—he who had lived closest to his Lord. How he must have cherished the memory of that last night with the Saviour—the night before the crucifixion! He must have recounted its details again and again to the early Christians.

Hear him telling how Jesus had shared with them the bread that represented His broken body—and the pure juice of the vine that represented that lifeblood with which He purchased our forgiveness. They hadn't understood it then. But later it meant so much. "This do in remembrance of me," He had said. And we are told that the early Christians so valued the privilege of communion that they made it a part of most every meeting.

But one thing about that memorable Thursday evening had left a scar upon John's heart. It must have been hard to talk about. You see, sandals were worn in those days, and the streets were dusty. It was the custom for a host to provide a servant to wash the dust from the feet of his guests. But on this Passover evening, at this gathering of the disciples with their Master, who was the host? Somehow no one had thought to arrange for a servant.

Suddenly came the awkward moment. No servant was present. To each of the men came the conviction that he should perform this duty. But each in his heart responded, "No! Not me! The man next to me maybe. Or he who reclines across from me. I'm not the one to perform this demeaning service!"

And while they hesitated, each waiting for someone else to move, Jesus Himself, the Lord of heaven and earth, took a towel and knelt down and began to wash their feet!

They were crushed with sudden guilt. Jesus, their Lord, their Creator, was doing what they should have done—what they were too proud to do. And the memory was a scar upon every heart!

Jon Dybdahl, writing in *Insight* magazine, tells how he and his wife arrived in Thailand some years ago as young missionaries. They were eager to learn the language and become acquainted with the new culture.

One of the first things Jon learned had to do with proper foot etiquette. In Thailand one does not wave his foot around or point to anything with his foot. His habit of crossing his legs with his right ankle resting on his left knee and his size-thirteen shoe waving around in space was considered terribly rude. It could even be unlawful. At least he realized how serious it was when he had to be told by a bailiff in a courtroom to keep both feet flat on the floor during court proceedings.

This aversion to feet carried over into all conversation. One could freely discuss, even with a stranger, most any medical problem—even the details of dysentery. But not feet. Feet were even lower than dysentery. Any mention of feet, or even the lower leg, was taboo.

As time passed, Jon was eager to tell the people about the cross of Calvary. But the story didn't go over as he had expected. After all, to people who believe in reincarnation with multiple deaths and births, what was so special about this Man's one death and resurrection? Surely He must have done some terrible thing in a previous life to experience such a horrible death. How could you explain the cross to a Buddhist?

Then something happened. Witaya, a friend who was a devout Buddhist, came to visit Jon. He said that an acquaintance of his, a monk, was creating a hall of world religions on his monastery grounds. Would Jon be willing to visit him and suggest appropriate scenes and scriptures to depict the Christian religion? Jon agreed to go.

On the appointed day he set out on his motorcycle and prayed for wisdom. Then an idea grew into a conviction.

Jon and the monk visited leisurely and toured the buildings and grounds. They came to the hall of world religions. Jon admired the murals already completed, and they sat down. The monk expressed his own ideas and then said, "Ahjawn [teacher], what do you think the essence of Christianity is?"

Jon referred the monk to John 13, found it for him in his Bible, and then slowly read to him in the Thai language about how Jesus washed the feet of the disciples. The monk said nothing as he read, but Jon could feel a strange, awesome quietness and power. When he finished, the monk looked up with utter incredulity and said, "Do you mean to say that the Founder of your religion washed His students' feet?"

The monk's face wrinkled up in shock and amazement. He was speechless and so was Jon. They were both caught up in the drama of the scene. Then the look on the monk's face turned to reverent awe. Jesus, the Founder of Christianity, had actually *touched* and *washed* dirty fishermen's feet!

Yes, friend. Jesus washed the feet of the men who were too proud to wash His! Their love for Him had been great enough to talk about. It had been great enough to lead them to pledge, to promise, to vow that they would even die for Him. But not until that Thursday night, with guilt stabbing at their hearts, did they get a clear picture of what Jesus had been trying to teach them all along—that love is something you do!

Doing What Comes Naturally

We stand in awe before the mighty Niagara, deafened by the roar of its spectacular plunge. And we say, "What power!"

We wait helplessly for the onslaught of the hurricane, unable to turn it back. Or we are caught by surprise as a funnel cloud dips down to earth and sends a tornado on its mindless, unpredictable path of destruction.

No man on earth can shout at the hurricane and divert it. Or expect the tornado to obey a red light. And no power ever tapped by man can reverse the mighty Niagara and send its waters pouring back up the falls!

We don't like to admit it. But we are powerless before the forces of nature. We can *talk* about the flood, the earthquake, the volcano. We can clean up the debris, submit our insurance claims, mourn our losses, and write it all into memory. That's about all.

But how does nature generate all this power? Does the Niagara accomplish its spectacular fall by trying? Does the tornado grit its teeth and vow to destroy?

And what about our sun, that mighty nuclear furnace in the sky? How does it produce the power to send bursts of flame leaping hundreds of thousands of miles out into space? Are millions of little sunburned men continually shoveling fuel into its fiery fissures to feed the flames?

No, it is the sun's nature to fling its spectacular flames into space. It is the nature of water to fall. It is the nature of wind to blow. No hurricane was ever set spinning by a fleet of jet planes flying in counter-clockwise formation!

Nature is simply doing what comes naturally. And it is doing it spontaneously, effortlessly, and without trying!

What if tomorrow morning we should walk outside and find it difficult to keep our feet on the ground? What if we should see trees growing upside down—and balls falling up? What if nature should stop doing what comes naturally?

And how repelled we would be by the sight of nature pretending to be what it is not! What if the weeds in our backyard should pretend to be roses?

It is true that our entertainment-minded generation spends millions of dollars to watch people pretend to be what they are not. But in real life we don't like it. We have a word for it. We call it phoniness!

Nothing is more repulsive to the non-Christian world than the Christian whose religion is obviously artificial, mechanical, and anything but natural. We are repelled by the sight of a Christian who transparently is trying very hard to be what he is not.

On the other hand, we are fascinated, we are irresistibly drawn, by the Christian with a light in his face and a spring in his step— the man or the woman whose religion is obviously without effort, completely natural.

Unfortunately, some have decided that all Christians are only pretending, that they are just good actors. Is it true?

I hold in my hand a straw. It bends and breaks easily. That is its nature.

But now I hold a piece of steel spring. Under pressure it can be bent. But it does not break. It snaps back. That is its nature.

Can God do something with a man to make him behave like steel instead of like straw? Can God effect a change in a man so that it is just as natural for him to behave like steel, to stand firm and even unbending under pressure—and do it just as naturally as he once behaved like straw?

Yes, God is doing it every day. And there is no better example of such a change than a man called Peter. Peter, whose name means "a rolling stone." Peter, who has been described as "a shifting compound of loyalty to Christ and treacherous self-interest." Peter, the blundering disciple. Peter, who ran away when Jesus needed him and denied even knowing Him. Yet it was Peter, a new Peter, a man miraculously changed, who on the Day of Pentecost stood fearlessly before the enemies of Jesus and boldly charged them with His death!

Not long after Pentecost Peter and John were on their way to the meetinghouse. Just as they were about to enter, they were accosted by a cripple begging money. You would expect these busy men, now leaders in the new Christian church, to brush him off. Instead, they showed a keen interest in the beggar. And Peter said to him, "Silver or gold I do not have, but what I have I give you. In the name of Jesus Christ of Nazareth, walk." Acts 3:6, NIV.

And the man walked! The cripple walked and jumped and praised God!

This healing made a great impression on the people who saw it. But Peter and John, however spectacular the miracle had been, received no commendation from the rulers of the temple. This, in their eyes, was dangerous preaching. It could not be tolerated. It must be stopped!

So it was that Peter and John, for doing a good turn to a crippled beggar, were locked up in jail for the night. No attorney. No bail. No telephone calls.

The next day they were brought to trial. And the rulers, after considering the matter, decided on a verdict that they thought was surprisingly mild. They did not demand that Peter and John renounce their faith in Jesus. They did not order them to go back into the temple and apologize to the people. They did not require them to say publicly that they had misrepresented the facts when they said that Jesus had been resurrected. They only demanded that they *keep still about Jesus. Just keep still!*

A mild sentence indeed, to their way of thinking! So the response of these two fishermen-turned-preachers must have stunned them beyond words. For instead of thanking the court for their leniency, they said simply, without the slightest fear or hesitation, "Judge for yourselves whether it is right in God's sight to obey you rather than God. For we cannot help speaking about what we have seen and heard." Acts 4:19, 20, NIV.

Did you get it? *"We cannot help speaking."*

I am impressed and thrilled by the grand way in which these men—who showed up so poorly when Jesus was arrested and tried—I am delighted with the way they stood up so magnificently in this situation. Instead of giving way to cowardice and compromise, they faced this hostile court with quiet confidence.

But not only am I impressed by the fact that these apostles saw a hard and dangerous situation through with honor. I am more impressed by the ease and naturalness with which they did it!

We can only conclude that it had become *just as natural* for Peter and John to be courageous as it had once been natural for them to act cowardly!

When these men answered the court in such gallant fashion, there was no bluster. There was no gritting of teeth to generate courage, no whipping up of the will. There was no clenching of fists or squaring of jaws. They spoke as if courage and loyalty had become second nature with them, as, in fact, they had. They saw their task through with such a beautiful ease, not because the task was easy—for it was not. They saw it through because they had experienced a miracle, a change of nature. And now they were only doing what came naturally!

Howard Welklin says it so beautifully. Listen!

"I walked through a rose garden and took time to look a lovely red rose full in the face. It was possessed of a beauty that had power to lift the heart and fill the eyes with wonder. I looked at this exquisite flower for a moment, and then I said, 'You may relax now. You can't go on being that beautiful all the time—it would give you a nervous breakdown!'

"But the rose only smiled and said, 'I am not putting on a show. I look like this all the time—even when no one is around to look at me. It is my nature.'

"A mockingbird developed the habit of singing early each morning just outside my bedroom window. One particular morning he was really giving a concert. The little artist was singing as if he were practicing for an appearance in heaven. After I had listened for quite a while, I raised the curtain and said, 'You may rest your voice now. There is nobody here but us and a couple of neighbors. There is no need for you to exert yourself so strenuously just for us.'

"But the mockingbird said, 'Really, I didn't even know you were home. You see, it is just natural for me to sing as I do.'

"I looked up at a mountain. I saw it stabbing the clouds and wrapping a mantle of mystic whiteness about its shoulders. I asked how it managed to climb so far toward the stars. 'It must be a terrible strain,' I concluded.

"But the mountain replied, 'Oh no! It is as easy for me to be tall as it is for a molehill to be low.'

"In the same way it is as easy for a giant Sequoia to climb to a height of three hundred feet as it is for a toadstool to hug the ground. It is as easy for the eagle to mount toward the sun and bathe his plumage in the fleecy clouds as it is for a bat to cling to a stalagtite deep in a cave!"

The transformation in Peter and John was not the result of long practice in being courageous. They had practiced cowardice—until the miracle happened. It was a miracle that could not be explained. The work of the Holy Spirit could only be experienced—and witnessed.

Peter and John, at last, had made an unreserved surrender to their Lord. And now thousands were witnessing the results. Thousands saw that they were not acting artificially. They were doing what came naturally—as naturally as breathing. And thousands were drawn irresistibly to the Saviour who could change men as Peter and John had been changed.

That is the only kind of Christianity that is worthwhile. If Christian behavior is awkward and unnatural, if it is obviously drudgery, there is no charm in it, no music in it, nothing to attract. But there is nothing in this world so beautifully irresistible as a life that naturally and spontaneously reflects the character of the lovely Jesus. Such a life is a breath of heaven!

Such a life can be yours, friend. And when it is, *love will be something you do.* But *love will also be something you are!*

Section Eight
The Dark Centuries

Avalanche of Terror
Red Stairs to the Sun

Avalanche of Terror

The high Sierras was a paradise of snow that Wednesday afternoon. At Heavenly Valley there wasn't a cloud in the sky. Lake Tahoe was deep blue. The whole landscape was white, and hundreds of skiers were on the slopes. It was a day in God's country. Nothing less.

But at Alpine Meadows, sixty miles north, all was not well. Eight feet of snow had fallen since Monday, and concern had turned to worry that the mountain of snow above the resort might break loose. At three o'clock those responsible began placing avalanche road guards and warning hikers and skiers out of the danger zone. They had an idea the snow was about to give way. And it did—at 3:45!

The snow broke loose atop Beaver Bowl and thundered down the mountain for three quarters of a mile to the Alpine Meadows Lodge. It crushed a ski patrol cabin, buried the parking lot, and caved in a wall of the lodge. Trees four and five feet in diameter were torn up and strewn about, and tractors were flipped over the blown-apart structures.

Under all that snow were eight people!

"They never knew what hit them," said Nick Badami, chairman of the Alpine Meadows board. "They heard a roar at the last minute, and things just let go like an earthquake!"

It would be a mistake to underestimate the power of an avalanche. It ranks with a major earthquake or a tidal wave in destructive potential. The power of the air pushed in front of an avalanche has been compared to that of a couple of locomotives.

They say there is little hope of surviving more than a half hour under the snow—unless you have few injuries and a good pocket of air. But a team of seventy searchers, with dogs and sophisticated probes, worked late into the bitter cold night. By Friday they had found six bodies. Two were still missing. One of them was Anna Conrad, a 22-year-old employee of Alpine Meadows. Hope was not realistic.

But the story has a surprise ending. On Monday Anna Conrad was dug out of the snow! After five desperate days, after 115 hours under the snow, the plucky and cool-headed young woman was alive, alert, and talking!

And it's true that she didn't know what hit her. Only after her rescue did she learn that there had been an avalanche!

We often wish that our knowledge of the future were not so limited. But have you ever thought how merciful it is that God has not given us the unlimited view of the future that we wish were ours?

And let me ask you this. Have you ever thought what a crushing burden our God must carry—able to see every disaster before it happens? Knowing the suffering—the death toll—and every tragic detail? Feeling the heartache and pain of centuries—all at once! Wanting desperately to stop it—but knowing He must wait a little longer, till all the universe knows what is wrong with sin. It must not be easy to be God!

There was singing and shouting everywhere. This was a very special day. Jesus was riding into Jerusalem just as the kings of Israel had ridden before Him. This must be His finest hour. Shouts of triumph were echoing across hills and valleys.

As the procession reached the brow of the hill, ready to descend into the city, Jesus stopped, and the crowd with Him. The sun, low in the west, was lighting up the pure white marble of the temple walls and sparkling on its gold-capped pillars. The people, proud of their temple, were spellbound with the vision of glory!

But suddenly, like a note of wailing in a grand triumphal chorus, Jesus wept! His body rocked to and fro like a tree before the tempest. And the wail of anguish that escaped His lips came from the depths of a breaking heart. Many wept with Him, in a grief they couldn't understand.

Jesus was only days away from Gethsemane and the cross. But He did not weep in anticipation of His own suffering. It was the sight of Jerusalem that pierced His heart.

The eye of the Saviour looked ahead not many years to the day when Jerusalem would be besieged by armies. He saw starvation and death on every hand. He saw Calvary—where He would soon be crucified—set with crosses in such great numbers that there was scarcely room to walk among them. He saw the bodies of the dead lying in heaps in the valley. He saw the magnificent temple ablaze, and then destroyed forever, with not one stone left upon another, just as He had predicted. See Matthew 24:2.

Is it any wonder that Jesus wept?

The Saviour could see all the way to the end. He had looked down the long, dark centuries, and now He told His disciples of a time of trouble and persecution so severe that God would in mercy shorten it. See Matthew 24:21, 22.

This is the same period of persecution spoken of in more detail in the book of Daniel and the book of Revelation. See Daniel 7:25; 12:7 and Revelation 11:2, 3; 12:6; 13:5. It is a period extending over 1260 days, or 1260 literal years. (You recall that in symbolic prophecy a day represents a literal year. See pages 74, 75.) The persecuting power was fully in place by A. D. 538, so that the period would end in 1798, with the persecution ending a short time before that.

Notice now, if you will, the twelfth chapter of Revelation. Here, beginning with verse one, we see "a woman clothed with the sun, and the moon under her feet, and upon her head a crown of twelve stars." The woman is about to give birth, and a dragon stands ready to destroy the child as soon as it is born. The woman gives birth to a male child, who is caught up to God and to His throne.

It is not difficult to get the picture here. This beautiful woman, of course, represents the faithful church. Compare 2 Corinthians 11:2 and Ephesians 5:25–32. Satan is the dragon. See Revelation 12:9. He stands waiting, determined to destroy the child. But he fails, and Jesus, the Man Child, is caught up to God and to His throne.

What would the rebel leader do now? Jesus was out of his reach. The throne of God was secure. He determined to turn all his hatred toward the church. He would hurt Jesus by destroying His people. Heaven was safe, but the earth was in great jeopardy. For we read, "Therefore rejoice, you heavens and you who dwell in them! But woe to the earth and the sea, because the devil has gone down to you! He is filled with fury, because he knows that his time is short." Revelation 12:12, NIV.

And the apostle Peter describes the mood of the fallen angel this way: "Your enemy the devil prowls around like a roaring lion looking for someone to devour." 1 Peter 5:8, NIV.

Like a roaring lion. Not a lion in a zoo, whose borders are marked by wire or water, reducing his threat to little more than his awesome roar. No. This lion is on the loose, able to prowl wherever God does not restrict him. He is not content to station himself before the church and hurl threats as did the giant Goliath. He is on the move. And his roarings are not idle threats. He is bent on destroying the followers of Christ.

So what happens? The woman flees into the wilderness, where she is relentlessly persecuted by the dragon, Satan. There, for 1260 years, more than twelve centuries, God protects her from extinction. See Revelation 12:6, 13–18. The persecution of the church is so overwhelming that it is described as a flood. Verse 15. But the earth helps the woman. Verse 16. The high mountains, the remote places of earth, provide her with protection. And she does survive. For in verse 17 we see her again—down in our day—still under Satan's attack, but still clinging to the faith of Jesus and still loyal to the commandments of God.

So much for the prediction, as we find it in the twelfth chapter of Revelation. This is what Jesus saw as He looked down the dark centuries. Did it happen that way? Yes, it did!

The powers of evil arrayed themselves against Jesus in the person of His followers, and it was not long until a storm of persecution was unleashed against them. It began under Nero, about the time of Paul's martyrdom. Christians were falsely accused of the most dreadful crimes. And natural calamities, even earthquakes, were charged against them. Great numbers were thrown to wild beasts or burned alive in the amphitheaters. Some were crucified. They were hunted like beasts of prey. Thousands found shelter only in the catacombs.

But under the fiercest persecution these Christians remained firm. Those who gave their lives were replaced by others equally loyal. Satan saw that he could not destroy the church by violence. He resolved now to work from within the church instead of from without.

Now the church was in fearful peril! Compromise proved a more effective weapon than death. The church, desiring to be popular, courted the pagan world. Pagans in great numbers came into the church and brought their idols and their superstitions and their pagan ceremonies with them. The church became corrupt. No longer could it be represented by the beautiful and pure woman of Revelation 12. The woman of Revelation—the small nucleus of Christians who held firm to the faith of Jesus and the apostles, could never accept the heresy and corruption that had come in. She had no choice now but to go underground, to flee into the wilderness. And there she would remain, hidden from view, through the long dark centuries—more than twelve hundred years.

Only God knows how many were martyred during those dark years. And during that time the persecution did not come from without. It was Christians persecuting fellow Christians. All through history some of the worst atrocities have been committed in the name of religion. It seems there is no terror so fearful as terror in the name of God!

But all through the dark centuries the light of faith, the light of truth, never went out. Hidden away somewhere in the wilderness, somewhere in the high mountains, God had His faithful ones. There were the Waldenses, for instance. In the Piedmont valleys of northern Italy, surrounded by the lofty mountains that hid them from their enemies, they worshiped God for a thousand years and never surrendered their faith.

Today you can crouch down on your hands and knees and enter the Chiesa de la Tanna—the church of the earth—where for many years the Waldenses sang and prayed and shared their testimony without fear.

But at last came the day when two hundred and fifty of them were caught in that very cave by soldiers who built a fire at its opening. As the oxygen was consumed, they sang praises to God until breath was gone, glad to give their lives rather than renounce their faith.

Yes, the torch of truth, even in the strongest winds of persecution, was never wholly extinguished.

It was in France—enlightened France—that some of the darkest deeds of all history took place. France had been heading for trouble for a long time. In 1572, it was the scene of perhaps the blackest and most horrible of all the fiendish acts of all the dreadful centuries—the St. Bartholomew's Day Massacre. A bell, tolling at dead of night, was the signal for the slaughter. Christians by the thousands, sleeping quietly in their homes, were dragged away without warning and murdered in cold blood. The massacre continued for seven days in Paris, and throughout France for two months. Some seventy thousand of the very flower of the nation perished.

Finally, in the late 1700s, came the French Revolution. The people took over. The atrocities of all their lifetime had been committed in the name of religion, and in their ignorance they blamed the Bible for it all. The Bible was banned. A dancing girl was brought into the legislature and worshiped as the Goddess of Reason. The worship of God was abolished by law. But little did unhappy France foresee the results of casting off the restraints of the divine law.

The people had learned cruelty all too well. Now the gutters ran red with blood. The galleys and prisons were filled. Spies lurked in every corner. The guillotine was long and hard at work every day. But the knife of the deadly machine was too slow for their work of slaughter, and long rows of captives were mowed down by cannons firing grape-shot.

Even atheistic France saw that she was ruining herself. Three years and a half after the Assembly had abolished the Christian religion and set aside the Bible, a resolution rescinding those decrees was adopted by the same Assembly. France had had enough. And the watching world stood aghast at the frightful result of rejecting the Bible and its principles!

At last, in 1798, the 1260 years came to an end. In most of Europe the persecution had largely ceased a quarter of a century earlier. The Reformation had become established. Bible translators had done their work. Printing presses were making the Scriptures available to all. Light was dawning!

Satan, in his fury, had unleashed a veritable *avalanche of terror* upon the church in the wilderness. Buried beneath it, still clinging to truth, she was left for dead—like Anna Conrad. But, like Anna Conrad, the church did not die. She emerged from her long and tortuous ordeal alive, alert, and talking. From the debris of centuries she emerged to stand like the Alps for her Lord, to speak in a voice heard round the world. And truth triumphed with her. For truth, safe in her hand through the long centuries, came out of the smothering avalanche untainted, needing only to be polished and presented again to those who had been so long without it!

I like the way Dr. J. B. Phillips has translated John 1:5. Listen! "The light still shines in the darkness and the darkness has never put it out."

The light still shines. The darkness has never put it out! It never could! And it never will!

I think of that winter night when the Roman legion was encamped by a lake in Armenia. There are several versions of the story. But evidently forty soldiers had refused to recant their faith. And they were sentenced to die out on the frozen lake.

Banded together in the numbing cold, they began to sing. The stern, pagan commander, on watch from his comfortable tent, heard the words:

> Forty wrestlers, wrestling for Thee, O Christ,
> Claim for Thee the victory
> And ask from Thee the crown.

Strangely moved by this unusual testimony, that hardened soldier, so used to cursing and frantic pleas for mercy, listened intently. These were men of his own company, men who had angered the authorities by their faith. These were his forty heroes, distinguished soldiers. Must they die?

He moved out into the cold, gathered driftwood from the shore, and built a huge fire with flames leaping high into the night. Perhaps this would lead them to renounce their faith and thus save their lives. But no. Again the sound of the refrain met his ears, weaker now:

> Forty wrestlers, wrestling for Thee, O Christ,
> Claim for Thee the victory
> And ask from Thee the crown.

Then suddenly the song changed:

> Thirty-nine wrestlers, wrestling for Thee, O Christ—

And all at once, as the song still floated in across the ice, one of the prisoners climbed up the bank and dropped by the fire, a shivering mass. The song of the forty was no more. One of the heroes had disavowed his faith.

On the shore, clearly outlined against the fire, stood the commander. Strange thoughts were surging in his breast. Then suddenly his fellow legionnaires saw him take one brief look at the pitiful specimen before him and throw off his own cloak. Before they could stop him, he raced down the bank and across the ice to the freezing prisoners, casting back the words, "As I live, I'll have your place!"

In a few moments the song, with a fresh note of triumph, was wafted again to the soldiers who had gathered, fearful and awe-struck, on the silent shore:

> Forty wrestlers, wrestling for Thee, O Christ,
> Claim for Thee the victory
> And ask from Thee the crown!

Who knows how soon you—or I—will need a courage like that?

Red Stairs to the Sun

Petra! The rose-red city half as old as time, carved out of solid rock! And out of this mountain fortress, red stairs—red stairs to the sun!

Stairs carved by generations long forgotten. Stairs that led to the high altars of sun worship. Stairs that for centuries felt the endless tread of fascinated, compromising feet. Climbing to worship a strange, forbidden god.

Red stairs rising from the city of the dead. Silent crimson symbol of the worship of the sun!

Can you imagine our thoughts—our excitement—as we left the Jordanian desert, approached a precipitous mountain range, and then entered the Siq—a narrow, rocky corridor leading into Petra?

Those vertical, towering walls were so close we could almost reach out and touch them—both of them—at the same time. Far above us was a narrow strip of blue that told us the sky was still there. And we knew that just a little way ahead—at the other end of the Siq—was Petra, the rose-red city half as old as time!

No wonder Petra was practically an impregnable fortress. For there was no other entrance to the city. Any invading army had to pass through the Siq virtually single file—and risk a hail of rocks from the defenders above.

It took us thirty minutes to go through the Siq. And then, bursting into view was the ancient, magnificent treasury building, a masterpiece carved out of solid rock.

And then the amphitheater, the palaces, the temples, the tombs, the dining halls, the homes.

We surveyed them all on horseback and marveled at these wonders of a past civilization. But we were looking for the red stairs. They were what we had come to see.

Yes, out of this unique and fabulous city of the dead, rise the red stairs that once led to the high altars of sun worship. And as I stood atop those red sandstone steps, it seemed that I could feel the very heartbeat of the great controversy of the ages.

Why? Because here was an ancient center of sun worship—the forbidden worship that for centuries challenged the true God. Here was the altar. And beside it the virgin pool, in which young women were bathed before being burned upon the altar as human sacrifices to the sun.

It is not difficult to understand why a worship like that of Petra, the worship of the sun instead of the God who made the sun, should call for a divine rebuke of some kind. You would expect God to act, to respond to this challenge. Here was a civilization that actually burned its children to its gods. You wouldn't expect God to remain silent. Especially when His own people became involved!

In the days of the prophet Elijah sun worship had filtered across the borders of Israel. The most degrading cults had infiltrated the chosen nation. King Ahab had married Jezebel—a name ever since associated with all that is licentious and vile. And the people followed their weak leaders!

And what happened? "They left all the commandments of the Lord their God, . . . and worshipped all the host of heaven, and served Baal." 2 Kings 17:16, KJV.

Here is a very important point. Not only did they turn to the worship of Baal, the sun god. But the worship of Baal also involved turning away from the commandments of God. It's always that way. False worship is not something extracurricular on the side, in addition to true worship. It's a choice. It's one or the other. The difference between true and false worship, then as now, was a difference in attitude toward the commandments of God. There's a dependable clue—if you want to tell them apart.

Imagine how God must have felt. Here was a world He had created—a race lured into revolt by His enemy. Here was a people for whom He would one day give His life. But now His own nation had gone tramping, tramping after other gods!

So it is that in the days of Elijah we see the most dramatic confrontation of all time between sun worship and the worship of the true God—the most dramatic up to that time, that is.

It was about 870 B. C. Elijah returned from seclusion and appeared before King Ahab, demanding that the prophets of Baal, the sun god, meet him atop Mount Carmel. There was to be a showdown. It was to be determined, once and for all, who was the true God.

And so they climbed Mount Carmel—450 prophets of Baal, one lone prophet of God, and a multitude to witness the outcome.

An altar was built by the prophets of Baal, and all day they begged that heathen deity to send fire to consume their sacrifice. But nothing happened.

And then you remember that Elijah repaired the broken altar of the Lord, placed a sacrifice upon it, covered the sacrifice and the altar with twelve barrels of water, and prayed a simple, heartfelt prayer.

And God heard! Immediately fire descended and consumed not only the sacrifice, but the altar and the stones and the water as well. For He who made the atom knows how to control it!

It was there on Mount Carmel, standing alone before the mighty prophets of Baal and a rebellious people, that Elijah cried out, "How long will you waver between two opinions? If the Lord is God, follow him; but if Baal is God, follow him." 1 Kings 18:21, NIV.

How long are you going to waver between two opinions? The New English Bible says, "How long will you sit on the fence?" It was a call for decision. It was a call to choose between the worship of the true God and the worship of the sun god.

But now something interesting. Right at the close of the Old Testament is this prediction: "I will send you Elijah the prophet before the coming of the great and dreadful day of the Lord: And he shall turn the heart of the fathers to the children, and the heart of the children to their fathers, lest I come and smite the earth with a curse." Malachi 4:5, 6, KJV.

Elijah? Coming back in our time? What do we have here? Reincarnation? Does this mean that we can expect to see the prophet Elijah himself, with his long flowing robes, standing in Times Square in New York City, or walking up and down Washington's Pennsylvania Avenue, or Market Street in San Francisco? Or Picadilly in London? Or Tokyo, Sydney, or Paris?

Actually Malachi's prophecy was to have a double application. It was to be fulfilled twice. Elijah would return down here in our time, before the *second* coming of our Lord. But he was also to come into the picture before the *first* coming of Jesus to this earth.

The disciples of Jesus understood Malachi's prophecy to mean that Elijah would appear before the Messiah came. And when they became convinced that Jesus was the Messiah, they wondered why they had seen nothing of Elijah.

So they asked Jesus about it one day, and He told them that Elijah had already come and they hadn't recognized him. Then He made it clear that He was referring to John the Baptist. See Matthew 17:10–13. But when they asked John if he was Elijah, he said he was not. See John 1:21.

Confused? It all clears up when we read the announcement of the angel to Zacharias, the father of John the Baptist—before John was born. "And he shall go before him in the spirit and power of Elias, to turn the hearts of the fathers to the children, and the disobedient to the wisdom of the just; to make ready a people prepared for the Lord." Luke 1:17, KJV.

There you have it. Some of the exact words of the ancient prophecy are repeated. And John the Baptist, the angel said, was to fulfill it.

But no reincarnation. Elijah himself was not to reappear. John was to give a message, he was to do a work, in the spirit and power of Elijah. It was the message, not the man, that would reappear.

And was John's message similar to that of Elijah? Yes. He spoke in the same spirit and with the same power. He was fearless in denouncing hypocrisy. His message, like that of Elijah, was a call to repent, to reform. It was a call back to the commandments of God. It was a call to decide. A call to choose.

But was John's work in any sense a confrontation with sun worship? On the surface it seems that it was not. Yet if we dig a little deeper, some interesting facts appear.

The Roman Empire was then in power, you remember. Rome ruled the world. The Jewish people were chafing under Roman rule. Herod, a Roman-appointed ruler in the palace in Jerusalem, attempted to destroy Christ soon after He was born. And interestingly enough, Herod by birth was an Edomite. And it was the Edomites who had inhabited the ancient fortress of Petra, with its red stairs to the sun. Sun worship was in his blood.

Furthermore, the entire Roman Empire was riddled with sun

worship and God's people were not immune from its influence. So John preached to Jews and Gentiles alike.

The Roman Empire, I say, was riddled with sun worship. It was in A. D. 321 that the Roman Emperor Constantine actually decreed that Sunday, the ancient pagan holiday devoted to the worship of the sun, should be observed by all in his empire. In fact, in his decree, he even called Sunday "the venerable day of the sun."

That was only 321 years after Christ. But sun worship was not dead, even in the days of John the Baptist.

But now, according to the prophecy, the message of Elijah is to be repeated again just before the second coming of Christ. And just as a message given in the spirit and power of Elijah was to prepare the way for Christ's *first* coming, just so a message similar to that of Elijah will prepare the way for the *second* coming of our Lord.

Just like the messages of Elijah and of John, it will be a call to repent, to reform. It will call men back to the commandments of God. It will be a call to decide. A call to choose.

We can expect—in our day as in Elijah's day—a decisive confrontation between true and false worship. And sun worship will be involved!

You say, "No one worships the sun today. Sun worship is long dead!"

I'm not so sure!

You remember we've mentioned that during the early centuries after Christ things began to change. Compromising segments of the infant church permitted pagan influences to creep in, to corrupt and adulterate the pure teachings of Jesus. Compromise took over. Truth was confused and distorted.

Then came the Dark Ages. Copies of the scriptures were scarce and not readily available to the people. And without the safeguard of God's Word, rites and ceremonies—little things—crept into the church that would have shocked Peter or Paul.

Let's take a look at some of these little things—things that have little moral significance. They aren't necessarily a matter of right and wrong. But I want you to see what happened.

Have you ever wondered what chocolate eggs and bunny rabbits have to do with the resurrection of our Lord?

According to an ancient legend, an egg of tremendous size fell from heaven into the Euphrates River, and some fish nosed it up on the bank. That's where egg rolling started. Doves came down and settled on it until it hatched out Venus—known in the East as Ishtar, the great virgin-mother, the goddess of love and fertility, also called the "queen of heaven."

Easter eggs. Bunny rabbits. Fertility, you see.

Now listen. Ishtar, it is said, gave birth to a son, Tammuz, without a father. Here in heathen mythology, centuries before Christ, we find a counterfeit of the virgin birth. Imagine!

Certain of the male gods of fertility became sun gods. They all died every winter and had to be resurrected to restore the fertility of plants, animals, and man.

Now Tammuz, the legend says, was killed by a wild boar. And the worshipers devotedly mourned for his death for a month every year. Did you ever hear of a forty-day fast before a festival of resurrection?

Even in Jerusalem there were those who wept for Tammuz. And they made cakes to the queen of heaven, the Bible says. See Jeremiah 7:18. Did you ever hear of hot-cross buns?

Tammuz was supposed to have been resurrected on the birthday of the sun. That was December 25. Did you ever hear of that date? Since no one knew the exact date of Christ's birth, later Christians took the birthday of the sun.

In Babylon, however, the resurrection of their fertility god in their New Year festival was celebrated about the time of the spring equinox. Did you ever hear of a resurrection festival on the first day of the week after the first full moon following the spring equinox? We call it Easter.

But that isn't all. Remember the red stairs of Petra? These people went up to their housetops every day to burn incense to their sun god. And they also worshiped at their high places, such as the one atop the red stairs. Picture it. Those people climbing to the top of those red stairs early in the morning to watch the sun rise and to worship it.

Sound familiar? Tell me. Did you ever hear of Christians going to the highest place in each city to worship at sunrise? Once a year?

Now please don't misunderstand. These holdovers from paganism are nonessentials. There's nothing morally wrong with eating chocolate eggs or hot cross buns or putting bunny rabbits in a basket for the children. Or climbing to the top of a hill to watch the sun rise—so long as you don't worship it. Or giving gifts to each other at Christmas—even if it isn't the exact date of our Saviour's birth. I say again, these are only fringe issues. But here is the point. If these fringe areas of Christian worship have been so riddled with the trappings of sun worship, how do we know that some major area of our worship, something that does matter, has not been tampered with too? That's my question.

The fallen angel, during the long, dark centuries, did not spend all his time in persecuting the true followers of Christ. He was busy setting traps for the rest of the world too. What he could not immediately destroy he determined to corrupt.

He found endless opportunities to devise new falsehoods, to think up new distortions of truth. And his work was relatively unobstructed, for the Scriptures were not available to the people at large. Their knowledge of God's Word was limited to whatever the religious leaders chose to share with them.

This was Satan's hour. And he didn't miss a single opportunity. Little by little, and ever so subtly, he brought paganism, disguised as the faith of the apostles, into the mainstream of Christianity. And far more than fringe issues were involved. He had no intention of letting sun worship die!

Was it a fringe issue when the observance of "the venerable day of the sun" was not only decreed by a Roman emperor but maneuvered into the church, where it became so much a part of the Christian culture that millions today have never thought to question its right to be called God's day of rest?

The prophet Daniel predicted that the same power that drove the woman of Revelation into the wilderness would also tamper with the divine law and attempt to change it. See Daniel 7:25 and Revelation 12:6. Is it possible that Daniel's prophecy was long ago fulfilled—and with few voices raised in protest?

Satan was far from idle during the long, dark centuries. He used his time to strengthen and expand his whole deceptive system. The whole culture of those centuries was literally laced with unsuspected error.

And sun worship made it easy. The birth and the journey and the death of the sun each day, repeated over and over—this is what dominated the life of the sun worshiper. The sun gods were continually dying and being resurrected. It was not difficult, then, to promote the idea that life is like that—dying and being resurrected but never ending. "Ye shall not surely die." Genesis 3:4, KJV. Remember? That's where it all started. And that is what ties so much of the fallen angel's error together.

If a man never dies, then he must live on forever. If a man never dies, then it must be possible to communicate with the dead, wherever they are. And if such communication is possible, then Satan and his demons have only to impersonate the dead— and they have a direct line to the soul. With that direct line in operation, it is only a short step to control of the minds of men and woman. And control is the name of the game!

If the people, in general, had had the Scriptures in their hands during the long centuries, if they had had some way to check the truthfulness of what they were told, it would not have been so easy to deceive them. As they opened the sacred pages for themselves they would have discovered that Jesus called death a sleep. See John 11:11–14. They would have learned that the dead know nothing (Ecclesiastes 9:5, 6), that there is no work or knowledge or wisdom in the grave (verse 10), and that a man's thinking completely stops when he dies (Psalm 146:4). How, then, could there be any communication with the dead?

They would have found that one who has died knows nothing about what is happening to his loved ones (Job 14:21), and that a man never comes back from the dead to haunt his house (Job 7:10). They would have seen clearly that a man doesn't go anywhere when he dies—not to heaven, not to hell, not to purgatory (Acts 2:29 and Psalm 115:17). They would have seen that the Christian's hope is in the resurrection (1 Thessalonians 4:16, 17 and 1 Corinthians 15:16–22, 51–55). They could have grasped that hope, and it would have brought a light into the darkness of those weary years (1 Thessalonians 4:13, 18).

One of the cruelest inventions of Satan is the doctrine of an eternally burning hell. Out of the Dark Ages have come the most horrifying descriptions—picturing God as a cruel tyrant who delights in punishing endlessly, through all eternity, for even the smallest of sins. God has been made to appear more lacking in mercy than the worst of our terrorists—more cruel than the maddest of mad dictators!

It is no wonder that many were driven insane by the thought of themselves or their loved ones enduring such torture. It is no wonder that thousands became infidels because they could not reconcile such a teaching with the idea of a God of love!

Yet the teaching of an eternally burning hell is not in the Bible. No one is being tortured now in the flames of hell. No hell is burning now. There will be a hell someday. Revelation 20:9. It will be real and it will be hot. Malachi 4:1. But it will be quick. Psalm 37:20. And when the fire has done its work it will go out. Psalm 37:10; Obadiah 16; Malachi 4:1-3. It is inevitable, for the good of the universe, and for the good of sinners themselves, that God must finally deal with rebellion. But He will do it in the kindest way He can!

I say again, there is no ever-burning hell. Nor will there ever be. But how could the people of those dark, weary centuries know—without the Scriptures? How could they know that the whole thing originated in the mind of the fallen angel who is determined to defame the character of God?

Thank God, the dark centuries came to an end! And thank God, the Scriptures are now at our fingertips!

But remember—Satan is not dead. Sun worship is not dead. The final clash between true and false worship will come in our day—and sooner than we think!

But in the meantime—even at this very moment—the call of Elijah rings in our ears: "How long will you waver between two opinions? If the Lord is God, follow him; but if Baal is God, follow him."

It isn't a moment too soon to decide where we will stand!

The Truth About 1844

You've heard about 1844. The Millerites. The people who said the world was ending—for sure—on October 22. You've heard how they made pure white ascension robes for the event—and climbed the high hills to wait. How some climbed apple trees— and even barns—to get a better view. And how some went stark mad.

That's what you've heard. But would you like to know the truth about what happened in 1844?

The amazing, exciting, sometimes heart-wrenching story of 1844 begins about twenty-five years earlier, with an honest, highly respected farmer by the name of William Miller. For some years, influenced by friends, he had doubted the Bible. To believe in a Saviour from sin seemed only superstition. He thought that decent, law-and-order patriotism would bring out the best in a man.

But now he wasn't so sure. He had volunteered for army service in the War of 1812 and had been commissioned as a captain. In 1815, discharged from the army at the age of 33, he returned to farming near Low Hampton, New York.

As he reflected on his army service, he was troubled by the low morality of the men who had served under his command. It seemed that love of country had brought out the worst in men, rather than the best. And when, a year out of military life, he caught himself swearing just like any other soldier, he was alarmed.

He was almost in despair over his weaknesses. It seemed it would be so good to just throw himself into the arms of a Saviour and trust Him for forgiveness. But did such a Being exist? He turned to the Bible to find out. And there, in its pages, he found Jesus—a Saviour and a Friend.

The Scriptures now became his delight. He began to study

201

carefully, comparing scripture with scripture. By the year 1818, two years later, he had reached some startling conclusions.

He had come across the prophecy of Daniel which says, "Unto two thousand and three hundred days; then shall the sanctuary be cleansed." Daniel 8:14, KJV.

Here, he realized, was the longest time prophecy in the Bible, a period of 2300 years—for you recall that in symbolic prophecy a day represents a literal year. (See our earlier chapter "Decoding Bible Prophecy.") And he discovered from Daniel 9:25 that the period began with a decree of Artaxerxes in the year 457 B.C. Subtracting 457 from 2300, he was stunned. Something of great importance was going to take place in about twenty-five years. And what could it be?

He knew that the portable temple in which the ancient Hebrews worshiped was no longer in existence. And the magnificent Jewish Temple of Jesus' day had been destroyed in A.D. 70. He reasoned that the prophecy must refer to the cleansing of the earth by the fires of the last days. It must mean that Jesus would return, that the world would end—in about twenty-five years. And the world didn't know it!

Imagine, if you can, how he felt. The conviction deepened that he had stumbled upon information that the world desperately needed. But he wasn't a preacher. He was a farmer. Yet a voice burned within him, "Go and tell the world!"

For years he resisted the call. What if he were wrong? What if he had made some mistake? He didn't want to mislead anyone. He checked and rechecked his figures and shared his convictions privately. But that was all.

Actually there was internal evidence, within the prophecy itself, that sealed the accuracy of his calculation. For the first 69 weeks, or 483 years, of the 2300-year period would reach to the Messiah. Daniel 9:25. And the crucifixion would take place halfway through the seventieth week Daniel 9:26, 27. Miller's beginning date had to be accurate, for the sixty-nine weeks reached exactly to A.D. 27, the year of Jesus' baptism, when He began His public ministry as the Messiah. And the crucifixion followed in the spring of A.D. 31—three and a half years later. To have used any other beginning date for the 2300 years would have left these two significant dates wandering meaninglessly in history.

And we would have been robbed of irrefutable proof, mathematical proof, that Jesus was who He said He was. Unquestionably Miller was right in his calculation.

Finally, in August 1831, after thirteen years had passed, he promised the Lord that he would preach about the second coming—but only if he received an invitation to do so. He felt quite safe, for certainly no invitation would come.

But within an hour a nephew arrived unexpectedly with a message: The Baptist minister in nearby Dresden would be unable to speak the next day. Would he come and talk to the people about the second coming of Christ?

Miller was horrified. But he would go. How could he reject so definite a call?

From the start it was evident that this humble farmer had Heaven's blessing. For apparently his very first preaching series resulted in the conversion of about seventy persons!

The secret of his success was in his sound Bible preaching. And as ministers saw that his preaching built up congregations, he soon had far more invitations than he could accept.

Here was not an isolated revival. Nor was it confined to New England. It was a worldwide religious awakening. In Europe, for instance, Dr. Joseph Wolff, known as "the missionary to the world," began preaching, as early as 1821, that Christ was about to return. An English writer says that about seven hundred ministers of the Church of England were preaching "this gospel of the kingdom." In South America and in Germany, people heard the message.

In Scandinavia the preachers of the Lord's soon coming were opposed by the clergy of the state church, and some were thrown into prison. But where the preachers were silenced, God gave the message in a miraculous way—through child preachers, some of them no more than six or eight years old.

In 1833, a great meteor shower over New England fulfilled the prophecy of Jesus (Matthew 24:29) that the stars would fall from heaven as a sign of His soon return. This gave great impetus to Miller's preaching. At one point he would claim, and probably correctly, that he had seen at least six thousand conversions in the meetings he had conducted—and that about seven hundred of these were former infidels.

But the attitude of the organized churches toward his preaching, and that of the other ministers who joined him, began to change. The churches could find no fault with the clear, sound, persuasive Bible preaching of the Millerites, or with their calculations. It was the *event* they predicted that was resisted. The truth is that the popular churches, though founded upon their professed love of Christ, simply did not want Him to return—at least not in their day!

It was made to appear a sin to study the scriptures regarding the coming of Christ and the end of the world. The Millerites began to be pushed out of the churches. And sensing that they were not welcome, many began to voluntarily withdraw. It is estimated that fifty thousand withdrew from the churches in the summer of 1844—in New England alone.

The Millerites have sometimes been charged with irresponsible time-setting. Didn't they know that Jesus had said no man knows the day or the hour? See Matthew 24:36.

Yes, they were aware of what Jesus had said. But they reasoned that His words did not necessarily mean that no man would *ever* know. They thought that God was now revealing the time.

It is true that at least five definite dates for the end of the world were set by one or another of the Millerites, though not necessarily accepted by the leaders of the movement.

But this pattern of indecision is not at all surprising when we realize that the Millerites were still feeling their way in regard to the *exact* date that would mark the end of the 2300 years.

You see, if you simply subtract 457 BC from 2300 years, you get A.D. 1843. But the decree of Artaxerxes that marked the beginning of the time period was made in the *spring* of 457, not at the start of the year. This means that you have only 456 years and a fraction to subtract, and moves you to the spring of 1844. And then, when you discover that the decree did not go into effect until the *fall* of 457, you must move down to the *fall* of 1844. But even then, what exact date in the fall of 1844 would Christ consider appropriate for His return?

It was not until August 1844, as these Millerites, or early Adventists, continued to study the meaning of the types and symbols of the ancient Hebrew sanctuary service, that they realized that the Mosaic annual Day of Atonement had been in fact a cleansing

of the earthly sanctuary. And in the year 1844, according to the
Caraite Jewish calendar, the Day of Atonement would fall on
October 22. That date was then generally accepted, although Miller himself did not accept it until October 6.

Some writers have not resisted the temptation to circulate fanciful reports concerning the behavior of the Millerites on October
22 that have made interesting reading for many years.

But the late Francis D. Nichol, a specialist in this Millerite
study, really got to the bottom of the matter. He checked out
every wild tale about the ascension robes and other alleged fanatical behavior. And in every single instance he found the report
either untrue or greatly exaggerated. Then he put the results of
his research into a large volume called *The Midnight Cry,* which
effectively exposed the ascension-robe tales as nothing but myths
turned folklore.

One scholar after another who reviewed his book applauded his
work. One reviewer, writing in the *New York Herald Tribune,*
had this to say:

"Most laymen in New England and the Midwest have been
brought up on stories of the fanatical imbecilities of the Millerites—how they gathered and shouted, how they tailored ascension gowns of pure white muslin for the great day, how they
climbed hills and mountains, even barns and apple trees, in order
to get a good view of the event; and how many went stark mad
and had to be confined. . . . These stories have long since congealed into a folklore that is as firmly believed as is Henry Longfellow's verse about Paul Revere.

"Now comes Mr. Nichol," he says, "with a truly monumental
and enlightening study of Millerism, with especial regard to the
allegedly insane acts of its cohorts. . . . He discovered—what
every infidel knows—that the greatest persecutors of all were the
other Christian sects."

He goes on to applaud the book, and then concludes with a
light touch: "Though I admire the book and found it of intense
interest, I regret it must largely dissipate the more lurid of the folk
tales about the Millerites, wondrous stories cherished for years."

A lot of good stories lost! And what journalist likes to lose a
good story?

I need not tell you that the disappointment following October

22 cut the Millerites very, very deeply. One man wrote, "Our fondest hopes and expectations were blasted, and such a spirit of weeping came over us as I never experienced before. It seemed that the loss of all earthly friends could have been no comparison. We wept, and wept, till the day dawn."

And then imagine, if you can, the crushing embarrassment of meeting friends and neighbors the next day. "Oh, are you still here? I thought you were leaving this world yesterday. What happened? Why didn't you go?"

God, for His own reasons, had permitted the movement He had so remarkably blessed to end in bitter disappointment. And as the night of October 22 wore away and turned to dawn, not a soul knew why!

Isn't the Cross Enough?

The cross of Calvary—remember—had stood like a giant billboard of defeat. There on that despised instrument of death hung the limp, lifeless body of One who had claimed to be the Son of God, One who had claimed to have power over death. But now He had died like any other man. And the message seemed clear. Whatever the mission of Jesus had been, it had misfired. And tears were everywhere. The people were left without a Healer. Israel was left without a Messiah. And no one read the situation more gloomily than the men of Jesus' own inner circle. Hope itself had died on that cross!

But Sunday morning everything changed. The dark enigma of the cross gave way to the wonder of the resurrection. The tomb of Jesus was empty. He *did* have power over death. He was exactly who He claimed to be. Trusting in Him had been no mistake. Out of the ruins of Friday's despair rose a faith stronger than death, a church that centuries of persecution could not destroy, a light that could never be put out!

And now, eighteen centuries later, it had happened again. A movement so evidently blessed and guided by God had fizzled in the sight of all the world. The year 1844 stands out as the year of the great mistake, the year when thousands waited for their Lord to appear—and He didn't show up. He left them waiting—without a word of explanation. And the disappointment and embarrassment could never be measured by words!

October 22, 1844, like the cross of Calvary, was read by the watching world, and by all concerned, as a giant billboard of defeat!

But, in spite of apparent failure, some good had been accomplished. The experience served as a sort of dry run of the real second coming. It was a living demonstration of how men and women will act when Jesus really does return. It showed clearly who loved their Lord and who did not. It showed who really wanted Him to return and who did not. The false among the professed believers were quickly separated from the true.

The Millerites, by their individual responses to this experience, had soon divided themselves into four groups. One group, the hypocritical and the insincere, those who had simply been frightened into joining up with the believers, lost no time in renouncing their faith.

A second segment of the Millerites concluded that they must have made a mistake in reckoning the time. And a third segment decided that Christ had really returned after all—not physically, of course, but spiritually.

Then there was a fourth group—a group that held fast to their faith and continued to pray and search the Scriptures, determined to discover where they had gone wrong.

Light was not long in coming!

In this group that continued to pray and search was a layman by the name of Hiram Edson. On the very morning after the disappointment, as he reviewed what had happened—after all, he could think of nothing else—he was suddenly struck with a question that opened the door wide for an answer. In fact, as the next hour sped by, his mind was flooded with questions and answers moving into position. Could it be that Jesus had never intended to return to earth on October 22? Could it be that with all their focusing on the calculation of the prophecy, they had been wrong about the event? Daniel's prophecy had not said that Christ would return to earth at the end of the 2300 years. It had said only that the sanctuary would be cleansed. See Daniel 8:14.

It had been obvious all along that Daniel could not be speaking of the sanctuary, the portable temple, that God commanded the ancient Hebrews to build. Exodus 25:8. That sanctuary, the center of their worship as they traveled through the desert, no longer existed. And Solomon's magnificent temple, which replaced it, had now long since been destroyed. They had *assumed,* without giving it much thought, and without any Scripture proof, that the sanctuary to be cleansed was the earth. Their *assumption* had failed—not the prophecy!

They knew from their study that the ancient sanctuary of the Hebrews was a miniature representation of a sanctuary in heaven not built by men. See Hebrews 8:2, 5 and 9:11, 23, 24. Could it be the sanctuary in *heaven* that was to be cleansed at the end of the 2300 years? Had something important—terribly important— happened on October 22? Not on earth, but in heaven?

It was as if Heaven was dropping the missing piece of the puzzle into his mind—not all at once, but faster than he could comprehend it. Imagine the excitement as Edson, and others in his group, turned to the book of Hebrews again. For it is the book of Hebrews that tells us what Jesus has been doing since He ascended to heaven. Their excitement could scarcely be contained. Would they find that Jesus had done something *very special* on the day that to them had been so disappointing?

To many Christians divine history seems suspended between the cross and the second coming. They are not aware of any activity between those two events. Jesus said He was going to prepare a place for His people. See John 14:1-3. But should it take Him so long? Wasn't everything necessary for our salvation finished at the cross? Wasn't the cross enough?

Many Christian minds resist the suggestion that Jesus had anything more to do after the cross. Calvary, they say, was a full and complete sacrifice. And they consider it a sort of heresy to suggest that anything more was needed.

The Christians of the apostle Paul's day were troubled with questions too. They had expected Jesus to return right away— surely within their lifetime. They couldn't understand the delay. What was Jesus doing that He should be so long? The book of Hebrews was written to answer their questions—and ours. In order to explain what Jesus was doing, Paul talked about the two sanctuaries, one in heaven and one on earth—the one on earth a type of the one in heaven. And those to whom he was writing, being of Hebrew background, readily understood.

At the moment Jesus died on Calvary, the veil of the temple— the massive curtain that separated the temple's most sacred place from the sight of the people—was torn from top to bottom by an unseen hand. Matthew 27:51. The system of sacrifices had ended. No longer must lambs be slain to point forward to the Lamb of God who would come. For Jesus, the true Lamb of God (John 1:29), had given His life at that moment on a hill outside the city.

The system of sacrifices was over. But its types and ceremonies still have rich meaning as they help us to understand the activity in the temple in heaven since Jesus left this earth. Paul explained that when Jesus ascended to heaven, He became our High Priest. See Hebrews 4:14–16.

Jesus our Saviour? Now our High Priest? How is that? Was it not enough to be our Saviour? Was His sacrifice on Calvary not full and complete and sufficient?

This may startle you until you think it through. But without the work of Jesus as our High Priest, you and I could receive no personal benefit from His sacrifice!

Suppose, if you will, that the United States Congress votes a large amount of money for the poor. Are checks simply mailed out to every name in the phone book? Of course not. Do government agents walk down the streets and leave huge boxes of food at every house? No, you say. A lot of money meant for the poor would go to the rich. It must be determined who is eligible for this aid. Billions of dollars appropriated by Congress don't help a poor family one bit until there is money in the pocket and food in the kitchen. The money appropriated by Congress must reach the individual who needs it. It must be personally applied.

Just so, Jesus has made the perfect sacrifice. He made provision that everyone—every man, woman, and child in the world—may be saved. There is enough for all. But all will not be saved. Millions will reject His sacrifice. And God will save no one against his will. Salvation is not automatic. The blood of Jesus, like an appropriation of Congress, must be personally applied to the individual—to the person who needs it and desires it. Jesus, then, as our High Priest, had something more to do.

Jesus, by dying in our place, by taking our sins to the cross and letting them crush out His life, by paying the penalty for every one of them—by this incredible act of love He earned the right to forgive us, and to give us life—never-ending life. When we accept the Lord Jesus as our Saviour, and His sacrifice, His death, in place of ours, our names are written in a very special book—the Lamb's book of life. It contains the names of all who have ever made a commitment to their Lord. Everything depends upon our names being written there—and remaining there. See Daniel 12:1 and Revelation 3:5; 20:15.

At this point we may be tempted to say, "I'm all right. I'm forgiven. I'm saved. I have eternal life. My name is in the book.

Nothing can touch me now!" And we may quote the words of Jesus, "I give them eternal life, and they shall never perish; no one can snatch them out of my hand." John 10:28, NIV.

Sounds like a foolproof situation, doesn't it? And certainly no combination of men and demons can snatch us out of the Saviour's hand—against our will. But we are free to take ourselves out of His hand at any time—if we choose. It isn't a matter of once-saved-always-saved, as many have thought.

An Air Florida jetliner slammed into a bridge and plunged into the icy waters of the Potomac. Stewardess Kelly Duncan was one who struggled in the water. A line was thrown out to her, and she grasped it. But then she let go, too weak to hold on. At that point was she a casualty or a survivor? Who could say? What if she had not grasped the line again? What if a man watching from the shore had not jumped into the icy water and rescued her? Or what if she had resisted rescue? I think you can see that it would hardly be appropriate to say that she was saved, to call her a survivor, when first she grasped the line. There was time for that when she reached shore—living, breathing, and happy to be alive.

Just so, the status of our relationship to our Lord at the end of the way is what counts. When we set foot on the shore of God's country, then it will be time to say that we are saved. And when that time comes, not one of us will call it something *we* achieved. We shall be forever aware that we were *rescued*—the strong hand of the Saviour bringing us in when we were too weak to hold on. Only the decision was our own!

Our decisions all along the way are what count—not just at the beginning. Accepting Christ does not make us robots. A commitment to Him does not take away our power of choice. We are always free to choose another master. We can accept Jesus today and reject Him tomorrow—if we choose.

Jesus declared, "He that shall endure unto the end, the same shall be saved." Matthew 24:13, KJV. And He counsels us, "Hold that fast which thou hast, that no man take thy crown." Revelation 3:11, KJV. The apostle Paul was keenly aware that it was possible for him to preach to others and ultimately lose out himself. See 1 Corinthians 9:27.

Do these scriptures rob us of the quiet assurance that a Christian should have? Not at all. They only protect us from a false assurance, from resting comfortably in a relationship that has never existed—or that we have long since lost.

The more we probe the Scriptures, the more we see that the Christian life is a relationship with our Lord—a relationship that is maintained and grows as the days go by, or a relationship that is lost through carelessness. Jesus said to His Father, the night before He died: "Now this is eternal life: that they may know you, the only true God, and Jesus Christ, whom you have sent." John 17:3, NIV.

There is no joy in the world like the joy of knowing Jesus—a living, breathing, two-way relationship that defies description. Men cannot touch it. Demons cannot touch it. Circumstances cannot touch it. There is no security like it, no place of safety like it, no assurance like it. Truly it can be called the beginning of eternal life!

But there is nothing more tragic than for a person to spend years promoting the name of Jesus, working long, weary days, always confident that one day his work will be acknowledged and rewarded—only to find himself in the group to whom Jesus will say at the end, "I never knew you!" But it will happen to millions!

One day Jesus was talking about the time of final reckoning. And this is what He said: "Not everyone who says to me, 'Lord, Lord,' will enter the kingdom of heaven, but only he who does the will of my Father who is in heaven. Many will say to me on that day, 'Lord, Lord, did we not prophesy in your name, and in your name drive out demons and perform many miracles?' Then I will tell them plainly, 'I never knew you. Away from me, you evildoers!' " Matthew 7:21–23, NIV.

Think of it! Years of work! Work punctuated with prophesying and miracles and casting out demons! Years of assurance that everything was all right. But it was a false assurance, a deceptive assurance. For Jesus says, "I never knew you!"

Why? Why was there no saving relationship? Because they did not bother to do His Father's will!

Evidently it isn't enough to say, "I believe in Jesus." Evidently Jesus expects faith in Him to be demonstrated, not just talked about. There is no better illustration of this principle than the experience of the ancient Hebrews as they were about to be freed from Egyptian slavery.

Because of the stubborn king's refusal to let God's people go, God had found it necessary to let severe judgments fall upon the land. These judgments had been increasingly disastrous. But in every case there had been adequate warning, with opportunity to escape the plague. Repeatedly God had made a difference between the Egyptians and the Hebrews, with the homes of the Hebrews being spared.

But now the last and most severe judgment was about to strike. The destroying angel would pass through the land, and the firstborn in every home would die—unless the blood of a lamb had been sprinkled on the doorpost. And this time it would be different from before. The homes of the Hebrews would not automatically be spared. If the blood was not on the doorpost, their firstborn too would die.

You may have read the poem about the little girl who couldn't sleep that night. She kept asking her father if the blood was on the doorpost, and repeatedly he assured her that it was. Finally, at her insistence, he carried her out to show her that everything was all right. And the blood was not there!

A householder could say, "God knows I'm a Hebrew. He knows where I live. He knows I'm a descendant of Abraham. He knows all about me. He knows I believe. He has spared me before. He will spare me again. I don't need to bother with slaying a lamb and putting its blood on the doorpost!"

But God had asked the Hebrews to demonstrate their faith. And nothing less would do!

We are now ready to rejoin the little group of Adventists as they prayed and searched the Scriptures day after day, and often far into the night, to discover what had really happened— happened in heaven—on the day of their crushing disappointment.

Two sanctuaries. The one on earth a type of the one in heaven. Even the furniture in the ancient sanctuary was patterned after the great original in heaven. (See Hebrews 9:1–5 and Revelation 11:19). And if this was true, ought not the duties of the ancient priests, especially the high priests, give them a clue as to what the work of Jesus as our High Priest in heaven's temple might be? See Hebrews 8:1–5.

The high priest in the desert sanctuary, we are told, once each year went alone into the most holy place, where the presence of God was manifested (Hebrews 9:6–12). This was for a very special service, the high point of the year.

You see, all through the year, when the people sinned, they had brought innocent lambs as sacrifices, to remind them of how the true Lamb of God would one day have to die for their sins. Day by day, throughout the year, by means of the blood of innocent animals, their sins were transferred, in type, to the sanctuary. But there must be some disposition of these sins. The sanctuary must be cleansed of the symbolic contamination of the sins of the people. For this reason, once each year on the Day of Atonement, the high priest alone carried the blood of the sacrificial victim into the most holy place. By this ritual the sanctuary was cleansed. It was a service carried out because of the uncleanness—that is, the accumulated sins—of the people. See Leviticus 16:16.

The Day of Atonement was a most solemn occasion. It was a day of judgment, for any person who had not confessed his sins of the past year was cut off from God's people.

The little group of struggling Adventists learned from their Bible study that the sanctuary in heaven was also to be cleansed—not by the blood of animals, but by a better sacrifice, the sacrifice of Jesus Himself. Not once a year, but once for all, on the antitypical Day of Atonement. See Hebrews 9:22–26.

The conviction now was overwhelming—to Hiram Edson and the others who so tirelessly studied and prayed—that Jesus had never intended to return to earth on October 22. He *couldn't* return then. For although Calvary was a perfect work—a provision big enough for the whole world—there was something more He must do: The blood of His sacrifice must be individually appropriated to those found still eligible.

On October 22, 1844, the great Day of Atonement began in heaven. Jesus entered the most holy place to begin a work of judgment, concerning which the book of Revelation speaks. See Revelation 14:7. Heaven's books were then opened. See Revelation 11:18; 20:12; Daniel 7:9, 10. For before Jesus could return with His reward (Revelation 22:12), before the day when men and women are finally saved or finally lost (Matthew 25:31–34), the books of record must be opened—the books that reveal, without bias and without error, what each individual has done with Jesus.

No man heard the gavel as Heaven's court was called into session that October day. No bell tolled, no siren sounded. The sun rose and set as on every other day. Only by the Scriptures could men know that something of vital significance had taken place. Something *had* happened that day. While men and women waited in joyful anticipation and then wept in bitter disappointment, while the day and the night wore away apparently without incident, heaven's books had been opened. The hour of God's judgment had come!

Yes, God had chosen to reveal, to them and to us, through Daniel's book and the book of Hebrews, the very year and day when Jesus began his final review of the records of men. There is no need for any of us to come down to the end of the way and say we didn't know!

But bouncing around in a thousand minds are other questions about God's reckoning with men. Now that we know the *when* and the *where,* we ask the *why.* Why does *God* need a judgment, an investigation? Doesn't He know beforehand what the results will be? Doesn't He know who are His?

And why do *we* need to be judged—if we have once identified ourselves with Him? If one cross is enough, why isn't one commitment enough to assure us of a safe landing in God's country?

No Doomsday for Robots

An aging man sat in the door of his tent at noon. Looking out over the quiet of the upland plains, he saw three travelers approaching. Just before reaching his tent they halted, as if to decide what direction to take. Then, as they seemed to be turning away, the man hurried after them and urged them to stop for refreshment. While they rested in the shade, he himself selected their food and then stood courteously beside them as they ate.

Abraham at first saw in his guests only three weary travelers. Little did he suspect either their identity or their mission. Two of them, he soon learned, were angels on their way to the city of Sodom. And when the angels had gone their way, Abraham discovered that the third traveler was the Son of God.

Sodom was about to be destroyed. God knew the situation in that city. He knew how wicked it was. He didn't need to investigate the facts. But He did not want His act of destruction to be misunderstood. He said, "I will go down and see if what they have done is as bad as the outcry that has reached me. If not, I will know." Genesis 18:21, NIV.

On His way He had stopped to talk it over with Abraham. Abraham was His friend, and He wanted him to know. Abraham had a special interest in Sodom, for Abraham's nephew, Lot, was there with his family. And man of compassion that he was, Abraham was concerned for all the city's wayward inhabitants. Read the moving dialogue as Abraham obtains from God a promise to spare the city if only fifty good people could be found there. But what if there weren't quite fifty? Forty-five? Forty? Thirty? Twenty? God promised to spare Sodom if even ten good people could be found there.

The angels, arriving in Sodom, saw for themselves how frightful the situation was. They told Lot about their mission. He visited his married daughters and pleaded with them to leave the city. But it was a warm, balmy evening without the faintest smell

216

of doom. They thought he was talking nonsense. "Go home, Dad! You'll feel better in the morning!"

At dawn the angels led Lot, his wife, and the two daughters who lived at home, out of the city. It might be more accurate to say they were dragged out, so reluctant were they to leave. And then the fire and brimstone fell!

That was the best even angels could do, even God could do, in Sodom—four reluctant refugees. Hardly that—Lot's wife didn't make it very far!

God didn't need to be informed of the wickedness of Sodom. The investigation was for the sake of Abraham. He must understand.

Just so, God does not need an investigation, a judgment, to discover who will be saved and who will be lost. He knows the details of all our lives. He knows what the results of investigation will be—not because those results will be manipulated, but because He knows us all. The investigation is for our sake. He wants us to understand what He has done with our nephews in Sodom, our friends in Babylon, our sons and daughters in New York. And one day He will give us the opportunity to look into the books and see that He has done everything divinely possible to save them.

On one hand, God does not need the judgment. But, on the other hand, He *does* need it. He needs it because the fallen angel, for thousands of years now, has peddled everywhere his charges against the character of God. And God, in answer, has allowed Himself to be placed on trial. He has placed His character on trial before the universe. He invites us, He invites the angels, He invites the unfallen worlds to review the facts. For only as the details of His dealings with this rebel world are open to all—only then can the character of God be fully vindicated and Satan's charges forever laid to rest!

Judge Wapner, on ABC's "The People's Court," which televises actual small-claims proceedings, often has to remind a plaintiff or a defendant that once he renders his decision, it is final. They have nothing more to say. They must keep quiet. His decision is not subject to their approval.

But God is a different kind of judge. First, as the books are opened to the view of unfallen beings, He reaches His verdict.

Then, at a later time, He submits His verdict to us for our understanding and approval. And finally, at the very end, before the execution of His verdict, He submits it to the lost. And the Bible tells us that every knee, every knee on earth, will bow in approval of all that He has done! See Philippians 2:10, 11.

Have we anything to fear from a Judge like that?

We turn then to the question, Why do Christians need a judgment? They have publicly identified themselves with the Lord Jesus Christ. They had said, "I believe." They have witnessed for Him, promoted Him, recommended Him. Isn't one commitment enough?

If people were robots, a lot of problems would disappear. Robots have no moral responsibility. They cannot sin. But neither can they develop a character to be admired. They cannot choose. They are the slaves of programmers and deprogrammers. Whatever goes wrong, the blame can be passed along to something or somebody. There is no doomsday for robots. But, then, neither is there any heaven.

But people are not robots. People can choose. And because they can choose, God has a problem—especially with Christians. Let me explain.

Jesus, by dying in our place, paying the penalty that was ours, earned the right to give us eternal life. When we accept Him as our Saviour, when we accept His sacrifice, we have a right, a legal right, to live forever. It is ours at that moment. The apostle John says, "God has given us eternal life, and this life is in his Son. He who has the Son has life; he who does not have the Son of God does not have life." 1 John 5:11, 12, NIV.

But here is God's problem: He cannot—He simply cannot—let sin into heaven again. Here He has given eternal life to those who have accepted Him. But they still have freedom of choice. They still have the right to choose. And people do change their minds, you know. Their priorities change. Love wanes. Commitments grow stale. For a time they may have had a living, vital relationship with the Saviour. But that relationship may have deteriorated to the point where it has long since become nonexistent. Can God take all these people into heaven, equipped with immortality, without examining the ultimate status of their relationship? Never!

There is only one way can God handle this problem. The eternal life He places on deposit for a new Christian must be conditional. It must be revokable. It must be dependent on what happens to the relationship entered into at the first. You see, then, why the experience of every Christian must be investigated.

This does not mean that God is going back on His promise—or didn't mean what He said. The conditional element is right in the scripture. "God has given us eternal life," says John. But he adds, "and this life is in his Son. He who has the Son has life; he who does not have the Son of God does not have life."

When Jesus is no longer in the life, when the relationship has dulled and has been pushed into second place, when it has deteriorated until a person has imperceptibly eased the Saviour out of his life and never missed Him—does that man or woman still have the Son? Does that person still have eternal life? If he does—if she does—then God is in real trouble!

But God has made no such mistake. The books have been opened. Questions are being asked. A name may be written in the book of life. But should it remain there? Does Jesus still have the heart's best affection? Is the blood still on the doorpost? Is the first love still strong and vital? Or is the heart firmly attached to Sodom—or Babylon—or New York—unwilling to let it go? Can this person be trusted with never-ending life?

We may think of the decisions of heaven's court as being arbitrary. But they are not. It is *our* decisions that determine the verdict. Heaven simply recognizes them.

The residents of Sodom had been making decisions all along the way. Lot's married daughters were no exception. They were choosing the comfortable way, the popular way. God waited. Maybe they would change. But when they refused to be rescued, what more could God do?

Those who refused to let go of Sodom were destroyed with it. Those who refuse to come out of Babylon will be there when her plagues fall. And those who refuse to bail out of a doomed planet will go down with it!

Is it because God wants it that way? No. He will weep over every soul that refuses rescue. He takes no pleasure in the death of the wicked. See Ezekiel 33:11. But He must honor their choice. There is no other way!

The judgment need not be the stuff of nightmares. If we have made Jesus our Friend and Saviour, what have we to fear? We will be judged by One who risked His own eternal life rather than see us miss out. Will He try to find some way to condemn us? No. His consuming passion, all along, has been to find a way to save us. It is not *His* decisions we need to fear. It is our own. And they are under *our* control!

Tolling like a mighty bell over this wayward planet is the call of God, "Repent!" And the bell tolls loudest just before it is forever silenced. That is what makes me restless. There is so little time—and so much at stake!

The bell still tolls. It is the Jonah of today for the Ninevehs of today. It is the Daniel of today for the Babylons of today. It is the rumbling of Vesuvius for the Pompeiis of today. It is Christ weeping over the Jerusalems of today. The bell still tolls. But it is God's last call!

God is reckoning with the cities. And you—and I—we are the cities. Oh Detroit, with your humming dynamos, with your idols of steel and chrome, God says, "Repent!" New York, with your jungles of cement, with your long fingers of light reaching high into the sky, God says, "Repent!" Washington, with your graceful avenues, with your equitable system of justice, with your government for the people and by the people, God says, "Repent!" San Francisco, Los Angeles, London, Paris, Tokyo, splattering your streets and your skies with crimson neon, God says, "Repent!"

Where will you stand when the bell tolls no longer, when never another heart will be moved, never another mind impressed? Where will you be when a rejected Saviour calls out in inconceivable disappointment, "Oh strange planet in rebellion, how long and patiently I have knocked at your towers of glass and urged you to let Me in. I would have saved you from the burning. But you would not!"

Today—you can hear it now—the bell still tolls!

Their Picture in God's Album

It had been a beautiful autumn. And there's something about a New England autumn that holds you spellbound. For a few exciting weeks a divine Artist empties His paint pots over New England and splashes color with a happy abandon that takes your breath away. It's as if the Creator had stood facing the Atlantic, dipped His mighty brush in pure glory, and swept it low across the landscape from north to south!

But to the fallen angel, in late 1844, the skies were nothing less than ominous. God was making bold moves. And Satan would respond with countermoves on all fronts. Time was running out—and he knew it!

The fallen angel is a diligent student of Bible prophecy. He knew the significance of the year 1844. He knew that Bible prediction is tied to no specific date beyond that year. His warfare against God would soon be cut short—and the thought made him furious. Yet he had anticipated this, and he comforted himself with the thought that some of his best strategic moves were already in operation.

History reveals that the early nineteenth century marked the beginning of a number of movements destined to destroy the faith of millions. Karl Marx and the *Communist Manifesto*. Charles Darwin and his theory of evolution, which would all but destroy faith in the Bible and its account of Creation. Add to this the revolutions of 1848, involving France, Italy, and Austria. The smoldering tension in America between North and South. A couple of false prophets. And appearing just fourteen years before the little group of Adventists discovered the truth about the ministry of Jesus in the sanctuary in heaven—a religious movement with *human* priests and temples *on earth*. Is it difficult to detect the strategy of the fallen angel in all of this?

But as the winter of 1844 approached, the rebel leader was especially disturbed about the little group of Adventists who were spending a lot more time with their Bibles than he liked. They hadn't faded away as he had hoped. And since he had often listened in on their discussions, he knew why!

Yes, their disappointment had been real and deep. It had not been easy to pick up the pieces of their broken dream while the world watched. Fixing a roof—mending a fence—laying in a supply of fuel for the winter—harvesting potatoes. All the little things that couldn't be put aside longer—now that they were going to be here through another winter after all.

How could they have missed it—these sincere followers of their Lord, living, as it were, only a step from heaven? How could they have made such a mistake? How is it that they checked and rechecked their calculations of the 2300 day-year prophecy, but failed to question the event? I would like to submit that it was because they loved their Lord so deeply. They were so anxious for Him to return, so anxious to see Him, that they would have resisted any suggestion that they were wrong about the event. It was their crushing disappointment that had forced them back to the Scriptures to discover the truth.

It had been that way with the disciples of Jesus. Again and again He had told them of His forthcoming death. He didn't want them to be taken by surprise. He wanted to spare them this crushing blow to their faith. But they were so sure nothing tragic could happen to their Lord that they resisted any mention of His terrible ordeal to come. His words just didn't register.

But in spite of their misunderstanding of the Saviour's mission, and out of the very experience that had snuffed out their hope, came the great early thrust of the gospel that turned the world upside down. And now, down in the time of the end, out of what looked like a mistake, out of the most crushing disappointment, would come the great final thrust of the everlasting gospel that would reach to the ends of the earth!

Now, suddenly, like an avalanche of light, things began to fit together. Scripture after scripture opened to the understanding of this little group.

They saw now that not only had their disappointment been *permitted* by a God who was leading all the while. Their disappointment had been *predicted* in the tenth chapter of the book of Revelation. Verse 8, of that chapter, spoke of a little book *open* in the hand of the angel. Evidently a book that had been closed. What book could this be but the little book of Daniel, sealed till the time of the end? See Daniel 12:4.

This little book of Daniel would be "eaten"—that is, studied, assimilated. And at first it would be sweet as honey, but afterward would turn bitter. See Revelation 10:9, 10.

How better could their experience with the prophecy of Daniel be described? The sweetness of looking for the coming of their Lord, followed by the bitterness of disappointment when He did not appear when they expected Him. It was like finding their picture in God's album!

And now, were they who had walked so closely with their Lord—were they to just fade away in embarrassment? No! They were overjoyed—and awed—as they read verse 11: "Thou must prophesy again before many peoples, and nations, and tongues, and kings." KJV.

Prophesy again? Little did they know what God had in mind for them. Their disappointment was not to be the end. It was to be the beginning of a mighty movement that was to go to all the world with a message for all people!

Again and again this unique people emerges in the book of Revelation. In the fourteenth chapter, symbolized by three angels flying in the midst of heaven, they would find the message they were to communicate to all the world. And early in that message is the announcement that the hour of God's judgment "is come." Verse 7.

Do you see the perfect timing? Here was a message that no previous generation could give. The Reformers could not give it. For only on and after October 22, 1844, could it truly be said that the hour of God's judgment *is* come!

In verse 12 of this same chapter these people are described as keeping the commandments of God and the faith of Jesus. And in chapter 12, verse 17, they arouse the furious anger of Satan because they still hold to the commandments of God and have the testimony of Jesus.

What is the testimony of Jesus? Revelation 19:10 ties the testimony of Jesus with the spirit of prophecy. Could it be that these people, as they set out to communicate their message to the world, would have the advantage, the special help, of the gift of prophecy?

Through the eyes of the apostle John (Revelation 11:19) these people would look into the temple in heaven and see there, in a golden chest, the great original of the Ten Commandments. And if God saw fit to so emphasize the importance and sacredness of His law, should not that emphasis be transmitted to the world?

Would such attention to law make them legalistic? Hardly! Not a people who loved Jesus so much, and wanted so much to be with Him.

Rather, they would see in that law a transcript of the character of the lovely Jesus—and a definition of how those who love Him will act. And they would never forget that above that law, in heaven's temple, they saw the mercy seat and forgiveness!

This little group, so lately disappointed but now infused with new life and a new commission, was to become the nucleus of the Seventh-day Adventist Church, which was formally organized in 1863.

And what a package God would give them for the world! God's last call to man! A prophet/messenger among them, with a special knowledge of the future—when the world is crying out to know what is coming! A health message, and a worldwide network of hospitals—an answer to the problem of health care that would actually reduce the risk of death from our worst killers! With their emphasis on divine law—an answer to the escalating problem of crime. An unexcelled system of education. A call to worship God as Creator—in an age that looks to accident and chance for its beginnings and for its future. In a day when death and disaster have gone berserk, an answer to the haunting question "Why?" And when a rising chorus of voices is saying, "We would see Jesus," a demonstration of His love and an invitation to know Him! What a message for a jittery world!

As an Adventist, says a southern California attorney, "you would have in your hands a package of such immense value that if you could commercially package this thing and offer it to the world, you could make the Vanderbilts look as if they needed public assistance!"

And all this out of a crushing disappointment!

October 22 had seemed to hold such promise. But the day had ended in embarrassment and tears. Hope had all but died, and faith had shuddered with the blow. The day had passed without incident—or so it appeared. But somewhere beyond the stars, out of the reach of human vision, something *had* happened. God had opened the books. And now the world must know!

Storm Warning

On September 21, 1938, a hurricane of monstrous proportions struck the East Coast of the United States. William Manchester, writing about it in his book *The Glory and the Dream,* says that "the great wall of brine struck the beach between Babylon and Patchogue [New York] at 2:30 P.M. So mighty was the power of that first storm wave that its impact registered on a seismograph in Sitka, Alaska, while the spray, carried northward at well over a hundred miles an hour, whitened windows in Montpelier, Vermont.

"As the torrential forty-foot wave approached, some Long Islanders jumped into cars and raced inland. No one knows precisely how many lost that race for their lives, but the survivors later estimated that they had to keep the speedometer over 50 mph all the way."

For some reason the meteorologists—who should have known what was coming and should have warned the public—seemed strangely blind to the impending disaster. Either they ignored their instruments or simply couldn't believe what they said. And of course if the forecasters were blind, the public was too.

"Among the striking stories which later came to light," says Manchester, "was the experience of a Long Islander who had bought a barometer a few days earlier in a New York store. It arrived in the morning post September 21, and to his annoyance the needle pointed below 29, where the dial read 'Hurricanes and Torandoes.' He shook it and banged it against a wall; the needle wouldn't budge. Indignant, he repacked it, drove to the post office, and mailed it back. While he was gone, his house blew away."

That's the way we are. If we can't cope with the forecast, we blame the barometer. Or ignore it. Or throw it away!

Only once in history has a worldwide storm warning been is-

226

sued. The forecaster was Noah. God Himself had told him to warn the world of a global flood. And Noah showed his own faith in the forecast by beginning at once to build a huge ship in which all who believed the warning could escape.

There were no barometers in those days. A barometer had never been needed. There had never been a storm—or even any rain. See Genesis 2:5, 6.

But human nature then was exactly what it is now. The people laughed at Noah, called him a fanatic, a man deranged, made his boat a tourist attraction—and were caught by surprise!

But now, as we near the windup of history, once again the Creator of our world has issued a warning of global peril more dangerous than any natural disaster. This time, crowding the junction of time and eternity, we are warned against a storm of deception and false worship that will sweep the world. At its center are whirling a thousand evil winds—a low-pressure system that has been developing for centuries. And its danger, its deadly peril, is measured not by any man-made barometer, but by God's own Word!

The book of Revelation is the barometer. And you don't have to be a meteorologist or a scientist or a theologian to read it—regardless of all the fallen angel's propaganda to the contrary. Would God issue a warning on which your eternal destiny depends—and make it incomprehensible? Never!

Haven't you been told that Revelation is a closed book, a sealed book, a book so mysteriously symbolic that it can't be understood? Of course you have. But that isn't what God says. He calls it a "revelation." And a revelation is something revealed—not something hidden from your understanding.

At the beginning of the book (Revelation 1:3) a blessing is pronounced upon those who read and act upon what is written in its pages. And at the end of the book (Revelation 22:18, 19) is a serious warning against adding to or taking from the words of its prophecy. Evidently we are supposed to understand it. And evidently we can!

God's last call to men—the worldwide warning of which I've been speaking—is found in the fourteenth chapter of Revelation. Because of its urgency it is represented as given by three angels flying in the midst of heaven, each angel entrusted with a segment of the message that is God's last special communication to the human race.

These angels are symbolic. They are not flying over our heads with a megaphone. God sometimes does communicate with men through angels. But He usually uses people, not angels, to sound His messages. And this worldwide call of the three angels is no exception. Their words are being communicated by the human voice, by printing presses, by radio and TV, by satellite—all around the world. No one must be missed!

Here is the message of the *first* angel: "And I saw another angel fly in the midst of heaven, having the everlasting gospel to preach unto them them dwell on the earth, and to every nation, and kindred, and tongue, and people, saying with a loud voice, Fear God, and give glory to him; for the hour of his judgment is come: and worship him that made heaven, and earth, and the sea, and the fountains of waters." Revelation 14:6, 7, KJV.

First of all, the everlasting gospel. Not something new or strange. It's the same gospel found all through the Scriptures. In the Old Testament it is the Lamb of God who *would come* to die in our place. In the New Testament it is the Saviour who *did come* to take our sins upon Himself so that we could live. All the way through, it's Jesus. All the way through, it's the message that we cannot save ourselves. All the way through, it's Jesus doing for us that which we cannot do for ourselves.

And why is the everlasting gospel so in need of emphasis today? Because men and women are still trying, as they have all through the centuries, to save themselves, to accomplish their own salvation, to get by without a Saviour, without a cross, without depending on God.

First the gospel. First the protection. First the way out. Then the fearful warnings. Warnings that would not be needed if the gospel were fully accepted. Warnings for those who have refused the gospel, refused the protection, refused the way out. Warnings desperately needed because in opposition to the principles of the everlasting gospel is a false gospel that will yet sweep the world!

"Fear God, and give glory to him," says the angel. And what could be a more appropriate message for a generation that is giving glory to science, to technology, to material things, to each other, and to self? God has been left out—not needed any more, some say.

And why is the message so urgent at this time? Because the hour of God's judgment is come—has come. And you understand now what that means. Jesus is finishing up His work for men and women. Time is running out!

And now listen: "Worship him that made heaven, and earth," says the angel. Do you see how precisely God has tailored His message to this generation? God knew away back there, when He sent His angel to the apostle John, exiled on the lonely island of Patmos—God knew away back there that this generation would reject His claim to be the Creator of heaven and earth. God knew that men today would look everywhere else for our origins. They would credit long ages of evolution, long ages of accident and chance, with putting us on this planet. They would not want the responsibility that goes with acknowledging God as their Creator. No wonder the angel calls on this generation to accept that responsibility—to worship Him that made our world and us!

I think you can see that evolution and the everlasting gospel are incompatible. How can we worship Jesus as Saviour while we reject Him as Creator—when they are one and the same Person? See John 1:3, 10, 14 and Hebrews 1:1, 2.

Now the message of the *second angel:* "And there followed another angel, saying, Babylon is fallen, is fallen, that great city, because she made all nations drink of the wine of the wrath of her fornication." Revelation 14:8, KJV. Babylon! The symbol of all false worship. The purveyor of a false gospel, a counterfeit of the everlasting gospel. Like an unfaithful wife, she has been unfaithful to her Lord. And how far has she fallen? Revelation 18 tells us that she has become the habitation of devils!

In chapter 17 Babylon is described as the mother of harlots. Babylon has many daughters who, like herself, have fallen. Not all at once, but little by little. Once they were lovers of the true gospel. But they have compromised here and there, substituting a man-made gospel for the flawless sacrifice of Jesus—until finally they bear the name of their Lord but none of His character.

Millions of God's own people have become unwittingly involved with this counterfeit. They have been deceived by the propaganda and show of a false worship. And now the Saviour Himself calls them out: "Come out of her, my people, that ye be not partakers of her sins, and that ye receive not of her plagues." Revelation 18:4, KJV.

But now back to Revelation 14 and the message of the *third angel.* Here, in verses nine to eleven, is the most fearful warning in all of the Scriptures. Please don't fail to read it for yourself. It is a warning against the worship of the beast and his image and the receiving of his mark.

The beast—a vast, worldwide system of worship that is antagonistic to God, to His law, to His gospel, and to His people. It is the same power that the prophet Daniel describes as persecuting God's people and attempting to change God's law. Daniel 7:25. It is the same power that the apostle Paul describes as sitting in the temple of God and convincing himself and millions of others that he *is* God! 2 Thessalonians 2:4.

The image of the beast—a similar combination of religious and political power that joins hands with the beast in attempting to accomplish its sinister purposes. Both the beast and its image, of course, are tools of the dragon—Satan, the fallen angel—who is determined, one way or another, to gain for himself the worship that belongs to the Son of God!

And *the mark of the beast*—here is an act of allegiance to the beast that will clearly mark a man or woman as choosing the authority of the beast over the authority of God. It will not be a literal mark. And no one has received it yet. No one will receive it unwittingly. Every man will know, when the time comes, that he is choosing sides. And by receiving the mark, or by refusing to receive it, he will decide his own eternal destiny!

Some *will* refuse it. Some will refuse to go along with Satan's rebellion against God, for listen to verse 12: "Here is the patience of the saints: here are they that keep the commandments of God, and the faith of Jesus."

Here are the people who, in spite of all the threats of the dragon and the beast and its image—in spite of everything—have held to the faith of Jesus and remained loyal to all God's commands.

Here are the people, pictured in Revelation 12:17, who emerged from more than twelve long, dark centuries of persecution—still keeping the commandments of God and having the testimony of Jesus. It is because of their unbending loyalty to God and His authority that the special wrath of Satan is aroused against them.

Here are the people described in Revelation 10, who after crushing disappointment, would "prophesy again."

Here, then, are the people commissioned to deliver God's last call to the human race, the message of the three angels. They are a people of prophecy who appeared on the scene at the right time specified in the prophecy. For it is no coincidence that the message of the first angel announces to the world that the hour of God's judgment "is come"—an announcement that could not be made at any time previous to 1844.

From its earliest days the controversy between God and Satan, on this earth, has been between true and false worship, between the true gospel and a counterfeit gospel, between the authority of God and the authority of the dragon. And now, in our day, the issues will come out in the open. And every person will decide. There will be no neutral ground!

The issues will be clear to all. While a quiet minority are holding fast to all of God's commands, the worshipers of the beast, in contrast, will be violating them all. The rebellion against God, in its final days, will be total!

What a time of woe and wonder! A people quietly loyal to their Lord. Guided by a prophet/messenger. In constant communication with heaven. Visited by angels. Satan angry. Making war on those he cannot distract from their loyalty to God. And three angels sounding God's last call to the inhabitants of this planet. Sounding a warning that neither men nor demons can stop from going to all the world. For all the world must know. All the world must realize what the controversy is all about. In every country on earth men and women must have the opportunity to step out from the rebel camp and take their stand beneath the blood-red banner of Calvary!

This, then, is the storm that soon will break over our heads. Will you believe what the barometer says? To throw it away, or ignore it, or bang it against the wall to try to manipulate its forecast is to play games with your own destiny. It is to be caught by surprise, caught unprepared by a tempest the fury of which cannot be imagined!

But to believe the barometer, to believe the book of Revelation, to believe every word that God has said, and by His grace live accordingly, is to place yourself in the happy and secure and enviable position where every promise in the book is yours. And just one of those promises would be worth a million dollars in a storm like that!

Listen to this: "He that dwelleth in the secret place of the most High shall abide under the shadow of the Almighty. . . . Surely he shall deliver thee. . . . He shall cover thee with his feathers, and under his wings shalt thou trust. . . . Thou shalt not be afraid for the terror by night; nor for the arrow that flieth by day. . . . A thousand shall fall at thy side, and ten thousand at thy right hand; but it shall not come nigh thee. Only with thine eyes shalt thou behold and see the reward of the wicked. Because thou hast made the Lord, which is my refuge, even the most High, thy habitation; there shall no evil befall thee, neither shall any plague come nigh thy dwelling. For he shall give his angels charge over thee, to keep thee in all thy ways." Psalm 91:1–11, KJV.

A Prophet in the House

The editor of a large city newspaper was talking with a Seventh-day Adventist minister. He said, "I listen occasionally to the Voice of Prophecy. Now and then I glance at the *Signs of the Times,* which someone sends me. I keep a Bible in my desk. I listen and read as a newsman."

And then, "I wonder if you Adventists realize what an edge you have on the rest of the world. You have sources of inside information that are a real scoop—*advance information.* You know ahead of our best reporters what's going to happen."

And then a penetrating question: "What are you doing with it? Why don't you capitalize on it more? How can you keep quiet? Why don't we see you holding more public meetings warning the people of coming events?"

What did that editor mean? Inside information—advance information—ahead of our best reporters—a real scoop? Do Seventh-day Adventists know something the rest of the world doesn't? Do they have sources not available to our best reporters? What kind of edge—what kind of advantage—do they have?

Adventists are known as careful Bible students. They believe that the book of Revelation is written especially for our day and that it is meant to be understood. The book of Revelation is filled with sound, straight, sometimes startling information about our day, and Adventists have been sharing what they have learned from their study. But is there something more? Have they some other advantage?

The ancient king of Syria was at war with Israel. But he was having trouble, for the king of Israel seemed to know all his moves ahead of time. He called his servants together and demanded to know who was spying for Israel. And one of the servants replied, "None of us . . . but Elisha, the prophet who is in Israel, tells the king of Israel the very words that you speak in your bedroom." 2 Kings 6:11, 12, NIV.

233

It was an advantage—a distinct military advantage—to have a prophet in the house. Again and again the kings of Israel and Judah were instructed by prophets when to go to war and when not to go. Sometimes they disregarded the divine counsel—with horrible results!

Jehoshaphat, king of Judah, who spoke these words of counsel: "Hear me, O Judah, and ye inhabitants of Jerusalem; Believe in the Lord your God, so shall ye be established; believe his prophets, so shall ye prosper." 2 Chronicles 20:20, KJV.

The land of Egypt survived a seven-year famine famously because Joseph, sold into Egyptian slavery by his jealous brothers, warned the king of the coming famine and told him how to prepare for it.

Nebuchadnezzar, king of Babylon, was given a dream that outlined world history from his day to ours. But he forgot the dream, and none of his psychic counselors could tell him what it was. It was the prophet Daniel, a young Hebrew captive, who told him the dream and what it meant.

Years later, at Belshazzar's wild feast, there wasn't a soul who could read the fiery writing on the wall. But Daniel could—and did!

A young widow was ready to prepare the last bit of food for herself and her son—and starve. But the prophet Elijah appeared just then and asked her to feed him first. She did, gave him refuge in her home—and that tiny bit of food lasted all through the famine. And when her son took sick and died, Elijah prayed for him and his life was restored.

It has always been an advantage to have a prophet in the house! Wouldn't it be the same today? The prophet Amos wrote, "Surely the Lord God will do nothing, but he revealeth his secret unto his servants the prophets." Amos 3:7, KJV.

God has always spoken through His prophets. In times of crisis He has given special guidance through a prophet. Before the worldwide flood there was Noah. At a time of widespread apostasy in Israel there was Elijah. Before Jesus began His ministry on earth there was John the Baptist. To write down the book of Revelation there was the apostle John.

I ask you, In a time of crisis such as the world has never

known, when Jesus is about to return and the world is about to end abruptly, will God send no special messenger, no special guidance for His people and for the world? Is that reasonable?

Solomon, the wise man, said, "Where there is no vision, the people perish." Proverbs 29:18.

We have an abundance of prophets today. They make the headlines all the time at the check-out counter. But they seem to be mainly concerned about the activities of movie stars. Does God have some special interest in the movie industry? Is that the information without which we would perish?

The presence of false prophets proves one thing—that a true prophet is nearby. For the fallen angel and his helpers never bother with counterfeiting when no genuine exists. (Ever see a counterfeit $3 bill?)

Have Seventh-day Adventists had a prophet among them all these years? Is that the edge, the advantage, the real scoop the editor was talking about? Probably so. For Ellen White (born Ellen Harmon), who bore every mark of a true prophet, acted as a messenger of God from December 1844, when she received her first vision, until her death in 1915.

A girl of seventeen, she was one of those who were so bitterly disappointed when their Lord did not return on October 22, 1844. About fifty days later she was given her first vision—the first of more than 2000 visions during her lifetime. And to say that her counsel has given the Seventh-day Adventist Church a distinct advantage, in many ways, would be an understatement!

The famed John Harvey Kellogg, world-renowned surgeon and director of the huge Battle Creek Sanitarium, at its peak around the turn of the century, once spoke in a unique way of that advantage. He was in New York at the time, talking with Dr. David Paulson, who was just completing his medical training. The year was 1895. He said, "Do you know how it is that the Battle Creek Sanitarium is able to keep five years ahead of the medical profession?"

Dr. Paulson said he didn't know. Dr. Kellogg explained, "When a new thing is brought out in the medical world I know from my knowledge of [Ellen White's writings] whether it belongs in our system or not.

"If it does," he said, "I instantly adopt it and advertise it while the rest of the doctors are slowly feeling their way, and when they finally adopt it, I have five years start on them.

"On the other hand," he continued, "when the medical profession is swept off their feet by some new fad, if it does not fit [what she has written] I simply do not touch it. When the doctors finally discover their mistake, they wonder how it came that I did not get caught."

Think of it! He was talking about a woman who had no medical training whatever. She was not a nutritionist. She had had only three grades of education!

What she wrote on the subject of health was often directly contrary to what was believed in her day. She penned in 1864, "Tobacco is a poison of the most deceitful and malignant kind, having an exciting, then a paralyzing influence upon the nerves of the body. It is all the more dangerous because its effects upon the system are so slow, and at first scarcely perceivable. Multitudes have fallen victim to its poisonous influence. They have surely murdered themselves by this slow poison."—*Spiritual Gifts,* vol. 4, p. 128.

Can you imagine how she must have been ridiculed for saying that? Do you realize that at that time the medical world regarded tobacco and cigar smoke as an effective cure for lung diseases? One doctor even emphasized that a person should be careful to inhale deeply so that the lung surfaces would be bathed with the smoke!

Ellen White never heard of cholesterol. But in 1868 she warned that those who ate flesh food were "liable to acute attacks of disease and to sudden death."—*Testimonies for the Church,* vol. 2, p. 61. She said that animal fat would "make a diseased current of blood."—*Counsels on Diet and Foods,* p. 393. And today we clearly understand about cholesterol and saturated fat and coronary artery disease and heart attack and sudden death.

She did not understand the reasons behind all that she was told to write. In one instance she said, "The whys and wherefores of this I know not, but I give you the instruction as it is given me."

If Ellen White did not understand the whys and wherefores of all that she wrote, neither did Seventh-day Adventists—to whom much of her counsel was especially directed. And yet in a day when her statements were ridiculed, a day when she spoke in complete opposition to the medical thinking all around her, a day when science had not begun to confirm what she had written—they followed her counsel anyway!

Was this a blind conformity, a mindless following of a leader? No. They had simply checked out her divine credentials as a prophet of God and found them in perfect order. And that was enough!

What has been the result? Seventh-day Adventists have enjoyed a tremendous advantage healthwise. Because of her counsel against the use of tobacco, they have largely escaped lung cancer. And, most likely because of her counsel against the use of flesh food, they have also escaped, to a significant degree, certain other types of cancer as well.

Adventists definitely live longer than the general population. This is all borne out by careful scientific studies.

Some have mistakenly thought that Adventists, in their vegetarianism and their non-smoking, were simply conforming to some strange church taboo. This is not true. They have simply followed divine counsel given for the purpose of protecting health. And it has paid off.

The counsel of Ellen White was an invaluable advantage to the church in its early days. The worldwide network of Adventist hospitals and related health-care institutions number nearly 500; their excellent system of Christian education, including 76 universities and colleges; their 50 publishing houses around the world—all can be credited largely to counsel given through her. Not only was she divinely instructed as to what institutions should be established, but also when and where.

Sometimes, however, the messages she was given for individuals or groups were messages of reproof, and here was an area of her work that she did not enjoy. Like the Bible prophets, she was called upon to point out the sins of individuals. Some accepted reproof in a right spirit and corrected their course of action. Others did not. And with these she was not popular.

But it was the same way in Bible times. The world has never been very good to its prophets—except to its false prophets. Messengers of God were popular only when they prophesied smooth things. See Isaiah 30:10. Jeremiah spent time in a dungeon because what he predicted was not what the people wanted to hear. Jesus called Jerusalem the city that killed the prophets. See Matthew 23:37.

The timing of Ellen White's messages was often no less than fantastic. Sometimes a letter of counsel would arrive just as a committee was wrestling with a difficult problem. Often the letter had been written weeks before the problem developed—and mailed from as far away as Australia.

On one occasion, in vision, she was shown a group of men, in committee, discussing a publishing problem. She heard what was said and one particularly distressing remark. Five times she tried to relate the vision, but each time, as she began to speak of it, her memory of the vision was taken away. Finally, *at three o'clock one morning,* she was awakened and instructed to relate the vision in an early-morning meeting. This time she had no trouble remembering it. Several spoke in response, and then one man rose and said, "I was in that meeting last night."

"Last night!" she exclaimed. "I thought it happened months ago!"

He confessed that *just before the meeting adjourned at 3:00 A.M.* he had waved a paper over his head and made the very remark she had heard him make in vision. But he took the opportunity to step over onto the right side of the issue.

But it was not always like that. In the year 1902, after church leaders had repeatedly disregarded divine reproof, two Adventist institutions burned to the ground. Fire Chief Weeks, who directed the fighting of a number of big fires in Battle Creek, later remarked that he had fought every one of the Adventist fires and his score was zero. They simply couldn't be controlled. He said there was something strange about them. The water from fire department hoses had acted more like gasoline than water!

It is no accident that the Adventist Church around the world remains united in its belief in, and presentation of, basic Bible truth. Its doctrinal teachings were not formulated by Ellen White. Rather, they were arrived at through long sessions of Bible study and prayer by the early pioneers. She sat in on these discussions, but, not being a theologian, it was difficult for her to understand the problems. Again and again, however, when they reached an impasse in their understanding of certain scriptures, she would be given a vision either confirming their conclusions or pointing in a new direction. Such remarkable guidance, recognized by these serious and careful students as the work of the Holy Spirit, was an invaluable advantage.

And then, through the years, whenever fanaticism erupted somewhere, whenever some false teaching crept in, appropriate counsel always arrived at the hour it was needed. Compassionate person that she was, she wept over these problems and pleaded with those in danger. When pantheistic ideas slipped into a book unnoticed and were circulated among Adventists, she was shown in vision the peril of those innocent-sounding ideas, which, if followed to their natural conclusion, would have led to the worship of nature instead of nature's God.

For many months she watched the developing crisis, quietly counseling those caught up in the subtle error. For weeks it was difficult for her to sleep. Then, one night in 1903, she saw in vision a ship about to collide with a gigantic iceberg. And a voice cried out, "Meet it!"

She recognized her orders. There was not a moment to lose. And meet it she did—fearlessly. The church shuddered under the blow, lost an institution and a few of its most talented physicians and ministers—just as Jesus lost His most talented disciple. But the church went straight on—shaken but unscathed, and free from the subtle danger that would have destroyed it!

It is impossible to estimate fully the advantage of having an all-wise Lord guiding through a prophetic voice!

Yet today, as in Bible times, there are those who don't want the voice of a prophet that close. They don't want God that close, sending them messages in the handwriting of a prophet when they wander from a safe path. So they have looked for problems—for some excuse not to listen to the voice they find disturbing.

Some have made much of the fact that Ellen White frequently borrowed material from a variety of other authors, including historians. Yet Bible writers often borrowed from one another. Are they to be condemned? Jesus, in His teaching, sometimes repeated what others had voiced before Him. Is He to be condemned because the golden rule did not originate with the Sermon on the Mount—and because the command "Thou shalt love thy neighbor as thyself" had previously been communicated through Moses? See Leviticus 19:18.

Does truth cease to be truth just because someone has said it before? Is truth to be spoken only once—and denied to every subsequent generation? Are we justified in demanding that God show His prophets supernaturally, in vision, that which they can find in any good library?

As the author and originator of truth, has He not the right to draw it from whatever human source He chooses? Is He obliged to seek permission to quote the writings of an earlier prophet when He is inspiring a later prophet to write something? Did such duplication make either God or His prophet a plagiarist? And what about the writings of historians? Has God no right to the facts of history? Is history the sole property of historians?

Add to this the fact that in Ellen White's day writers, especially religious writers, borrowed freely from each other.and considered it a compliment to be borrowed from.

Jesus could have chosen highly educated men as His disciples. Instead, He chose humble fishermen willing to be taught. Ellen White was chosen for the same reason. With only three grades of education, she felt keenly her lack of ability as a writer. But listen to this from her son W. C. White—a statement made in 1933:

"In her early experience when she was sorely distressed over the difficulty of putting into human language the revelations of truths that had been imparted to her, she was reminded of the fact that all wisdom and knowledge comes from God and she was assured that God would bestow grace and guidance. She was told that in the reading of religious books and journals, she would find precious gems of truth expressed in acceptable language, and that she would be given help from heaven to recognize these and to separate them from the rubbish of error with which she would sometimes find them associated."

Ellen White, then, in her borrowing, was simply following divine instruction. Did God have no right to so instruct her?

The remarkable thing is that when she did borrow, she never borrowed false teaching. How is it that she immediately recognized even a phrase of doctrinal error? How could this be—unless the Holy Spirit was guiding?

At this point I want to bring you a statement that is uniquely appropriate—not only for what it says, but because of who says it. In Ellen White's extensive library was a book called *The Great Teacher*, by John Harris. She greatly prized the book and borrowed from it rather freely. But listen to what John Harris himself says, on pages 33 and 34 of that very book:

"Suppose, for example, an inspired prophet were now to appear in the church, to add a supplement to the canonical books— what a Babel of opinions would he find existing on almost every theological subject! and how highly probable is it that his ministry would consist, or seem to consist, in the mere selection and ratification of such of these opinions as accorded with the mind of God. *Absolute originality would be almost impossible.*" In John Harris' opinion, there would be *"little more, even to a divine messenger, than the office of taking some of these opinions, and impressing them with the seal of heaven."* (Italics supplied.)

You may say, "I prefer to live by the Bible alone. The Bible is enough for me."

Yes! *Sola Scriptura*—the Bible and the Bible alone—was the great cry of the Reformation. But there is a problem. Let me explain. Suppose, if you will, that the captain of a ship follows the chart carefully—most of the time. But the chart calls for him to take a pilot aboard for the treacherous entry into a certain harbor. Is he following the chart if he refuses to take a pilot aboard at that point? The captain of a large troopship did that, hit a mine, and lost his ship!

The Bible, in Revelation 12:17, describes God's last-day people as keeping the commandments of God and having the testimony of Jesus. And what is the "testimony of Jesus"? On two occasions the apostle John fell at the feet of the angel to worship and was told to worship God instead. Two parallel scriptures, with very similar wording—Revelation 19:10 and 22:9—record these incidents. Read these two scriptures carefully. Notice that the first says, "of thy brethren that have the testimony of Jesus." KJV. And the second says, "of thy brethren the prophets." KJV. Evidently the testimony of Jesus is something the prophets have. And Revelation 19:10 adds that "the testimony of Jesus is the spirit of prophecy." Putting these scriptures together, it seems clear that Revelation 12:17 can only mean that God's last-day people would have the gift of prophecy operating among them.

I ask you, then, Are we really following the Bible if we reject not concerned with assassinations and plane wrecks—however tragic. Rather, her visions were concerned with the great conthe gift of prophecy which the Bible says would be present among His people in the last days? Are we following Jesus if we reject a prophet/messenger to whom the Revelation of Jesus has introduced us? The truth is that Seventh-day Adventists *without the gift of prophecy* could not claim to be the people pictured in Revelation! Nor could any other group. The gift of prophecy must be present!

Adventists have sometimes been charged with putting Ellen White's writings above the Bible. But is a prophet placed above the Bible when that prophet is held so accountable to the Bible that she would be immediately rejected if she wrote anything contrary to it?

The Bible is the great standard by which every would-be prophet must be measured. And Ellen White had more to measure up to than any prophet before her. Let me explain.

The Holy Spirit is the real Author of the Scriptures. The Holy Spirit spoke through all the Bible prophets. See 2 Peter 1:20, 21. And the Holy Spirit never contradicts Himself. He will never tell a prophet anything contrary to what He has told the prophets before him.

A prophet today must be measured by the Bible prophets—all of them—because they came first. Moses was first to write, and every prophet that followed must agree with Moses or be considered fraudulent. Daniel had to agree with Moses, Isaiah, Jeremiah, and more. Paul had to agree with all the Old Testament prophets. And John in the book of Revelation must agree with all the rest. Still more was demanded of Ellen White, for her writings, if she was inspired by the Holy Spirit, must measure with what the Holy Spirit said in all of Scripture. What a test! And she met it!

One of our modern psychics—probably the most popular of them all—was asked on television whether or not her predictions agreed with those of the Bible. She responded with a look of utter surprise and said, "I don't know. I never thought of that!"

Strange, isn't it?

Ellen White's vision were not concerned with the activities of the movie stars—though of course God loves them all. They were not concerned with assassinations and plane wrecks—however tragic they might be. Rather, her visions were concerned with the great controversy between Christ and Satan—from its beginning to its end. Also revealed to her was the strategy of the fallen angel—all the way through! This, you will agree, is an invaluable advantage!

The first chapter of Ellen White's book *Patriarchs and Prophets* describes in detail how sin originated in heaven with the defection of Lucifer, heaven's highest angel. It answers the questions that have haunted us all: How did sin begin? Why was it permitted? Why didn't God destroy Lucifer when first he rebelled? Are other worlds involved—or only this one? Why doesn't God step in and do something about all the trouble we're in? Why is it taking so long? It's all there!

Later in the same book is a chapter that describes in great detail the Flood of Noah's day. It reads like an eyewitness account. It will hold you spellbound—and you'll never doubt again!

The book *The Desire of Ages* is unquestionably the most beautiful book ever written on the life of Christ. Like a telescope, it gives you more detail. Palomar's giant mirror does not add a single star to the sky. But oh how many more it enables you to see! It is that way with this book. With additional detail you are able to understand the conflict between Jesus and His enemies. You see how the fallen angel hounded His steps all the way from Bethlehem to the cross. And when you read the chapters about Gethsemane and Calvary it will break your heart! You'll see what Calvary was all about!

Her book *The Great Controversy* is the most amazing book you will ever read. It begins with the destruction of Jerusalem in A.D. 70, follows through the Dark Ages and the Reformation and down to our day. But it doesn't stop there. Without a ripple it moves on into the future and spotlights the issues in the crisis ahead of us as the great controversy of the ages reaches its final wind-up. It makes you an eyewitness to the upheaval of all nature, the roar of the tempest, mountains and islands disappearing, the cities falling, the earth convulsed as if about to break up. The sun shining at midnight. A hand holding the Ten Commandments against the sky. The quiet joy of God's waiting people and the agony of those who waited too long to repent!

And then comes the hour of ultimate triumph as the Lord Jesus pierces the skies and rides a cloud of glory, escorted by every angel of heaven, to history's finish line! And it isn't science fiction!

What an advantage—what a coveted advantage—God has provided for this dangerous, jittery day! A prophet in the house!

Section Ten
Creator on Trial

Looking for Adam

Anna was only four years old the night Fynn found her on the fog-shrouded London docks. Fynn was six feet two and 225 pounds. She wouldn't tell him where she lived, but announced that she was coming home to live with him. So he took her home. His mother was used to taking in strays—whether dogs or cats or people.

But little did Fynn know how this tiny child would dominate his life. At four she possessed an irresistible charm. And already she had a very special acquaintance with Mister God. But by the time she was six she was a theologian, a mathematician, and certainly a philosopher. Fynn considered himself well educated, but when he tried to answer Anna's questions, he found himself continually going to the foot of the class. He tells the story, which happens to be true, in his delightful book *Mister God, This Is Anna.*

One evening they were sitting on the railway wall, watching the trains go by. Anna was drinking lemonade. Suddenly she started to giggle. She giggled until she got the hiccups. When finally she had settled back to normal, Fynn asked her what was so funny.

"Well," she said, "I just thought, I could answer a squillion questions." *Squillion* was a word she had invented for numbers too big to express any other way.

"Me too," Fynn said, not surprised at all.

Anna leaned forward in her excitement. "Can you do it too?"

"Sure," he said. "Nothing to it. Mind you, I might get about half a squillion wrong."

She was disappointed. "Oh, I get all my answers right."

This was going too far. A little correction was in order. He said firmly, "You can't. Nobody can answer a squillion questions right."

"I can," she said. "I can answer a squillion squillion questions right."

"That's just not possible. Nobody can do that."

"I can—I really can."

Fynn was ready to scold her. He turned her to face him. But he was met by a pair of eyes that were calm and certain. "I can teach you," she said.

And before he could say another word she was off. "What's one add one add one?"

"Three, of course."

"What's one add two?"

"Three."

"What's eight take away five?"

"Still three." Where was she leading him?

"What's eight take away six add one?"

"Three."

"What's a hundred and three take away a hundred?"

"Hold it," he said. "Of course the answer's three, but you're cheating a bit, aren't you?"

"No, I'm not."

"Why, you could go on asking that kind of question until the cows come home."

At that Anna exploded into a roar of laughter, and he wondered what he had said that was so funny. Then he realized that asking questions till the cows come home was certainly the same as asking a squillion questions!

But she turned the thumbscrew one more turn. "What's a half and a half and a half and a —" He put his hand over her mouth. He didn't need to finish. He had the message.

She finished off with,"And how many question sums is *three* the answer to?"

Duly chastised, he answered, "Squillions."

He turned away to watch the trains. And after a moment or two she put her head on his shoulder and said, "Isn't it funny, Fynn? Every number is the answer to squillions of questions!"

That was the beginning of a game they would play for many months. Start with the answer. Find the question. Any number, any sentence, anything you could say was the answer to something. For Fynn it was not only a game, but an education in reverse. He had been taught the old-fashioned way—question first, answer second. But this tiny redhead was teaching him a new approach. She was teaching him to walk backward until at last he bumped into the question!

Walking backward, of course, is not always the safest way to proceed!

But Anna's game is not really new!

This generation is looking for its beginnings. It is looking for Adam, the first man. But it doesn't want to find him in the book of Genesis!

Millions today are sincere in their search. But other millions are unwilling to accept any answer that involves a Creator. They would gladly spend millions of dollars to search for the answer in outer space. They would happily accept some ancient legend—or some dusty artifact. But not a Creator! They are playing Anna's game—the answer first, and then the question. They have found an answer they like. They have decided that evolution is the answer to a squillion questions. And they like the game.

There are those who enjoy bobbing like corks on the sea of uncertainty. They like the mystery of it. If they knew something for sure, they couldn't speculate anymore. And speculation is fun. They like to have their minds boggled by the brilliant spinning of scientific myths.

All this to escape a Creator!

All this to escape moral responsibility? It was Aldous Huxley who said, "The philosopher who finds no meaning in the world is not concerned exclusively with a problem in pure metaphysics, he is also concerned to prove that there is no valid reason why he personally should not do as he wants to do."—*Ends and Means,* p. 315.

Yes. Doubt is seldom intellectual. It is usually moral. Human nature wants to do what it wants to do. And it tries to make its doubt sound intellectual.

You see, if there is a Creator, then we are responsible to that Creator. But if we are only sophisticated animals, if we arrived here by chance, then we have no responsibility. We can do as we please.

But you say, "I don't see how it matters what we believe about our beginnings. After all, it doesn't seem reasonable that God could create this world—and us—all in six literal days. Can't I still believe the rest of the Bible?"

No, you can't. Not very well. The Bible claims to be the inspired Word of God—not just a part of it inspired, but all of it inspired. See 2 Timothy 3:16. And if the first seven chapters of

Genesis do not tell the truth, if they are not reliable, then none of the Bible can be trusted. It is not even a good book—if it is a book of lies!

It matters—it matters very much—what we believe about how we got here. For what we believe about our beginnings determines what we believe about *God*. If He has lied to us about how we arrived here, if His claim to be our Creator is false, then is He a God worth worshiping?

It determines what we believe about *Jesus*. For if we simply evolved upward from some lonely cell in the sea, if we were not created in the image of God (Genesis 1:26, 27), if we have not fallen from that high position, then there is no sin, and no need of a Saviour. The mission of Jesus becomes pointless, and the cross only a meaningless drama!

What we believe about our beginnings determines what we believe about the *future*. For if we write the book of *Genesis* off as myth and legend, we are not likely to take the book of *Revelation* seriously.

What we believe about Genesis determines what we believe about divine *judgment*. For if we believe that the first judgment of the human race, in the days of Noah, never happened, are we not likely to quiet our restless conscience with the false assurance that the second judgment, which we are approaching at breakneck speed, won't happen either?

We could go on and on. I think you can see that what we believe about our beginnings could well determine our *destiny*.

And in the meantime, he who rejects the Genesis account of Creation is left without hope. For if Genesis goes, Calvary must go. We cannot reject the Creator without rejecting the Saviour, for they are one and the same Person. John 1:10, 14. Without a Saviour, there is no forgiveness. And without forgiveness, we are doomed to a life of utter despair!

Is it any wonder that the fallen angel, in his war against God, aims his sharpest arrows at the first seven chapters of Genesis? It's the Creator who is challenged, who is placed on trial before this generation!

God knew what the focal point of the controversy would be. He knew that nothing in all Scripture would be more attacked than these ten words: "In the beginning God created the heaven and

the earth." And notice that He didn't try to bypass a confrontation by hiding that statement away where only the persevering
would find it. He didn't give us a long introduction and finally get
around to saying it. He put it right up front—in the first ten words
of the Bible—so that anyone who sincerely wants to know the
truth about our beginnings can find it in an instant. No one can
say he couldn't find it, or that he missed it, or didn't have time to
search farther.

Why, then, is this generation, a generation so obsessed with
piecing together our beginnings—why is it looking everywhere
else? There can be only one answer. It wants to find Adam. But it
doesn't want to find him in the book of Genesis!

Recently there have been a number of reports of unrest among
scientists. Not a few are realizing that man is just too complex to
have sprung unannounced from a puddle of chemicals sparked by
random lightning bolts. Here and there we find what one writer
calls "a sheepish resort" to the idea of a Creator.

In fact, the magazine *Science News* ran an article breathlessly
talking about certain qualities in our environment without which
life could not exist, and concluding that "it seemed as if the universe knew we were coming." The article pointed out that the
creation-by-God theory would solve all the problems. But the
author didn't foresee any great turn in that direction—because of
what he called the present "unpopularity of God in scientific circles."

Dr. Carl Sagan is probably the most fascinating astronomer of
our time—and the most fascinated by what he is doing and what
he dreams of doing. He is unquestionably the most enthusiastic
spokesman in the search for life on other worlds. Like many other
scientists, he hopes to find clues to our own beginnings in outer
space. He is not afraid to speculate, not afraid to dream.

But of course when we are seeking solid information, serious
evidence, we have to park our imaginations at the door and let the
facts speak without any help from us. In such a spirit Dr. Sagan
asks, "Wouldn't we look silly if we expended a major effort listening for radio messages or searching for life on Mars if, all the
while, there was here on Earth evidence of extraterrestrial life?"

Looking for Adam? And a voice from a neglected Book on the
shelf says, "Here I am—right here!"

Remember the old childhood game where you go about the room searching for some object another player is thinking about—and you are guided by the clues "cold" or "hot" or "warm"? Listen! When you pick up the Bible, it burns your fingers!

You say, "I believe the Bible. I believe that God created this world in six days. But it doesn't say how long those days were. Each day could have been a billion years."

It is true that the book of Genesis does not say that the days were twenty-four-hour days, just like ours. But it comes very close to saying that. Scanning the first chapter of Genesis, you will see that each of the days of Creation week consisted of an "evening" and a "morning"—the dark part of the day coming before the light part. Evidently they were just like our days, marked by the rotation of the earth.

But suppose the days of creation week *were* each a billion years long. The idea poses some problems. For instance, God created trees and vegetation, including grass, on the third day of Creation week. There was no sunlight available until the fourth day. You men with your lawns, you know how hard it is to keep grass growing, even with a good start. Could anyone tell you that grass planted on the third day would have survived the "evening" of the fourth day—half a billion years—before getting any sunshine?

My friend J. R. Spangler poses another interesting question. He suggests that the Fourth Commandment, if the days were each a billion years long, would have to read, or at least be understood, this way (compare with Exodus 20:8–11): "Remember the sabbath day, to keep it holy. Six billion years shalt thou labour, and do all thy work: But the seventh billion years is the sabbath of the Lord thy God: in it thou shalt not do any work. . . . For in six billion years the Lord made heaven and earth . . . and rested the seventh billion years: wherefore the Lord blessed the seventh billion years, and hallowed it."

How do you think that would work out?

Adam, we are told, lived 930 years, and then died. See Genesis 5:5. Calculating a billion years for each day, he hasn't died at all. In fact, he hasn't even finished his first day yet. His sons Cain and Abel haven't been born yet—let alone the rest of us!

It gets a little ridiculous, doesn't it?

But one more question: If the days *were* a billion years long, but now they are twenty-four hours long, when did they stop being a billion years long? In the afternoon of the sixth day? Was the sixth day a billion years in length for God—but a twenty-four-hour day for Adam?

Creation cannot be proven—nor can evolution. We can't put a planet into a laboratory and speed up time and see what happens in six billion years. Nor can we invite God to spend a week in one of our laboratories and demonstrate for us that He *can* make a planet and furnish it with animals, vegetation, and people, all in six literal days.

But God gives us all the evidence we need for a strong faith. He demonstrates every day that His Word can be trusted. On the other hand, He will not force any man to believe. Belief is a mind-set. Unbelief is a mind-set. We are free to choose what and whom we will believe!

Not so long ago a Sequoia National Park ranger strolled into a crowd of about three hundred who had made the climb from the Owens Valley to the granite summit of Mount Whitney. One of the hikers, simply awed by the sight of the two-mile plunge down to the valley floor, asked the ranger how the Sierra came to be shaped as it is. The ranger had had a smattering of geology, and he replied, "Well, this summit plateau is part of the old landscape that was lying here as kind of a rolling lowland millions of years ago. Then the whole Sierra was bowed up like an arch."

More people turned to listen, and he went on, "Then the keystone collapsed to form this great escarpment going down into the Owens Valley, with the White Mountains over there to the east making the other half of the broken arch. And later, through erosion and glaciation we got the final shaping of the land—the meadows and canyons and peaks and bowls—as you see them all around you today."

The ranger paused to let all that information sink in, and one of the hikers spoke up and said, "I don't believe anything you say. The Bible says the Lord made the world in six days, so nothing you say is true!"

The ranger replied thoughtfully, "Well, you're right—it says that." And he wandered off by himself to think about it. Months later he hadn't thought of a more suitable reply. "What could I tell the guy?" he shrugged. "Besides, maybe he was right!"

The truth is that some of the most sophisticated earth scientists are still probing, sifting and re-sifting the evidence, hoping to uncover the secrets of the Sierra's creation, not quite sure as they once were.

Wondering if there has been a mistake. I do not mean that there is any wholesale exodus from the Darwin camp. Far from it. Nor will there be any such widespread defection. The fallen angel will not allow his attack on God's creatorship to fizzle out. If anything, he will escalate it. But more and more scientists—serious, qualified scientists—are coming to realize that the evidence is not all on one side!

It was the ancient Job who said, "Go and ask the cattle, ask the birds of the air to inform you, or tell the creatures that crawl to teach you, and the fishes of the sea to give you instruction. Who cannot learn from all these that the Lord's own hand has done this?" Job 12:7–9, NEB.

Yes, a man may juggle his speculations with the skill of a drum major—and have millions at his feet. He may speak with a show of polished authority about what happened in ages past. He may pronounce with fanfare that there is no God. He may witness the decline of faith—and call it progress. He may write off the book of Genesis as myth—and declare that the man who believes it is gullible and unenlightened. He may spin his fables so cleverly that only a few ever notice the absence of the strong threads of fact!

But *all the while* the little honeybee, with the brain of a mathematician, keeps on dancing her strange dance—oblivious to the doubts of men.

All the while the birds take to the air better equipped for flight than any airliner ever was, able to fly unmapped oceans with their built-in instruments of navigation.

All the while the bats effortlessly operate their ultrasonic radar, reminding us that neither technology nor wisdom are exclusive with the human mind.

Doubt is in the air. Ether waves carry the speculations of men into the homes of millions. But *all the while* the female potter wasp, untroubled by the doubts of men, is doing her hanging act. You say you never heard of the potter wasp? Never heard of the eggshell that doesn't break but unwinds—into a miniature spiral staircase? You don't know what you've missed!

Book after book will tell you, with an air of authority, as if it couldn't be questioned, how this earth came to be. Its supposed history is traced through supposed ages by supposed experts. But *all the while* the birds and the honeybees and the potter wasps are challenging entrenched beliefs. Yes, and even the fleas!

Did you know that if you could jump as well as a flea can, you could start from a kneeling position at the base of the Washington Monument and sail right over the top with room to spare?

Where did the flea get its amazing ability? Why didn't it develop wings instead of spring? Was it afraid to fly? Did it have its eye on the Olympics? Or is there a Creator?

We are bombarded with tales of the magic of the ages, of happy accidents that exploded us ever upward—with never a need for intelligent direction, never a need for God.

But *all the while* the stars, oblivious to human pratings, speed on in their unerring orbits, keeping their appointments with a precision that boggles the mind. And no man can shoot them down!

Said the prophet Isaiah, "Lift up your eyes to the heavens; consider who created it all, led out their host one by one and called them all by their names; through his great might, his might and power, not one is missing." Isaiah 40:26, NEB.

And it was David who said, "The heavens tell out the glory of God, the vault of heaven reveals his handiwork. One day speaks to another, night with night shares its knowledge, and this without speech or language or sound of any voice. Their music goes out through all the earth, their words reach to the end of the world." Psalm 19:1–4, NEB.

No man can silence the message of the stars, or the voice of the beasts and the birds. No man can escape the grand chorus as all nature joins in the unmistakable refrain, "There *is* a Creator!"

But the One who flung the stars into their perfect pathways, the One who could make a world out of nothing and hang it on nothing (Job 26:7), is also the One who let men nail Him to a rough, splintery cross outside Jerusalem—so that you and I might live. And even the evidence of the birds and the beasts and the bats, of suns and worlds and racing constellations, convincing as it is, pales before the mighty argument of the cross!

You may remember the story of the unbeliever who rescued an

orphan boy from a burning building. Having lost his own wife and child, he desired to adopt the lad. Christian neighbors were skeptical about the wisdom of placing the boy in an infidel home. But the applicant won his case when he held up his hand, badly burned in the rescue of the lad, and said, "I have only one argument. It is this."

He proved to be a good father, and little Bobby never tired of hearing how Daddy had saved him from the fire. And he liked best to hear about the scarred hand.

One day with his new father he visited a display of art masterpieces. One painting interested him especially—the one of Jesus reproving Thomas for his unbelief and holding out His scarred hand.

"Tell me the story of that picture, Daddy," the little fellow pleaded.

"No, not that one."

"Why not?"

"Because I don't believe it."

"But you tell me the story of Jack the giant-killer, and you don't believe that."

So he told him the story. And Bobby said, "It's like you and me, Daddy." And then he went on, "It wasn't nice of Thomas not to believe after the good Man had died for him. What if they had told me how you saved me from the fire and I had said I didn't believe you did it?"

The father could not escape the sound reasoning of a little child. He had used his own scarred hand to win a small boy's heart. Could he continue to resist the scarred hand of the Man who had died for *him*—and say He didn't do it?

The mightiest argument of all is the cross of Calvary. The scarred hands of Jesus. Hands that were wounded in His encounter with the forces of evil—so that you and I could live!

What can we do but fall at His feet and say with Thomas, "My Lord and my God!"

When God Made Rest

How long has it been since you've taken a walk in the woods? Or spent an hour beside a secluded waterfall—just watching, relaxing, letting it tumble away your cares? How long has it been since you've backpacked deep into the wilderness? Have you forgotten what it is like?

Just thinking about it refreshes you. And looking through your favorite book of nature photos will set you planning for the first free weekend that comes your way.

It's all right to dream. Turning off the ignition and stepping into silence. Silence broken only by the sound of some little wild creature at home in the woods. A bird song that you haven't heard since childhood. You walk softly, slowly, listening after every step. You want to *see* the next bird that you hear. But a bluejay noisily announces your presence. Now all the forest knows you're coming. Your soft-pedal stalk seems rather ridiculous. You might as well let the twigs snap.

The hours slip happily by as you gather up memories to keep forever. There's plenty of time in the wilderness. Time to sit on a moss-covered log and get acquainted with beauty again—with life again. Time to climb the nearest mountain and stop to rest wherever there's an inviting rock beside the trail. Time to look down at where you've been—and up to where you've never been.

Time to mount your high-powered binoculars on a tripod and watch wildlife in action—creatures who wouldn't perform if they knew you were in the audience. Time to watch a coyote leap high in the air and come down mouth first, mouth wide open, coming up with a pocket gopher and a mouthful of dirt.

Time to watch a snowshoe hare, his nose twitching. Moose dunking their heads in a beaver pond. A brown mink hiding fish for its dinner in a tiny pool beneath a rock. A sandhill crane catching mice and insects. Time to watch a swift, graceful fox and see the mischief in his eyes as he turns your way. A little black

257

bear that seems to be daring you to come one step closer. You feel as if you're cheating, seeing it all so close!

There's time to follow any trail you choose—or no trail at all. You have no appointments in the wild. You don't have to go anywhere. Says Les Blacklock, "If you want to get somewhere, don't follow a wildlife trail. Moose trails run into bear trails, bear trails into deer trails, deer trails into fox trails, fox trails into rabbit trails, rabbit trails into squirrel trails, and they go up a tree and into a hole."

Finally, as the sun drops low in the west, you are perched on a boulder beside a waterfall, eating your supper. Why couldn't you always live like this? You feel a little envious of Adam and Eve. But tomorrow it's back to the grind. Yet all this beauty, all this discovery, is stored in your mind, where nothing can take it away. And if you're wise, you have preserved much of it, too, on film.

But somehow you go back to work refreshed. You've left all your troubles in the wilderness. They seemed too insignificant to carry home. Who needs a psychiatrist—when a weekend with nature will do the trick?

Every chance you get you relive your days in the wild, dreaming now in reverse. Still feeling refreshed. Wondering why there is such healing of mind and body in just sitting on a granite boulder and admiring God's creation. What was all this beauty trying to tell you?

And then you realize that everything in nature was repeating the invitation of One who said long ago, "Come to me, all you who are weary and burdened, and I will give you rest." Matthew 11:28, NIV.

What does Jesus know about rest—and the need for it? More than you think!

Jesus was often weary after a long day of teaching and healing. He was weary after climbing the mountainside. He was weary after giving of Himself, days on end, without rest. He knew what it was to be tired—dead tired!

But Jesus knew about rest—another kind of rest—thousands of years before He spoke that memorable invitation. For it was Jesus—remember—who created our world. John 1:10. And it was

Jesus who rested when His work was finished. It is Jesus in the New Testament—and Jesus in the book of Genesis. And we read, "Thus the heavens and the earth were finished, and all the host of them. And on the seventh day God ended his work which he had made; and he rested on the seventh day from all his work which he had made. And God blessed the seventh day, and sanctified it: because that in it he had rested from all his work which God created and made." Genesis 2:1–3, KJV.

Rested? Was He tired?

Anna got off her chair and went over and sat on Fynn's lap. Fynn had little doubt what he was in for. Listen to the conversation as Fynn has recorded it in *Mister God, This Is Anna:*

"Why did Mister God rest on the seventh day?" she began.

"I suppose he was a bit flaked out after six days' hard work," I answered.

"He didn't rest because he was tired, though."

"Oh, didn't he? It makes me tired just to think about it all."

"Course he didn't. He wasn't tired."

"Wasn't he?"

"No, he made rest."

"Oh. He did that, did he?"

"Yes, that's the biggest miracle. Rest is. What do you think it was like before Mister God started on the first day?"

"A perishing big muddle, I guess," I replied.

"Yes, and you can't rest when everything is in a big muddle, can you?"

"I suppose not. So what then?"   "Well, when he started to make all the things, it got a bit less muddly."

"Makes sense," I nodded.

"When he was finished making all the things, Mister God had undone all the muddle. Then you can rest, so that's why rest is the very, very biggest miracle of all. Don't you see?"

This world may have been in a muddle when God started. But there certainly was no muddle when He finished, for we read, "And God saw every thing that he had made, and, behold, it was very good." Genesis 1:31, KJV.

Good. Very good. So good that even God couldn't find anything wrong with it!

But it may be that Anna was right when she said that rest is the biggest miracle. For do you realize what a miracle it was that God *could* rest on that first Sabbath day?

True, all that God had created was good, very good—so good it couldn't be better. But all was not well in the universe. Remember? Something had happened in heaven. Lucifer, heaven's highest angel officer, had challenged God's authority. And the peace and happiness of this planet were threatened even as it was being made!

Yet the Father and the Son had gone ahead with Their plan to create this earth and to make man in Their own image. They had gone ahead even though rebellion was loose in the universe. They had made Adam and Eve with the power to choose—even though that meant the possibility that they might choose wrong. They had refused to make man a robot, a mere machine programmed to worship its Creator. Instead, They took the terrible risk of making man free. And They knew the awful possibility that lay ahead!

How could God rest in a situation like that? How could He rest when He knew that man might rebel? How could He rest when He knew that sin might mar and ruin the beautiful world He had just made?

And yet He did rest! That's the miracle. He rested because Calvary already lay hidden in the divine heart. The Father and the Son had agreed together that if man should sin, and thereby bring upon himself the sentence of death, the Son Himself would come and die in his place. And so God could rest—even while the universe itself, and especially this planet, was threatened!

Can that sort of rest be ours? It can. We too can rest in spite of circumstances. We can rest in perfect confidence that God will take care of every problem, every emergency, foreseen or unforeseen.

Do you begin to see what that final day of Creation week was all about?

Why did God stop to rest? He wasn't tired. Why didn't He punch out at six o'clock Friday evening and get back to heaven for the weekend—or off to some galaxy for a new project? Why didn't He just say, "That's it"—and write us off as a job done, a job to be forgotten?

Why didn't He leave Adam and Eve to wonder where they

were and how they got there? Instead He gave them a beautiful twenty-four hours of happy fellowship with Himself, telling them how He had made them, explaining how He had made the world and the sun and the moon—and the stars too. Telling them that He had made the trees and the fruit and the flowers for their enjoyment and assuring them that this happy time of fellowship with Himself could be repeated week by week as long as they lived! Even forever!

Why did God give Adam and Eve all that beauty, with trees and flowers and birds—and exotic fruits to eat? Should they not have been satisfied with plain food and humble accommodations? Wasn't it enough to provide for their bare necessities? Why didn't He build them a barn to live in—and let them look out of stingy windows onto vast, empty expanses of dirt? Why didn't He start them out with a hundred sacks of wheat? Or why didn't He provide for their nutritional needs an oversize box of food capsules—five hundred for Adam, five hundred for Eve, and marked for refills on demand?

Why did God provide an environment that was beautiful as well as practical? Why did He provide for our happiness—and not just for our needs? Because that's the kind of God He is!

You can't drink in the incredible beauty of a rose without knowing that the God of the Bible is a God who cares. You can't look out over a deep blue lake, its waters mirroring the mountains and the clouds, without knowing that God loves beauty. You can't watch Him paint a sunset without knowing that He has gone the limit to provide for your happiness!

So God, in six days, gave us all that beauty. And then, as His crowning gift, He gave us a special day of fellowship with Himself!

Did He give us a day of rest simply because He knew we would be tired after six days of work? No. It's much more than that. The Sabbath is a day for tired bodies, it is true. But it's also for tired minds, anxious and troubled minds, questioning minds.

It's a day for letting our minds reach the stars, for saying, "God made them. Jesus made them. He's in control. I have nothing to fear. If He can fling the suns into their orbit, and keep them there, I'm safe in His hands!"

It's a day for watching a mighty waterfall, for thinking of all that power. For thinking how much power it took for your Saviour to make all the waterfalls, all the mountains, all the worlds and all the suns—and knowing that *all that power is available to help you in your struggle with sin!*

It's a day for sitting on a log and watching the little creatures of the wild, capturing all the beauty on the film of the mind, remembering who made it all, and who made you. Remembering that you are not a child of chance, but a child of your heavenly Father.

It's a day for aiming the lens of your eye at the most perfect scene you can find—the flawless blue of the lake, the snow-capped peak. Knowing that that's the kind of world God intended ours to be—the kind of world it will one day be again, because of His creative power!

It's a day for remembering. A day for remembering our Creator—the Creator who has been so carelessly challenged by this restless generation. God says to us, "Remember the sabbath day, to keep it holy. . . . For in six days the Lord made heaven and earth . . . and rested the seventh day." Exodus 20:8-11, KJV.

And remember the words of Genesis: "And God blessed the seventh day, and sanctified it." Genesis 2:3, KJV.

Sanctified it. What does that mean? It means He made it holy. He set it apart. He made it different. He made it perfect, beautiful, flawless. And how did He do that? He did it by putting His own presence into it.

And then God says through the prophet Ezekiel, "Moreover also I gave them my sabbaths, to be a sign between me and them, that they might know that I am the Lord that sanctify them." Ezekiel 20:12, KJV.

The Sabbath, then, is a sign, a pledge, that just as God made the Sabbath holy, He will also make His people holy.

But that's a big order. Can God do that? Can God give us characters as beautiful as a sunset, as flawless as the placid surface of a lake, as refreshing to others as a mountain stream or a waterfall? Yes, He can!

But how? How does He do it? The same way He makes a day holy. He makes a day holy by placing His presence in it. He makes a man holy by placing His own character in the man.

God can make characters as beautiful as anything we see in nature. And He doesn't stop with making them functional and utilitarian. He doesn't make men and women pious but hard to live with, uncomfortable to be around. He doesn't wash them and leave them unironed. He isn't satisfied with making men with characters straight as a tall pine, or sturdy as an oak. He makes them as beautiful as a mountain stream, as enjoyable as the chatter of a chipmunk.

Can He do it? He does it all the time. Says the apostle Paul, "Therefore, if anyone is in Christ, he is a new creation." 2 Corinthians 5:17, NIV.

A new creation. But remember this. A new creation requires the work of a Creator. If there is no Creator, if we are the children of chance, then all we've been saying is meaningless. A new creation isn't something we can accomplish by ourselves. It isn't something we can work at until we get it straight. Jesus said, "Apart from me you can do nothing." John 15:5, NIV.

God does not tell us to sanctify ourselves, to make ourselves holy, though millions have worn themselves out trying to do just that. Rather, the day of rest at the end of the week is to constantly remind us that He is the One who does it. "I gave them my sabbaths . . . that they might know that I am the Lord that sanctify them." Ezekiel 20:12, KJV.

Think what the character of Adam must have been before he sinned, before guilt marred his countenance, before he began to die cell by cell. Adam—created in the image of God!

Look at the incredible beauty of the rose. Yet, the rose wasn't made in God's image. Look at the majestic beauty of the rugged mountain peaks. But they weren't made in God's image. There's the fascinating beauty of a river tumbling down a cliff. But the river wasn't made in God's image. Adam was! Think what his character must have been like. Think what your character might have been, and still can be—because of God's creative power!

These are things to think about as we sit on a moss-covered log at the end of the week and wonder at the sights and sounds of nature. As we remember who made it all. And who made us.

But someone is saying, "Wait! All this sounds wonderful. But I never get to see all this beauty you're talking about. My world is made up of stuffy offices and crowded freeways. And I come home to a house too small for the family—too tired to go anywhere, even if I had the chance."

Yes, life today, for millions, is certainly not what God intended it to be. His plans have been pushed aside and His creation scarred by our uncaring hands. The world today—with its high-rise prisons, its concrete speedways, its slums and garbage dumps and polluted air, its fires and its floods and its dust storms—is no Garden of Eden.

And the characters of men, too, have been marred. Little is left of the image of God.

But God can restore the beauty of this planet. And He will. He promises, "Behold, I make all things new." Revelation 21:5, KJV.

All things new. Even people? Yes, even people. For people are the problem. It would do little good for God to fix up the planet without fixing up the people.

Remember the television commercial about the Mud Puddle Kid? He stomps gleefully through one mud puddle after another until he's a mess. But no matter. Mom has Mud-B-Gone detergent. That will solve everything. Just see how spotless his clothes come out.

But just keep watching. It doesn't solve everything. Hardly is the boy scrubbed up and dressed in fresh, clean clothes when he goes out to play again and heads for the nearest puddle. Will the problem ever be solved until the boy learns to stay out of mud puddles—or, better yet, learns to hate mud puddles?

But does even that completely solve the problem? Will things ever be as they should be until we are rid of the mud puddles?

God can forgive us and wash us in the blood of Jesus. This is essential. He can teach us to hate sin. This is essential too. But He isn't satisfied with simply having clean men in a polluted environment. The Lord Jesus never intended to pay the unspeakably high ransom He did for us—and then leave us forever in the hands of our captors!

It is not enough for us to be free, our chains unshackled by the blood of Jesus—and still be the slave of unhappy circumstances over which we have no control. God does not want a new environment with unrenewed people. Nor does He intend, eventually, to have new people with an unrenewed environment. It must be both. And thank God it *will* be both!

I ask again, Do you begin to see what that special day at the end of the week is all about? It's a happy reminder that we are not the children of chance, but children of the heavenly King!

It reminds us of what we have lost—and what can be ours again. It reminds us of characters lost—that can be ours again. It reminds us of the day when we will never stray again, never sin again, never weep again. The day when thorns will be gone and weeds gone and mudholes gone. The day when one pulse of harmony will beat again through all God's creation!

And God and man—once more—will be together!

The Tops of the Mango Trees

Missionary Goodwin lay on his camp cot and looked up through the corrugated metal roof. It had been a long and tiring day, but he was wide awake. The light of a full moon was shining through the machine-gun-riddled roof, for planes had strafed the school in a recent rebellion.

He kept thinking about Yekea. All week long his African friends had been saying, "Bwana, we *must* go to Yekea. We *must* go! There has been no missionary there for many moons. Please let us go!"

And he had told them, "There is no time. We have many things to do here before we leave. I don't see how we can take such a trip."

But several times a day during that week they had come to him with the same plea. And as they were finishing worship that Thursday evening they had made one last attempt. It was this final plea that kept ringing in his ears.

The quiet of the African night was broken only as the creatures of the bush began their activities. Finally, with his hands folded under his head, the missionary said, "Lord, what do You want me to do? Should we go to Yekea?"

Immediately the thought struck him as if he had been hit by a flash of lightning. "We *must* go to Yekea! We *must* go!"

He slipped into his bush clothes and went to where his friends were sleeping. He told them they would leave at four in the morning. Yekea was about seventy miles away. And the trip by truck, considering the tortuous track, would take about fourteen hours. And they would want to reach their destination before the Sabbath.

So it was that in Friday's predawn darkness the eager company left Talla Station and were on their way. They bounced and

266

creaked and ground their way up and down hills and across leveled grasslands. They forded rivers. And *just as the sun was touching the tops of the mango trees* to the west of the station, they arrived at Yekea.

As they drove into the play area near the school building that also served as a church, the place was teeming with people— almost as if an anthill had exploded.

The truck had hardly stopped when a man jumped onto the cab step, stuck his head through the open window, and began to count. "How many people are there?" he wanted to know.

"Nineteen altogether."

The man shouted, "They're here! They're here! They've come! Hurry, hurry, it's almost Sabbath and we are waiting for worship!"

Then he directed each of the nineteen passengers to certain homes that seemed already prepared to welcome guests.

The two missionaries were shown to a room in the home of the head teacher. In a long dug-out tub their bath water had already been drawn. That seemed strange. But after taking a quick bath and hastily putting their clothes away, they made their way to the meeting place. A man rushed up, saying how happy they were that they had arrived safely. Another spoke of how wonderful it was to have missionaries visit them again after so long a time. And just before the meeting began someone mentioned that they had been preparing for them for two days and hoped everything was satisfactory!

"Two days!" Pastor Goodwin exclaimed. "Brother, I didn't know I was coming until last night, after the tree hyrax began its evening song. How could you have known about it for *two days?"*

There was no time for an answer. The familiar Sabbath evening song "Day Is Dying in the West" was being sung reverently as they marched into the overcrowded building. The missionary's mind was a jumble of questions. What was going on? It was evident that these people had been expecting them. Everything had been carefully planned—even a baptism scheduled for the next day. Food had been prepared, places to stay arranged for, bath water drawn, and luscious fruit placed in their rooms!

During the song service he asked the one sitting next to him how they knew the visitors were coming. But again there was no time for an answer. The suspense was so great he doesn't remember what he preached about that evening. But after the service, as they made their way to their sleeping quarters, the head teacher explained the mystery.

On Wednesday night one of the dedicated teachers at the school had had a dream. In his dream he saw a large green truck pull onto the school grounds *just as the sun was touching the tops of the mango trees.* In that truck he saw two missionaries with seventeen African workers and family members. In his dream he was told to have everything prepared so that their guests could be ready to welcome the beginning of the Sabbath with them as the last bit of the sun sank beyond the western horizon!

Is it any wonder that the people at Yekea were not at all surprised—only overjoyed—as their guests arrived?

All around the world, every Friday evening—as the sun touches the tops of the mango trees, as it slips beyond yonder hill, as the ball of fire bursts through the clouds in another glorious sunset, as it slips beneath the curve of the earth and into the sea— devoted followers of Jesus leave their work and gather to welcome the Saviour into their hearts and homes for another special day!

Wafted toward heaven from homes around the world are the familiar words of the Sabbath evening song:

> Day is dying in the west;
> Heaven is touching earth with rest;
> Wait and worship while the night
> Sets her evening lamps alight
> Through all the sky.

> Holy, holy, holy,
> Lord God of hosts!
> Heaven and earth are full of Thee;
> Heaven and earth are praising Thee,
> O Lord most high!

Some sing it in other languages. And some can't carry a tune. But it matters not. It is all music to Heaven's ears. For it comes from hearts that have not forgotten their appointment with their Lord!

My mind goes back again to that first Friday evening when the

Creator stood beside the man and woman He had just created and watched with them the sunset that must have exceeded every other sunset in glory!

What an evening it must have been! A planet fresh from the Creator's hand! The hearts of our first parents still unscarred! An evening filled with indescribable happiness! Exciting prospects ahead! So much to learn, to discover! Other worlds to explore! The companionship of angels! Limitless possibilities! And never-ending life—if they were loyal to their Lord! And anything else was unthinkable!

But then something happened. One deliberate act of disloyalty changed it all. And a dark cloud of gloom and guilt rose over this planet. God and man were separated. And both were lonely!

I think of Adam, again and again through the long centuries of his life, relating to his children and his children's children how the Creator had spent that first unforgettable evening with them. His voice must have broken many a time as he told how that happy experience was intended to be repeated indefinitely. As long as the earth should orbit, every seventh day, as it rolled around, was to be a time of satisfying, fascinating communion between men and women and their Creator. But then had come the ugly interruption of sin and guilt. And Adam wept as he told them what might have been!

Actually, now that man was alienated from his God, the weekly appointments with the Creator, though no longer face-to-face, were even more important. For God had placed His presence, for all time, in the day on which He rested. And in those sacred hours men and women could find their closest communion with the Saviour. He longed for fellowship with them, just as they longed, in their heart of hearts, for fellowship with Him. And every Friday evening, at the sunset hour, He was saying to all who would listen, "I made you. I love you. Please come back!"

But as men forgot God, they forgot their weekly appointment with Him. And as they forgot that holy day, they forgot who made them. Soon they fell to speculating. They began to spin theories about their beginnings. And they have been spinning them ever since.

But there isn't a son of Adam today who needs to be in doubt. No man needs to speculate about his origin. The man who remembers that weekly appointment remembers his Creator. He is untouched by the mad race to find some meaning in life. He knows who made him. He knows who put him aboard this planet. And he knows why!

I think of another Friday afternoon—thousands of years this side of Adam. Jesus had let His life be crushed out by the weight of the world's guilt. His lifeless body had just been laid in a borrowed tomb. Faithful women followers stood by, weeping and wanting to honor Him in death as He should be honored. But the sun was slipping low in the west. The Sabbath would soon begin. And we read (Luke 23:52–56; 42:1) that while Jesus rested in the tomb, they rested according to the commandment—as they knew He would want them to do. Read those verses carefully. For if you want to find the day that God has blessed, if you think it might be eluding you, you will find it tucked between Friday's crucifixion and Sunday's resurrection. We call it Saturday.

The people of Yekea, so far removed from the swirl of sophistication in which most of us live and breathe, would find it difficult to understand how anyone would choose to miss his appointment with the Creator—and search to justify himself in that choice. To them it is a treasured privilege. It is a vital part of their relationship with Jesus.

But such a relationship the fallen angel is determined to destroy, wherever he can. He hates the Sabbath, because he wants to keep man separated from his God. He hates the Sabbath, too, because it reminds men of their Creator. And remember, God's creatorship—specifically the fact that Jesus, not Lucifer, created this world—is the focal point of Satan's seething jealousy.

The rebel chief suggests to us that to set apart one day in seven is all that God requires. All days are alike—twenty-four hours long. Just give God any day that is convenient. After all, if you owe a man five dollars it doesn't matter which five-dollar bill you use to pay your debt. Sounds so reasonable, doesn't it?

But the Sabbath is not a debt. We could never pay our debt to God. The Sabbath is an appointment. And appointments don't work out very well unless two people get together at the same time!

What if the people at Yekea had responded this way? "Two

days is too short notice. We need more time. We'll just prepare for our guests to arrive on Monday night. That will be more convenient."

Or, what if the missionary had said, "Lord, You know I need some sleep. We'll go Tuesday—next Tuesday"?

What a disappointment it would have been—for everyone!

Remember Moses at the burning bush? How he was told to take off his shoes because he was standing on holy ground (Exodus 3:1–6)? What made the ground holy? The presence of God. Then was it holy the day before? Or the day after? No. God wasn't there.

If this is true, then what happens when we try to keep an appointment with God—at a time of our own choosing, rather than His?

Far more than a twenty-four-hour day is involved here. The Creator has been challenged. The question now is what it has always been: What will you do with Jesus?

It was a long time ago—during World War II years. I was eating in the dining car of a train. And I noticed on the back of the menu an engraving of the Stars and Stripes in full color. As a loyal American I love the Stars and Stripes. So you can imagine my surprise and my perplexity as beneath the flag I read these words: "Just a piece of cloth." And then, "That's all it is. Just a piece of cloth. You can count the threads in it and it's no different from any other piece of cloth."

My patriotism would have rebelled if I hadn't read on:

"But then a little breeze comes along and it stirs and comes to life and flutters and snaps in the wind—all red, and white, and blue. And then you realize that no other piece of cloth could be just like it. Yes, that flag is just a piece of cloth until we breathe life into it. Until we make it stand for everything we believe in and refuse to live without!"

Here is an ordinary piece of red cloth. You can count the threads in it, and it's no different from any other piece of red cloth. But when I take this piece of red cloth and a piece of white cloth and a piece of blue cloth and sew them together into the Tricolor of France, Frenchmen would die for it! If I sew them together into the Union Jack, Britishers would die for it! Or if I sew these same pieces together into the Stars and Stripes, Americans would die for it—would not live without it!

Just so, God took an ordinary day. You could count the hours in it. It was no different from any other day. But then He breathed life into it. He made a Sabbath out of it. He made it stand for a relationship that makes life worth living—a relationship that millions have refused to live without!

Just a day. Or so it appears. A day marked off by the rotation of the earth. But it stands for something vital that we have lost. It stands for a living, breathing rapport with our Maker that has been broken. Yet, thank God, the separation can be healed. For that day at the end of the week, every time it rolls around, echoes the invitation of a loving and patient Creator, "Come to Me, and I will give you rest. I love you. I made you. I miss you. Please come back!"

And with the westering sun just touching the tops of the mango trees, who can resist an invitation like that?

Five Kilometers East

Two travelers, weary beyond words, were crossing the desert in the stifling heat. Their water supply was exhausted. They were pushing ahead with borrowed strength. And how much more would nature let them borrow? Their minds were discussing surrender to the sandy killer of men.

And then, at the farthest reach of their vision, their eyes latched onto a tiny patch of green. Could it be a mirage? No. It was real. The patch of green was larger now and more distinct. Something was growing there. And whatever it was, it was evidently getting water.

Water! The thought of it gave them courage to push on. It must be an oasis!

Using what must be the last of their strength, they dragged themselves into the haven of green. And there before their eyes, in this paradise of shade, was a well! And beside it a wooden bucket!

Hurriedly, expectantly, they let down the bucket. But it landed with a thud! The well was dry!

This was too much! They might as well just lie down in the cool, comfortable shade and admit that the desert had won!

And then they saw something else. A few feet away from the well, on the ground, was a piece of board. Someone, with a knife or some sharp instrument, had carved words into it. It said: WATER—FIVE KILOMETERS EAST.

Water! Five kilometers! Could they possibly make it? Could they summon up a few more ounces of strength? Of course they could. And did. Who would choose to lie down and die, even in cool comfort, with water only five kilometers away?

What about *living* water? Would we walk five kilometers for it? Or would we settle into the short-range comfort of a dry well and refuse to budge?

A woman of Samaria, you remember, met Jesus at Jacob's well

273

one hot noon. He offered her living water. And she became so excited that she forgot her waterpot and went to call her friends.

Abraham heard the call of God one day. He left his comfortable home and began a long walk that was still unfinished when he died.

Three wise men from a distant country followed a star for many a night to find the newborn King.

But the Pharisees in the days of Jesus were satisfied, content, and even proud of their dry wells. They decided to stay right where they were. They were quite comfortable in their situation. And they had enough self-manufactured shade to keep the light of truth from shining too brightly in their eyes.

Dry wells haven't *always* been dry. At some time or other they have yielded enough water to produce some flourishing vegetation—enough living green to attract weary travelers and lead them to linger nearby.

But if you discover that the well on which you depend has gone dry, there is only one thing to do. Move! Find another well! Five kilometers away—or five hundred!

It is said that a young Russian czar, many years ago, was walking in the royal garden one day when he noticed that out in a nearby field a palace guard was standing in all his pomp and ceremony.

Curious, the czar walked out into the field and asked the young soldier what he was guarding. He didn't know—except that orders called for a sentry at that spot.

The young czar looked up the records. He discovered that at one time Catherine the Great had sponsored acres of rare rose gardens. And on that spot a choice and beautiful rosebush had grown. Every week she permitted the peasants to come and view the roses. But she ordered a sentry to stand guard over that particular bush. The order was never rescinded. The rose gardens had long since disappeared. But a sentry still stood guard *over a patch of weeds!*

Things change in this deteriorating world of ours. Respectable neighborhoods become slums. Shiny new cars on the showroom floor are one day hauled away as junk. Roses are replaced with weeds. Wells go dry. And worship, once sincere, becomes only a hollow form!

Religion is especially vulnerable to the deteriorating influences

of our day. Everything about our practice of religion is susceptible to the inroads of compromise and carelessness. Principles are
abandoned little by little. Religious groups once pledged to follow
the Bible and the Bible only—willing to die for it—have reasoned
it away, a little at a time until they find themselves holding tightly
to nothing but tradition. Ministers who used to preach the gospel
of Jesus Christ have turned to preaching politics and protest. And
many a worshiper, when suddenly he discovers that the well is
dry, is stunned!

Edward Gibbon, writing in his *Decline and Fall of the Roman
Empire,* was describing how the zeal of ancient Rome faded after
Caesar's armies had subdued the world and later generations
were left with the inheritance of their fathers. And he penned
these memorable words: "They held in their lifeless hands the
riches of their fathers without inheriting the spirit which had
created and improved that sacred patrimony. They read, they
compiled, but their languor of soul seemed incapable of thought
and action."

It can happen to a nation. Could it happen to a church? Could a
church hold in its hands millions of dollars worth of buildings—
without inheriting the spirit of the pioneers who built them?

Never was there a people more missionary-minded than the
Waldenses. Remember them? For many centuries during the dark
ages of persecution they worshiped their Lord in the Piedmont
valleys of northern Italy, protected by the lofty mountains about
them. Early in life they were taught their mission. They copied
the Scriptures by hand. And then they went out, disguised as
merchants or peddlers, the precious manuscripts of the Bible
hidden in their clothing. They went into the cities, into the universities, into the homes. Cautiously the missionary would produce a
portion of the Scriptures. And then, with quivering lip and on
bended knee, he would read the precious promises. Often he
would be asked to read them again and again. Could it be true that
"the blood of Jesus Christ his Son cleanseth us from all sin"? As
light dawned upon their troubled minds, they would exclaim,
"Christ is my priest! His blood is my sacrifice!"

Sometimes the entire night was spent in this manner. The assurance of a Saviour's love seemed too good to be true. They
would ask, "Will God accept *my* offering? Will He pardon *me?*"

The answer would be read again from Scripture, until the

understanding could grasp it. And the response would come, "I may come to Jesus just as I am, sinful and unholy. 'Thy sins be forgiven thee.' *Mine, even mine,* may be forgiven!"

Joy filled the heart. All fear of prison or flame now was gone. They would gladly welcome death, if it would honor their Lord!

The messenger of truth went on his way, in many cases to be seen no more. He had made his way to other lands. Or he was wearing out his life in some unknown dungeon. Or perhaps his bones were left whitening on the spot where he had witnessed for his Lord. Such was the grand and untarnished devotion of the Waldenses!

But there is a sad postscript to that story. Not many years ago, near the little Waldensian village of Torre Pellice, a group of Christian youth gathered around their campfire to sing gospel songs and to tell mission stories.

Visitors from the surrounding valleys and mountains had drifted into the village, and now they approached the campfire with curiosity. Who were these young people? They heard them praying. They heard them singing about the second coming of Jesus, in which their own fathers had once so ardently believed. They heard them telling mission stories, and it brought a strange nostalgia for their own past.

On this night, after the singing and the stories were over, one of the Waldensian elders stepped from the shadows into the light of the campfire and spoke thoughtfully to the minister in charge, *"You must carry on!"*

And he continued, "We, the Waldensian people, have a great heritage behind us. We are proud of the history of our people as they have fought to preserve the light of truth high upon these mountaintops and up and down these valleys. This is our home. Here we have the great monuments of our faith. . . . Of all this we are proud."

And then this Waldensian elder, a layman in the church, said with conviction, "This is our great heritage of the past, but we really do not have any future. We have given up the teachings in which we once believed. We no longer believe that Jesus will soon come in the clouds of heaven. This belief we have abandoned. From all that I can observe, from what I have heard about your people, *you* must now carry on!"

And then he pointed to a nearby mountain. "If you look up here on the mountainside, you will see one of our Waldensian chapels. You will notice on this chapel, as on all our chapels, these words: . . . 'And the light shineth in darkness!' . . . But now beside these chapels we have built dance halls, thinking that in this way we might be able to hold our young people.

"Yet our young people seem to have no more interest in, or love for, the church. Their interest now is down in the bright lights of the big cities. No longer do they want to remain here.

"What a miracle it is that you still have young people who are interested in coming up here to our valley and in studying the history we love so much. But that is all in the past now. The sad thing is that we are not moving forward with courage for the future. *You* must carry on!"

Such is the haunting appeal of the Waldenses!

What a tragedy it is to stagnate, to fall asleep, to stand still when we might be moving into a future far brighter than the past! What a tragedy to abandon our beliefs—or water them down until we don't know what they are!

Not long ago a group of student leaders from across America were called to the White House. A government spokesman, in a carefully prepared speech, told them to be good students—not to bomb buildings, not to skip the country, not to give up on America. When he had finished, a student from Harvard stood and asked on what grounds these moral concepts were founded.

The official stood for a moment, flushed and embarrassed. Then he replied apologetically, "I'm sorry. I don't know."

Doesn't it make you wonder how many of our concepts today have no solid foundation? Is it possible that many of our popularly accepted beliefs are nothing but speculation—or nothing but tradition?

A few years back one of our airlines ran a two-page ad. Across the top it said this: "For 25 years you've been brainwashed into expecting the wrong things from your airline." The first paragraph said, "Airlines have been promoting a smile, a meal and a movie so hard, for so long, that most people have come to believe that a smile, a meal and a movie are what airline service is all about."

The ad went on to mention several things more important, including confidence in your airline. And it concluded, "There.

Now that you know what an airline should do for you, all you have to do is pick an airline that can do it. At the moment we can think of only one."

How do you choose a church? What do you expect from it? Do you look for a smile, a handshake, and a friendly word? Are you satisfied to find a choir, a convenient location, and a minister with charisma? Or do you get down on your knees and ask God to lead you to truth—and then search till you find it?

There are so many churches today. How could you ever make a safe and wise choice? And why are there so many denominations? One reason is the tendency of people to follow a leader— and then when that leader dies, to go no farther in their search for truth. Another reason—a sadder reason for many of the divisions in Christianity today—is the prevailing custom of distorting Scripture, wresting it from its context, to make it support some favorite theory. I need not tell you that some religious groups today are formed only for monetary return or to avoid paying taxes.

But the sincere seeker for truth need not go wrong. He has this promise: "If any one chooses to do God's will, he will find out whether my teaching comes from God or whether I speak on my own." John 7:17, NIV.

Jesus was here speaking of His own teaching. But it applies to anyone's teaching. God will guide the man or woman who is sincere, who is willing to follow truth wherever it leads.

Too many of us are willing to follow truth only if it fits in with our plans, only if it doesn't cost anything, only if it makes no demands of us. We want truth to agree with our preconceived notions. We don't mind if truth leads us to a Saviour. But we don't want it to lead us to a Creator.

But may I just say this. Any religion that has no Creator is a dry well. If we trust the theory of evolution, of accident and chance, for our past, we shall have to trust it for our future. And that means trusting our future to chance. If we deny the account of creation, as God has recorded it for us in Genesis, we shall likely deny the future as it is predicted in the book of Revelation.

A religion without a Creator is a religion without hope. For only a Creator can change our hearts. Only a Creator can restore in us the image of God. Without a Creator there can be no resurrection. Only the One who has conquered death can call our loved ones—or us—to life. And without a Creator, the new earth described in the last two chapters of Revelation could never be a reality.

Do we want to rob Jesus of His creatorship and leave Him powerless to keep His promises? Do we want to rob the Saviour of His power to save—and leave Him just a deluded teacher who promised castles that He could never build?

I say again, a religion without a Creator is a dry well!

People change. Bad people become good. And good people become bad. Churches change too. God's chosen people, became the nation that rejected Jesus. "He came unto his own, and his own received him not." John 1:11, KJV.

Those of the chosen nation who chose to *accept* Jesus had to break strong national ties and long-established customs and identify themselves with the newborn Christian church.

But, in time, the Christian church became a popularity-seeking church, a compromising church, and finally a persecuting church. The true church became the false church. It fell from its high position. It became Babylon, the symbol of all false worship. And God calls, "Come out of her, my people." Revelation 18:4, KJV.

There are times when it is not enough to believe, to know what is truth, to have right opinions, to silently place our sympathies on the right side. It was not enough for the ancient Hebrews, on that fateful night in Egypt, merely to believe. The blood had to be sprinkled on the doorpost. It was not enough for the Israelites to stand with the Red Sea before them and wait for a miracle. They must move forward!

It is not enough for you to say, "I believe." It is not enough to be a secret disciple of Jesus. You must step over onto the Lord's side. If we are on a sinking ship, it is not enough to *applaud* the lifeboat. We must *get into it*. It is not enough to agree that Babylon has fallen and is not what she once was. We must heed God's call and come out of her!

Today there may appear to be many options open to us. We may be confused by the multiplicity of voices all calling, "This is the way." But it will not always be so. Before Jesus returns the confusion will disappear. The issues will be plain and uncomplicated. There will be *only two camps*—those who choose to carry the banner of the fallen angel, and those who stand unflinching beneath the blood-red banner of Calvary!

Jesus said, "Other sheep I have, which are not of this fold: them also I must bring, and they shall hear my voice; and there shall be one fold, and one shepherd." John 10:16, KJV.

God's true sheep are scattered today—in many nations, many cultures, many communions—even in the fallen Babylon. And many are isolated, with no ties to any organized group. But the Saviour knows them all. And He says, "My sheep hear my voice, and I know them, and they follow me." John 10:27, KJV.

How can you tell if you are one of Jesus' true followers? You are His *if you follow Him*. If you live up to all the instruction He has given you. That's the way to tell!

I came across a delightful little story not long ago. A boy was herding his father's sheep. Not far away, across a little valley, a neighbor boy was herding sheep for *his* father. The boys were good friends. They often called to each other across the valley that separated them.

One day a severe storm came up very suddenly, and the boys, with their sheep, took refuge under the same huge ledge. When the storm was over and it was time to go home, the boys had a problem. They couldn't separate the sheep. Some of them they knew. But they weren't sure about others.

Finally, in desperation, and fearful that they would be scolded, they started for home—one down one path and one down another. And what happened? The sheep just separated themselves perfectly, every sheep following his own shepherd!

A great dividing is going on today. The sheep, day by day, are sorting themselves out, each one following his own shepherd. And if you want to know who a sheep belongs to, who his shepherd is, just watch to see whose voice brings a response. No man has to divide them, or judge them, or classify them, or put them over here or over there. By their actions, by their responses, the sheep are separating themselves.

If you find yourself at a dry well, follow Jesus! It may mean traveling five kilometers east—or west or north or south. But you can't go wrong. You'll find living water. And a well that never goes dry!

Section Eleven
Strategy at Showdown

Strategy at Showdown

It is said that a mysterious spell hung over the entire set where the movie *Close Encounters of the Third Kind* was being made. And a series of bizarre and terrifying events did nothing to relieve the mounting sense of fear.

For instance, a ghostly presence so terrorized the director and two of his associates that they were forced to pack their bags and flee in sheer panic from a hotel where they were planning the film.

At least a dozen times, we are told, the set was lashed by storms so fierce that some of the cast and crew believed there must be a mysterious force behind them. There were horrendous hurricane-type winds, with lightning and driving rain, that kept ripping apart a tent they were using. One member of the cast remembers thinking, "There are bigger forces here that are making us go the other way so that we can't shoot with the [tent]. Now we will have to shoot it their way."

When there wasn't a downpour, it was equally terrifying. For eerie cloud formations kept floating over the set. And those formations precisely resembled the one used in the movie to hide a UFO.

And when they came to the climactic scene depicting the landing of a UFO, suddenly a real UFO, with blinking and glowing lights, soared over the very set where they were filming. That's the story.

Said one of the actresses, "It was kind of hard not to think that there was something up there guiding the whole project." She said, "I found myself saying, 'All right. All right. Just don't hurt anybody and we will play your game.'"

And a vice president in charge of production says, "The presence of God was very much in evidence. . . . At times we felt as if something was guiding us along the way."

Was it the presence of God?

Early in production there was squabbling among the actors

because they were allowed to see only their own sections of the script. But soon cast and crew were united in a common fear—and then a common fascination. And we are told that "making the picture became an incredible spiritual experience."

A spiritual experience? A religious experience? Perhaps. But what kind of religion? Belief? But belief in what? Worship? But worship of whom? These are important questions!

Anything a man takes up with may become his religion. He may believe in God in the traditional way. Or he may believe in Eastern meditation or in astrology or in UFOs or in pyramid power. It is still a belief. He may worship God or worship money or worship the devil or worship himself. It is still worship.

Americans today are fascinated by mystery voices, by magic, by power to see the invisible, by pyramid power, by auras, by biorhythms, by monsters, by anything mysterious and unexplained. And some say it is all a good sign—because at least more people are willing to accept the supernatural.

But should we be cheered by the growing acceptance of the supernatural? Is it really a good sign?

It's a good sign *only if everything supernatural is from God.* But what if it isn't?

Can we safely lump all the supernatural together and say it is all from God? Can we put God and UFOs together in the same column and believe in both at once because both are supernatural? Are the acts of UFOs and the revelations of spirit mediums and the strange tales told by people under hypnosis—are we to link all these with God simply because they are supernatural?

A popular writer, who wishes he had been the author of the script for *Close Encounters of the Third Kind,* calls it "the science-fiction film we have all been waiting for." "In fact," he says, "we were waiting for it before we were born. The ghost in us, the secret stuff of genetics, was waiting. The Life Force was waiting, waiting to be born, waiting to be called forth."

Undeniably this generation was ready for just such a film, and for others of its stripe which have followed it. But who did the preparing? That's the question!

You can't open the Bible and read very far without discovering that God has an enemy. And so do we. That enemy turns up in the third chapter of Genesis. That's our first glimpse of him. You are well aware of the controversy that surfaced in Eden—and continues to this day. You know what his strategy was then (read again the chapter "The Strategy of Rebellion"). Is it any different now? No. It is exactly the same—except that it is intensifying on all fronts. The same use of disguise and the supernatural. The same challenge of God's authority and God's Word. The same lies. The same battle for the mind. The same bid for control and for worship. There is no change—only more urgency as the fallen angel sees that time is running out!

Now tell me. When Satan's first use of the supernatural was so successful, do you think for a moment he would abandon its use? Never! He hasn't changed his strategy a bit, except to intensify and multiply and diversify it—until today, as we near the end of time, the proliferation of Satan's supernatural tricks, many of them undeniable miracles, is well nigh overwhelming!

We don't need to be in the dark about Satan's use of the supernatural. We don't need to be unaware of what is going on. Nor will a self-imposed ignorance excuse us. For Jesus plainly warned us (Matthew 24:24) that false Christs and false prophets would use "great signs and wonders" in their work of deception. And the apostle Paul warned (2 Corinthians 11:14) that "Satan himself is transformed into an angel of light."

The apostle John speaks of "spirits of devils, working miracles" (Revelation 16:14) and of an agent of Satan bringing fire down from heaven (Revelation 13:13, 14).

Does this mean that even if we see fire come down from heaven it could still be a deception? That's what it says. And that's exactly what it means!

You say, "Then what chance do we have? How can we escape deception if that's the way it is?"

We won't escape deception by trusting our senses. We won't escape it by trusting our feelings. We won't escape deception by blindly following the supernatural, assuming that everything supernatural is from God. For that assumption is dead wrong!

Our only safety is in *knowing* what God's Book says—and *accepting* what it says!

Those who lose out in the final day will not lose out because of ignorance. Those who are the victims of Satan's almost overmastering deceptions in these last days will be men and women who have had contact with truth, who have known truth, but have rejected it. Listen to the frightening words of the apostle Paul:

"The coming of the lawless one will be in accordance with the work of Satan displayed in all kinds of counterfeit miracles, signs and wonders, and in every sort of evil that deceives those who are perishing. They perish because they refused to love the truth and so be saved. For this reason God sends them a powerful delusion so that they will believe the lie and so that all will be condemned who have not believed the truth but have delighted in wickedness." 2 Thessalonians 2:9–12, NIV.

How does Satan deceive men and women? By counterfeit miracles and signs and wonders. He uses the supernatural. That's his favorite tool—because it's his most effective tool.

And why does God permit these people to be deceived? It says He sends them a powerful delusion. He doesn't originate the delusion, you understand. He simply permits it. He doesn't stop it. And why? Because these people have refused truth; they have rejected truth. They have made it clear that they prefer lies. They have made their choice. He lets them have lies. He lets them believe lies—and be lost!

Do you see what a dangerous thing it is, what a fearful thing, to refuse truth? Do you see what a fatal mistake it is to push truth aside and blindly follow the supernatural?

How do you feel now about what happened on the set as *Close Encounters of the Third Kind* was being filmed? Supernatural? Yes, unquestionably. But was a divine presence guiding? Or did some other power, an alien and dangerous power, a power from beneath, have a special interest in what was going on?

Paul in 2 Thessalonians 2:11 speaks of "the lie." Did you notice the definite article, *the?* What is Satan's big lie? You find it right there in Genesis 3: "You will not surely die." It was there that the big lie started rolling, and it has snowballed until today almost everybody believes it. Almost everybody believes that you don't really die when you die. And what is happening? Satan and his host of helpers, all fallen angels, are going around impersonating dead people, taking advantage of men and women when they're lonely and confused, grieving over the loss of a loved one. That's what is going on!

I will never forget a certain Sunday a number of years ago. It was just two days after that memorable Christmas Eve when the astronauts of Apollo VIII read from the first chapter of Genesis—while they were orbiting the moon.

On that Sunday evening I was watching the Joe Pyne show. And Bishop Pike was a guest. The bishop was promoting his new book *The Other Side*. And of course they were discussing communication with the dead.

You may recall that Joe Pyne was not always as courteous to his guests as he might have been. But on this occasion he listened very attentively. And then finally he turned to his guest and said quietly, "Bishop, doesn't the Bible say somewhere that the dead don't know anything?"

The bishop, obviously taken back, replied, "I don't know." He reached for a pencil and said, "I'll go home and look it up."

A little later Joe Pyne opened the show to questions from the studio audience, and a young man stood in the dock. "And what is your question for the bishop?"

The young man replied, "I don't have a question for the bishop. I just want to tell him where the text is that he doesn't know is in the Bible. It is in Ecclesiastes, the ninth chapter and the fifth verse." And then he quoted it correctly from memory: "For the living know that they shall die: but the dead know not any thing."

The verse that follows is also interesting, for it says, "Also their love, and their hatred, and their envy, is now perished." KJV.

But evidently, all through his experience with the occult, the bishop did not feel it important to learn the Bible position on the matter. You recall that he was very perplexed about the strange haunting of his Cambridge apartment. I wonder what his reaction would have been if he had returned to the flat one day and found in front of his nightstand a Bible open to the seventh chapter of Job, verses nine and ten—and perhaps marked in red. It says, "He that goeth down to the grave shall come up no more. He shall return no more to his house." KJV.

Of course the haunter of an apartment would hardly want to call attention to a scripture that says the dead do not come back to their house!

In the bishop's perplexity about what was going on in his apartment, he asked counsel of Canon Pierce-Higgins and was advised to consult a medium.

If, however, the bishop had turned to the Bible for counsel, the advice would have been strikingly different—especially if he had come across this: "So why are you trying to find out the future by consulting witches and mediums? Don't listen to their whisperings and mutterings. Can the living find out the future from the dead? Why not ask your God? 'Check these witches' words against the Word of God!' he says. 'If their messages are different than mine, it is because I have not sent them; for they have no light or truth in them.'" Isaiah 8:19, 20, The Living Bible.

One gets the impression that God is not on very good terms with the world of the occult!

And it is difficult to rationalize away the startling statement that the dead do not know anything. Certainly the dead would find it difficult to carry on any intelligent communication if they don't know anything.

Is this just an isolated statement? No. It is consistent with the rest of the Bible—surprising as this may be to many who have thought otherwise. Here is an equally strong statement concerning death: "His breath goeth forth, he returneth to his earth; in that very day his thoughts perish." Psalm 146:4, KJV.

According to this, when a man's breathing stops, so does his thinking!

Was Jim Pike, after he died, really hovering near and worrying about his father? Was Arthur Ford chatting with a friend even before his funeral? Is Jack Kennedy even now working on some project somewhere? Is his peace being disturbed, wherever he is, by concern for his country and his brother Ted?

If you ask the Bible, the answer is No! "He passes off the scene. . . . He never knows it if his sons are honored; or they may fail and face disaster, but he knows it not." Job 14:20, 21, The Living Bible.

Are the dead still alive somewhere? I think you see the problem that is shaping up. The nature of the psychic evidence seems to say Yes. But the Bible says No!

Ruth Montgomery was undoubtedly sincere in her belief that her book originated with Arthur Ford and was dictated by him from somewhere in the unseen world. What convinced her? The nature of the information. Information that only he would have. Or so she believed.

One individual, after visiting a psychic, said enthusiastically, "When he saw where I had gone to that day, and when I would be back, I knew then he had a pipeline to God. How else could it be explained?"

That is the reasoning: If the information is right, if it checks out, then there must be a pipeline to God. No other test is applied. Countless messages from the spirit world are accepted simply because they contain information that supposedly no one else but a loved one would know.

But let me ask you: Are you sure that no one else knows those family secrets? Are you sure that no one else knows those intimate details that are so convincing? If evil spirits are all about us—out of our sight but watching us all the time—don't you suppose they know the family secrets as well as we do? If impersonators are in the spirit world—spirits willing to lie as psychics themselves admit—then do you see what can happen? Talented impersonators—plus convincing information—plus a willingness to lie—plus the advantage of being invisible!

And so, if you toss a ball across the wall into the unseen world and it comes back with a family secret written on it, it doesn't necessarily mean that Uncle Joe tossed it back. It may only mean that spirits can write!

How can we escape the conclusion that thousands today—it may be unwittingly—are playing games with the perpetrators of a giant cosmic hoax?

The strategy of the rebel chief, as we approach the final showdown, is just what it has always been. His goals are the same. He will sweep as many as he can into their graves, steeped in hatred and violence, with no chance to repent. He delights in war and bloodshed. Ten thousand innocent victims in a day bring no hint of remorse. He would destroy the whole human race in an instant if the restraining hand of God were removed!

And those he cannot instantly destroy, he is determined to deceive. He will impersonate, he will counterfeit, he will trick men into his unsuspected traps.

He has not yet run out of ways to convince the human race that it is safe to sin—because *the human soul can never die*. He counterfeits the resurrection with the cold and filmy apparitions of the séance. Or, wearing the white coat of science, he captures the imagination with visions of the near-dead, with tales of long, dark tunnels and bright lights and grassy slopes.

He counterfeits the real heaven that God has promised with a strange, eerie nowhere inhabited by radishes with wings, turnips with tails, and lettuce that laughs—this, believe it or not, a description of the afterlife attributed to Arthur Ford! How would you like to be a leaf of laughing lettuce—or a thought form—or just a beam of light?

The enemy counterfeits true divine healing with a show-business healing that demands the surrender of the mind as its price. He counterfeits divine prophecy by putting his own predictions into the crystal ball, into the mouths of mediums and astrologers and UFO contactees—and then fulfilling those predictions which are in his power to fulfill.

He counterfeits the cross of Calvary with talk of reincarnation and karma—a way for man to save his pride and pay for his own sins, even if it takes a thousand lifetimes to do it!

And with all this the rebel general hopes to keep men and women safely tranquilized until time has run out and it is too late to escape the vortex of deception into which he has led them. For control is the name of his game. And the worship of men he is determined to have—if not by choice, then by deception, by hypnotic maneuver, or by force!

Satan's big lie—that you don't really die when you die—is the key element in his propaganda. It is the basis of spiritualism. Spiritualism would collapse overnight without a belief in communication with the dead. But it isn't going to collapse—not until the day the Lord Jesus appears in the skies to set everything straight!

More than a century ago Ellen White wrote these startling words about the spread of spiritualism:

"I saw the rapidity with which this delusion was spreading. A train of cars was shown me, going with the speed of lightning. The angel bade me look carefully. I fixed my eyes upon the train. It seemed that the whole world was on board, that there could not be one left. Said the angel, 'They are binding in bundles ready to burn.' Then he showed me the conductor, who appeared like a stately, fair person, whom all the passengers looked up to and reverenced. I was perplexed and asked my attending angel who it was. He said, 'It is Satan. He is the conductor in the form of an angel of light. He has taken the world captive.' "—*Early Writings*, p. 88.

On another occasion she wrote these words: "Except those who are kept by the power of God, through faith in His word, the whole world will be swept into the ranks of this delusion."—*The Great Controversy,* p. 562.

My only comment is a question: Is it happening? Is the fulfillment of those words shaping up? I think you'll agree that it is!

Yes, everybody loves magic, it seems. And Satan knows it. There is something in the heart of this restless generation that says to those who would win its attention, "Entertain us. Amuse us. Mystify us. Startle us. Stun us. Dazzle our eyes. Light up the sky with mysteries. Make bread out of stones. Boggle our minds. Hypnotize us with decibels. Shatter our emotions. Give us the spectacular. Put us in a trance. Work us up to a frenzy. And we'll follow you anywhere—without asking why!"

That, I say, is the spirit of this generation. But never was a generation in greater peril. Never have men and women walked in paths so unsafe, so perilously near the edge of the precipice!

We have come to the time when we shall have to decide whether our religion will be magical or moral, whether it will be a religion of emotion or of responsibility, whether we want our eyes dazzled or our feet kept from slipping. We shall have to decide whether we prefer the supernatural performance of the showman or the quiet miracle of a new heart. We shall have to choose between Jesus the superstar and Jesus the crucified—the one a superficial, sentimental, nonexistent fiction, the Other an eternal reality, a living Saviour!

When we come to the final crisis hour, the hour in which our eternal destiny is decided, the hour from which there is no turning back—in that irreversible hour what will we do? Will we trust our senses—or the Word of God? Will we trust our feelings—or hold fast to a "thus saith the Lord"? Will we blindly follow the spectacular into eternal disaster? Or will we listen for the still small voice that says, "This is the way, walk ye in it"—and follow it safely home?

That is the decision we will have to make—and sooner than we think! We might as well make it now!

The Whisper of the Ax

An old jeep with its load of passengers bumped over a mountain road in northern Afghanistan. Suddenly, on the most remote stretch of the road—where no cars pass for weeks at a time—the jeep stopped dead. The driver, cursing, got out and began to tinker with the engine, without results. Then he slammed down the hood and grabbed his rifle.

Aiming at the only foreign passenger, he said, "God has punished me for carrying an unbeliever in this car. Say your prayers. Pray that a truck comes along with a driver that can fix this motor. If no truck comes, I will shoot you, and then the motor will start."

The foreigner prayed. A truck was heard approaching. The driver uncocked his rifle and said, "I see it is God's will that you live."

Have we come to a time when the will of God is to be decided by a stopped engine and administered by a rifle shot?

The earthiness of the sixties was more than a move back to nature. It was more than a concern for the environment, more than a rejection of materialism as a satisfactory goal in life. It was a parting of the ways with traditional morality. It was an embracing of permissiveness and situation ethics. It was an open and bold rejection of all absolutes in moral conduct.

But the permissiveness of the sixties was not to be the final chapter. It *could* not be. For if the predictions of the book of Revelation were to be fulfilled, there must come a change. There must be a moral backlash. Absolutes reminiscent of Puritan days would again be accepted—and an attempt would be made to force them upon others.

This is shaping up now. Permissiveness has had its day. And it hasn't worked. We are living in the backlash. It is apparent now that society, if it is to survive, if anything is to be done about the accelerating lawlessness that threatens us all, simply must have some absolutes. And the pendulum has swung so far to the right that there is talk of legislating morality—and permitting no deviation from the beliefs of whatever group may be in the driver's seat.

But trying to legislate morality doesn't work. It never has—and never will. The marriage of strong legislation with the weakness of human nature may produce the appearance of strength. The outward conduct may be changed. But the heart is not changed. And God says the heart is desperately wicked. See Jeremiah 17:9.

You can force a man not to swear in public—or punish him if he does—but that doesn't clean up his thoughts. You can force a child to listen to Bible reading and prayers in the school. But you cannot force him either to believe or to pray. You can force a family to go to church, but you cannot make them have a personal relationship with God. You can shoot a man and quite effectively stop his thinking. But so long as he lives you cannot make him think what you want him to think!

Yet more and more, according to the book of Revelation, we shall see the attempt to cure our moral deterioration with force. Coercion will soon be no stranger.

Even in the area of politics and government there is a growing dissatisfaction with what is seen as weakness. There is an increasing demand for tough talk and tough action. It is becoming easier to understand how a nation represented in Revelation 13 as having the characteristics of a lamb, could yet speak as a dragon—even in the area of morals, with church and state uniting to restrict the personal liberty once considered sacred to all.

Partly strong and partly weak. That is the prophet Daniel's description of our society. See Daniel 2:41, 42. Strong in military power. Strong enough to split the atom. Strong enough to speak as a dragon. Yet so weak in moral power that the might of the state is called in to do what the church cannot!

Will it happen? Certainly it will. God's Word has never failed!

But it will happen only as Christians disregard the clear counsel of the Lord they profess to worship. For Jesus said, "Render therefore unto Caesar the things which are Caesar's; and unto God the things that are God's." Matthew 22:21, KJV.

Those words of Jesus erect a barrier between church and state that we tamper with at our own risk. But that barrier is crumbling—and crumbling fast!

The change that we see today would have seemed impossible in the sixties. But it is happening. Permissiveness is giving way to movements that are antigay, antiabortion, antitax, and pro capital punishment.

I need not tell you that radio talk shows are one indication of the pulse of the people—of their reaction on current issues. One evening on a San Francisco talk show a gentleman called in. I don't recall what had happened to trigger the discussion. But this, in substance, is what he said: "God is not going to tolerate baby killing and homosexuality. And He isn't going to tolerate us if we tolerate them." Then he continued, "Now we'll forget the past because you didn't know better. But if it continues—I'm going to be ready with my gun!"

Now you would expect that such a comment would either be passed off as a crank call or that it would stir up a flood of protest calls from other listeners. But nothing like that happened. The discussion continued. And the frightening thing is that the actual *execution* of moral offenders was *not* discussed as an impossible option. I didn't hear a single voice protest that such a thing was unthinkable in a land like ours. Rather, the actual extermination of people who deviate from the Bible morality, as interpreted by the mood of society, was considered at least something to discuss!

A few years back homosexuality was more or less accepted as simply a preference of lifestyle. Now suddenly it was a sin not to be tolerated—with death as a possible punishment!

Now certainly it would be an ideal situation if everybody would live according to Bible standards of morality. And I am not forgetting that the ancient city of Sodom was destroyed with fire and brimstone for its moral deviation. It ought to make us nervous when one of our large cities welcomes and even honors those guilty of the same sin. But it was God who decided the fate of Sodom. I don't think we are qualified to play God!

It would be a wonderful thing, I say, if everyone would live according to the Bible. But *whose interpretation of the Bible?* That is the question!

Two guests were appearing on national television. They were

asked, "Why should *your* policies be enforced on the American people?" And one of the guests boomed out, "Because one of us is right. And the other is wrong!"

In religion, as in politics, power is the great temptation. The director of one group boasted, "If Christians unite, we can do anything. We can pass any law or any amendment. And that's exactly what we intend to do!"

And some of the causes being espoused by Christians today are not moral issues at all. They are purely political—in some cases little more than personal opinion.

Human nature finds it easy to make a moral issue out of a personal preference. I was told of a woman who considered it morally wrong to wear perfume—except the brand she used. We can hope legislation doesn't come to that!

The name of the game is power. Are we fast approaching the day when prophets will carry guns and the will of God will be interpreted by rifle? Or have we already entered it?

More and more of the world's political confrontations have religious overtones. It took only a band of angry Iranian students to plunge us into a frightening awareness of Moslem power. Afghanistan climbed out of the map and into common talk in one day. Ireland as an arena of religious conflict is no longer unique. Enemies, too often, are enemies simply because of their religion or lack of religion.

To the tribal mind of Afghanistan, communism means godlessness. "You have a book, we have a book," the Afghans will say to Christian visitors—referring to the Bible and the Koran. "But the Russians—no book!"

Jesus said to His disciples, "A time is coming when anyone who kills you will think he is offering a service to God." John 16:2, NIV.

Is it possible that those words of Jesus will be fulfilled again in our day?

There are many factors, many attitudes and trends emerging today, that could move us easily into a marriage of church and state and a loss of our cherished freedoms.

Ever since Jonestown there has been a critical awareness of the cults—and a call for both investigation and legislation of their activities. Legislators have held back for fear of violating the church-state barrier. But could one more disaster, one more Jonestown, tip the balance?

And what if the people, outraged by some tragedy, take the situation into their own hands? Already, in one city, residents banded together and attempted to drive a cult out of town!

How long will it be until your church or mine is labeled a cult, your belief or mine considered strange or odd and therefore a threat to society?

The right to differ, whether a man is right or wrong, is a sacred legacy that must be defended at all costs. But unfortunately, sometimes the most ardent and intelligent defenders of political liberty are the first to put chains on religious freedom. Molly Anderson Haley said it so well:

> Across the way my neighbor's windows shine.
>   His roof-tree shields him from the storms that frown.
>   He toiled and saved to build it, staunch and brown.
> And though my neighbor's house is not like mine,
>   I would not pull it down!

> With patient care my neighbor, too, had built
>   A house of faith, wherein his soul might stay,
>   A haven from the winds that sweep life's way.
> It differed from my own—I feel no guilt—
>   I burned it yesterday!

What strange reasoning, what manipulation of logic, leads men and nations to honor men's civil rights—but scorn their right to worship as they choose? Or not to worship at all? Yet that is the kind of intolerance that has painted crimson the pages of history!

And it will happen again—if we are to believe the book of Revelation!

A few decades ago many a mind rejected the predictions of Revelation 13. They seemed too impossible. Bigotry—religious persecution—in a nation founded on the principles of freedom? Never! It just couldn't happen!

But now—almost overnight, it seems—the calm and complacency is shattered by the not-too-distant clank of the chain. Erupting before our unbelieving eyes are movements, full-grown at birth, that could rapidly turn our cherished personal liberties into souvenirs of a past that has slipped away. The rumblings of Revelation have become a mighty crescendo in a symphony about to be finished. Already creeping into the thinking of this generation is the disturbing and ominous idea that those who won't go along with the religious views and practices of those in power, perhaps—just perhaps—ought to be eliminated!

Bigotry is surfacing like white fins in the surf. And if we aren't disturbed, we ought to be!

Yet all the while we witness a welcome return to morality. We seem to have entered some sort of religious revival. The backlash against the permissiveness of the sixties is real, and it makes us feel more secure. We just pray that the bandwagon of moral concern doesn't miss Washington. For God knows how much that city on the Potomac needs it!

Remember the march on Washington? Washington for Jesus? I was invited by nineteen respected ministers—some of them personal friends—to join in that march. But I had to decline. Why? There was so much about it that was good and commendable— and desperately needed.

But I couldn't believe that Jesus, in whose honor the march was held, would be walking in such a demonstration if He were here. The government in His day was desperately corrupt and in need of reform. Yet He made no attempt to correct the evils that were so obvious. He didn't reform that way. He never led a protest march. He was not a political activist. He knew that the problem was in the hearts of men. And He worked on the heart!

I have always been opposed to any attempt to legislate morality. It has never worked. And whenever the power of the state has been used to enforce the goals of the church, personal liberty has been violated and persecution has followed.

Don't misunderstand me. I don't believe those who organized the march on Washington had any such thing in mind. I feel sure of this—that when liberty is lost in America it will not be because the American people have suddenly become bigoted and cruel in nature. It will not be because they no longer believe in religious liberty. Rather, I am convinced that our freedom to worship as we choose will be voted away, legislated away, amended away, allowed to be eroded little by little by well-meaning Christians who do not realize what they are doing. They will sacrifice our liberties unwittingly in an attempt to solve our problems. In a backlash against decades of permissiveness, in a reaction against shrinking morality, in the belief that in a return to lost values is our only hope—in the pursuit of laudable goals, commendable aims, they will go too far. They will hope only to regain God's favor—and find out too late that they have been a party to the coercion of the consciences of men.

I feel sure that many of those who have set in motion the forces that are already snowballing dangerously, do not, even now, see where their steps are leading. They are only concerned with making our nation one that God can approve. They do not realize that while they mean only to weave a new moral fabric, they are really forging shackles for the mind!

And when they see the smoldering coals of persecution burst into flame in our beloved land, it will be too late to put them out!

In recent years we have witnessed a tremendous upsurge of fundamentalism in the United States. We have also witnessed it, again and again, in Moslem lands. We have stood aghast as we have seen, in countries far from our shores, the harsh punishment, the actual execution of moral offenders—and heard it defended as simply following the Koran!

We have thanked God that it couldn't happen here. But are we sure? Some of history's worst atrocities have been committed in the name of religion. There is no persecution so cruel as religious persecution. There is no terror so ruthless as terror in the name of God!

Is this what the book of Revelation is predicting?

Open your Bible, if you will, to the thirteenth chapter of Revelation. Look at it carefully, for it is extremely significant for our time.

Verse one. We see here a beast—the symbol of a nation, a kingdom, a power. In this instance it must be a combination of both political and religious power, for crowns suggest political power and blasphemy, an involvement in religion.

Verse two. The beast receives his power, his headquarters, and his authority directly or indirectly from the dragon, who is Satan.

Verses three and four. The beast receives worship that is virtually universal. And Satan also is worshiped—at least indirectly.

Verses five to seven. Blasphemy again is emphasized. This beast is attempting to exercise power that belongs only to God. It is a persecuting power, evidently the same power mentioned in

Daniel 7:25, where it is described as persecuting the saints and attempting to change God's law. Its power would extend over a period of 1260 years—a day in prophecy representing a literal year. This same period of persecution is described in Revelation 12:6, 14.

Verse eight. We can expect the whole world to worship the beast—except for those whose names are written in the Lamb's book of life.

Verse eleven. Here we see another beast, emerging at a later time. This is a lamblike symbol representing a nation professing to be Christlike and freedom loving, but which changes character and eventually speaks as a dragon. That is, it manifests the attributes of Satan. The symbols could also indicate that it begins as a Christian nation but later espouses the propaganda of the dragon—spiritualism.

Verse twelve. This second beast eventually, like the first beast, becomes a combination of religious and political power, for it causes the whole world to worship the first beast. And worship, of course, is a function of religion, not politics. Notice also that the first beast has suffered a severe wound, but has recovered.

Verse thirteen. This second beast is a miracle-working power, even bringing down fire from heaven. Again this suggests an involvement with spiritualism, the power of Satan.

Verse fourteen. By these miracles, counterfeit miracles, this second beast deceives the whole world and persuades the people to create an image of the first beast. When this image is formed, when a combination of religious and political power similar to that of the first beast has been created, then the second beast has forever abandoned its lamblike beginning, its Christian principles, and itself becomes a persecuting power!

It is significant also, in this verse, that a democracy or democracies must be involved. The image of the beast is not something imposed upon men by a dictator or monarch against their will. *It is the people who do it.* Notice the wording—"saying to them that dwell on the earth, that *they* should make an image to the beast." KJV.

Verse fifteen. The image of the beast, with power granted by the people, decrees death to all who refuse to worship the image of the beast. Here is what we have feared, what we have thought could never happen—legislation that would provide for the extermination of those who refuse to go along with the religious practices of the majority—or of those in power.

Verse sixteen. A mark is urged upon all—as a sign of allegiance to the beast and its image.

Verse seventeen. Those who refuse to receive the mark are not permitted to buy or sell.

Something very strange is predicted here—a Christian people, zealous for the morality of their neighbors, adopting the philosophies and methods of the dragon to bring it about. And it is the people—not the antichrist or the beast or the image of the beast or the dragon himself, though all these are the persuading influence—*it is the people who do it!*

It would seem that any threat to religious freedom would come from the non-Christian world. We expect it from atheistic dictators. But suddenly the threat seems to be coming not from the unbelieving world, but from a Christian element that in its zeal would like to use the power of the state to impose its own version of morality, its own interpretations of Scripture, along with its own political views, upon the nation and the world!

American presidents have been fond of praising the American people and expressing great confidence in them. Jimmy Carter was one whose speeches were liberally sprinkled with the expression, "the American people." He was confident the American people would understand this or that, would do this or that, would not permit this or that. And he was no exception. We have been educated to believe that the people are always right, that the majority should rule, that democracy is sacred. And certainly no better form of government is available on this planet—now.

But just as a monarchy is no better than its king, a dictatorship no better than its dictator, just so a democracy is no better than its people. The pulse of the people is not always a safe guide. If the heart is not right, the pulse will not be right!

It is difficult to see how a freedom-loving people could ever turn to force and coercion. But who knows what the response of the people might be, for instance, if the nation's economy should collapse? Is it possible that citizens might be willing to sacrifice some of their freedoms in exchange for relief from their economic problems? Is it possible that the majority would be willing to accept a measure of regimentation, a loss of some of their liberty, so long as their personal life-style was not seriously affected?

The people, in a severe economic crisis, would likely accept as a leader most anyone who would promise a way out. An aspiring antichrist would find them easy prey, delightfully vulnerable to his promises and propaganda!

Wouldn't it be a tragedy to step into an erupting fulfillment of Revelation—unprepared?

A citizen who was present at the execution of Marie-Antoinette, in the year 1793, said of the experience: "I was sitting so close I could hear the whisper of the ax!"

Friend, above the din of confused and quarreling voices, above the roar of jets overhead, above the hypnotic beat of rock and the booming of distant cannons and the clatter of jackhammers in the street—above it all, if you listen closely, you too can hear *the whisper of the ax!*

Forever Marked

"When I use a word, it means just what I choose it to mean, neither more nor less." Humpty-Dumpty was speaking—in *Alice in Wonderland*. But we still live in an unpredictable wonderland where words mean different things to different people. And some words—such as *love* and *loyalty* and *obedience* have had a real workout. It seems they can be stretched—or shrunk—to mean most anything.

But a certain farmer, in a story told by Steve Dickerson seemed to have the right idea. It goes like this:

Bill grew up on a farm. And there was never any question about his future. He would be a farmer like his dad.

He went to college and studied agriculture. That gave him the scientific know-how. But where would he get the money to buy a farm?

One day his father said, "Bill, I'm getting old. I'm almost ready to retire. I'd like to give the farm to you."

Bill was speechless. His problem was solved!

But the older man went on. "There's just one stipulation. I want you to run the farm strictly according to my directions for the first year. After that, it's yours."

That was fair enough. Dad was a good farmer. He knew what he was doing. And just think—after a year the farm would be his!

The two men spent the next few days going from field to field. Bill carried a notebook and wrote down just what his father wanted him to plant in each field. Then his father and mother left for a vacation.

Bill was curious. It would be interesting to see how his father's directions checked out with what he had learned at college. He got out his soil-testing kit and started around the farm again. As he went from one field to another, he was impressed with his father's wisdom. In each field his dad had scooped up a handful of soil and examined it carefully before deciding what to plant. And he had been right every time. Every time he had chosen the very crop that, according to what Bill had learned in college, would grow best in that particular soil!

Every time—until Bill came to the last field. His father had said to plant corn, but he must have made a mistake. The soil appeared to be sandy and poor. Plant corn! Why, Bill was sure that the slightest wind would tear the plants right out of the soil. And even if the stalks weren't blown over, he was sure that the corn would be sickly. Dad must have made a mistake.

Bill's analysis showed that the soil would be perfect for peanuts. Dad would want every crop to be a success. He would be pleased to see that all the money spent on Bill's education had paid off. So Bill planted peanuts.

Dad came back at harvesttime. He said the farm had never looked so good. Bill took him around and showed him the wheat and the potatoes and the alfalfa.

"But where's the corn?" Dad wanted to know. "I thought I told you to plant corn."

Bill said, "Well, yes, Dad. That was in this field over here. I went back and tested the soil in all the fields. You were exactly right in all except this one, so I thought you must have made a mistake. I was sure you would rather see a good crop of peanuts than a sickly crop of corn."

Dad shook his head sadly. "Bill," he said, "you haven't followed my directions in any of these fields. You've followed your own judgment in every case. It just happened that you agreed with me in all points except one. But as soon as there was any question, you did what you thought was best in spite of what I had directed you to do. I'm sorry, Bill, but you'll have to look elsewhere for a farm of your own."

How about it? Was Bill's father too harsh? Or was he absolutely right? Does it mean anything at all to follow directions—especially when they are God's directions—only when we happen to agree with them?

Most of us are not farmers. But our Father— like Bill's dad— has written down on slabs of stone, some specific directions for us. And on condition that we follow them, He promises not a farm, but a future beyond our wildest dreams—and never-ending life. We call those directions the Ten Commandments.

But millions today have brought out their own personal analyzing kits. They think it would be interesting to see how God's directions compare with what they've been taught at the university—or with their own philosophy of life and right and wrong. And what happens?

Millions today are improvising their own off-the-cuff morality to meet their moods. They have decided that God's directions are outdated and certainly not relevant for this "enlightened" generation. And even if they agree with God part of the time, they are sure that in some instances He made a mistake—or just didn't mean what He said. And so they are planting peanuts—and thinking how pleased God will be when He sees the crop!

Millions actually believe that God sometimes throws His Ten Commandments into reverse. They think it is all right to steal in an emergency. Or lie if it will keep you out of jail. Or commit adultery if, as Joseph Fletcher has suggested, having a child is the only way to get out of a concentration camp. Millions today follow God's directions when they agree with them—and ignore them when they don't seem to make sense.

But if we obey only when we agree, have we obeyed at all?

Jesus said, "Not everyone who says to me, 'Lord, Lord,' will enter the kingdom of heaven, but only he who does the will of my Father who is in heaven." Matthew 7:21, NIV.

Are we in danger of losing a fabulous future the way Bill lost a farm?

You see, God has the same problem today that He had with our first parents. He wanted to give them never-ending life. But He dared not give them immortality without first testing their loyalty. He must be sure that they could be trusted with a life that never ends!

How could He do this? What sort of test could He devise that would give Him absolute assurance of their loyalty—or tragic proof that they could not be trusted with the gift He wanted to give them? Promises were not enough. Promises are easy to make.

God could have put an active volcano, a crater of fire, on the edge of the garden. He could have told Adam and Eve that to jump into it would mean death. And they would undoubtedly have stayed away from it for sure. No man in his right mind is going to jump into a seething caldera when the heat of it, even at a safe distance, burns the whiskers off his face!

No! God must devise a test that, to human reasoning, seemed not to make sense. Obedience must stem from loyalty alone—nothing else!

Let me illustrate. The story is told of a railroad worker who lived near the tracks. He was off duty that day. He looked up from his work in the yard to see his little boy, four and a half, playing on the tracks. And a train was thundering toward him!

There was no time to reach him and snatch him away. He called, but Johnny did not hear. Then he called out at the top of his voice, for there was time for nothing else, "Johnny, lie down and don't move!"

Johnny obeyed instantly, without even turning to look his father's way. The train rushed over the motionless boy. And after the caboose had passed, the father gathered him up, his little heart pounding—but safe!

There was nothing in Johnny's short experience, his few short years, to qualify him to understand his father's strange command. But he didn't question it. He didn't ask why. He didn't delay. His father had spoken. And that was enough for him!

Just so, in Adam and Eve's experience there was nothing to qualify them to understand God's strange command. Why should the fruit of one tree, apparently just as beautiful, and as much to be desired as the others, have death within it? They didn't understand that the seemingly unimportant act of eating the fruit clearly revealed the weakness of their loyalty!

Now God, I say, has the same problem today that He had in the Garden of Eden. Millions have professed loyalty to God. But obviously not all could be trusted with never-ending life. How else can their loyalty be tested—except with a command that makes no sense to the human mind?

Now we are ready to turn to the book of Revelation. You recall that in the thirteenth chapter there are some very frightening predictions. A *beast*—representing a kingdom, a nation, a power. In this case it is evidently a coalition of religious and political power. A *second beast*—a nation with lamblike characteristics at the beginning, but later speaking as a dragon. This *second beast,* evidently a democracy, persuades the people to create *an image of the first beast*—a similar coalition of religious and political power. This *image,* this coalition, pronounces *a death sentence* upon all who refuse to worship the *first beast.* And those who refuse to receive the *mark of the beast* are not permitted to *buy or sell.* Frightening, you will agree.

But in the *fourteenth* chapter, the next chapter, symbolized by three angels, each with a message, we find God's last call to men (verses 6–12). And in the message of the third angel (verses 9–11) we find the most fearful warning in all of the Scriptures—a warning against worshiping the beast and his image or receiving his mark!

Now this is not something to play games with. This is serious business. It appears to be death-if-you-do and death-if-you-don't. And no middle ground!

I am aware of the widespread notion that the book of Revelation can't be understood. But I ask you, Would God include so fearful a warning in His last call to men—if He knew that the identity of the beast and the nature of his mark could not be understood?

But before we explore some clues as to what the mark might be, what about God? Does God have a mark too? Yes, He does. And could it be that in the final confrontation, in the still ongoing controversy in which every one of us will be involved, whether we want to be or not—could it be that the choice will be between two marks, with our choice revealing our loyalty either to Christ or to the fallen angel? Yes, it will be exactly that. And I believe that if we understand the nature of God's mark, it will be easier to understand the nature of Satan's mark.

The idea of God placing a mark upon His people is not new. You recall that in ancient Egypt, on that fateful night when the destroying angel was to pass through the land, every Hebrew householder was to slay a lamb and place some of its blood on the doorpost. The destroying angel, seeing that mark, that identification, would spare that home.

Then in the ninth chapter of Ezekiel, we find a symbolic vision that was shown to the prophet. Israel, in its idolatry, had reached the point where punishment could no longer be delayed. And in this vision Ezekiel saw six men with weapons of slaughter. One of them, however, had a writer's inkhorn—probably a case containing pens, a knife, and ink. He was commanded to go through Jerusalem, preceding the others, and place a mark upon the foreheads of those individuals who were sighing and crying in their concern over the depravity of God's professed people. Then the other five men were to follow him through the city, sparing only those who had the mark upon their foreheads.

Keep in mind that this was a symbolic vision. Israel's punishment would not be executed by six men, and there was no literal mark. The punishment, when God removed His restraining hand, would come from the Chaldean armies. This was the primary fulfillment of what the prophet saw in vision. A secondary fulfillment will take place down in the last days.

In the seventh chapter of Revelation we see four angels holding the winds of war and strife. They are commissioned not to let them blow in full force upon the earth until the servants of God are sealed, or marked, in their foreheads.

What will this mark be? What test will God administer to His professed people that will reveal, once for all, who is safe to take into His kingdom and who is not, who can be trusted with never-ending life and who cannot? It must be something that has no foundation in human reason, something that doesn't seem to make sense, a command that His true people will obey simply because He has spoken. Like Johnny on the railroad track— obeying without asking why. That's the kind of test to look for.

We find a number of clues. All through the Scriptures the fact that God is the Creator is held out as distinguishing Him from false gods who never created anything. And I need not tell you that God's creatorship is under attack today. From the beginning the fact that Jesus created this earth has been a focal point of Satan's jealousy. And in God's last call to men we are urged to worship Him who made heaven and earth (Revelation 14:6, 7)— again suggesting that the matter of God's creatorship is a key issue in the final conflict.

In the last verse of Revelation 12 we see Satan angry with the people of God, going to war against them because they persist in keeping God's commandments. And in Daniel's prophecy (Daniel 7:25) we see a persecuting power, evidently the same as the first beast of Revelation 13, attempting to make some change in God's law. The apostle Paul (2 Thessalonians 2:3, 4) describes the man of sin, the antichrist, as sitting in the temple of God and claiming that he *is* God.

God's authority, God's creatorship, God's commandments—these are the issues. And, as a test of loyalty, we can expect to find a command of God that seems not to be based on human reasoning.

With these clues in mind, scan with me the Ten Commandments, found in Exodus 20:3-17. The first three seem reasonable enough. If God is the true God, certainly we should not have any other gods or bow down to images of wood or stone. And certainly God should have our respect. The last six commandments are so reasonable that for thousands of years thay have frequently been incorporated into the laws of nations—even nations that do not worship the true God.

But one commandment—the fourth—is different. It doesn't fit into man's reasoning. There seems to be no moral principle involved. It seems arbitrary. And in a sense it is. Our year is marked off by the journey of our planet around the sun. Our month is marked off by the recurrent phases of the moon, and our day by the rotation of the earth. But our week has no basis in the movements of heavenly bodies. This weekly cycle is marked off only by the Sabbath.

The commandment would not be so troublesome if it simply asked for one day in seven as a day of rest. Most anyone would go along with the idea of a day off every seven days. Labor unions like it. Atheists like it. It certainly would not indicate any particular loyalty to God to take one day in seven for rest.

But the commandment specifies *the seventh* day. It is this specificness that makes it a problem, and often makes it inconvenient. Certainly the days are all alike, twenty-four hours long. What difference does it make which day we devote to rest and worship? It doesn't seem reasonable that God should specify a particular day. But He has. And there will always be those who love Him enough to obey without asking why!

Could this be the test we are looking for—a command that doesn't make sense to the human mind? It certainly fits. God, seemingly without reason, placed one tree in the center of the garden and declared it off limits to our first parents. Could it be that God has placed in the center of His law a command that doesn't answer easily to human reason—and that in these final days He will use it to measure the loyalty of every man, every woman, every child who professes to worship Him?

Yes, the Sabbath commandment is unique among the ten. There is no controversy about the other nine. Most any good citizens, Christian or not, will go along with them because they seem reasonable. But does any man, regardless of how often he goes to church or how much he puts in the offering plate or how spotless his moral character may be—does any man really obey God at all if he obeys only when he understands why, when he can see a reason, when he happens to agree with God, when a command makes sense? No, he doesn't. Like the farmer's son, he is really following his own judgment all the way!

Now I know that the identity of the day of rest may seem like a trivial matter. Surely, you say, there must be more important issues than quibbling about a day.

But we cannot always choose our challenges. The fireman cannot choose the location of the fires he fights. The soldier cannot choose where he will go to war. The lesson of the Falklands, for Britain, was this—that battles will not always be fought where they seem most likely.

Ted Koppel, hosting ABC's "Viewpoint" program before a live audience, was asked why the press did not give more time to Africa. Why did newsmen give so much coverage to the Middle East and not Africa? The answer, of course, is that the news goes where the fire is, where the war is, where an enemy has chosen to attack. Vietnam was an obscure place to many Americans, but that's where the challenge was. Iran was not at the top of our priority list, but that's where our hostages were held. The North Pole would have made the headlines if our hostages had been there!

Satan is angry with the people who persist in obeying God's commands. See Revelation 12:17. The prophet Daniel predicted that an attempt would be made to change God's law. See Daniel 7:25. Then I ask you, Will Satan focus his attack on the com-

---

*The publishers of this book will be happy to refer you to detailed evidence of what happened and the claims made by those involved. My own book, *A Day to Remember,* would be helpful.

mandments that men find reasonable and about which there is no controversy? Or will he zero in on the one which doesn't answer to human reason, the one which rests on God's authority alone? And wouldn't you expect the fallen angel to target especially the one that continually reminds men of their Creator? Of course!

Do you begin to see what the mark of God might be—and what the mark of the beast might be? If God uses the Sabbath commandment as a test of loyalty and if a faithful observance of that command marks a man as one who can be trusted to go God's way forever—then what might be the mark of the rebel camp? Could it be a substitute Sabbath, brought in from paganism during the dark ages when the Scriptures were not available to the people, a day of worship that rests, not on divine authority but on human authority? What could be more logical?

You see, the controversy isn't over a day at all. It's over authority. Whose authority will you accept? Will you accept the authority of God, or the authority of the beast as an agent of Satan? It matters not how trivial the command might appear. If God should say to you, "Go stand in the corner," and Satan should say, "Don't stand in the corner," it would probably seem downright ridiculous. But it would make a mighty big difference which command you obey, for it would mark you as a loyal follower of one or the other!

No one has the mark of the beast today. God will not permit any man to receive that mark until the issues are out in the open and every individual knows what he is doing. But when the issues are fully understood and he recognizes the critical and final nature of the step he is taking—*then,* if he deliberately chooses to obey a command of men in place of a command of God, if he yields to coercion and takes the easy way out when the going gets rough, he will have *marked himself,* by his action, as one no longer loyal to his God. The mark will be there. *In his forehead* if he believes the propaganda of Satan. *In his hand* if he knows it is false, but goes along with it anyway, because he can't take the pressure and ridicule of the crowd. The mark will be invisible to men. But angels will see it—and know where his loyalty lies!

And what of the mark of God? Even now our attitude toward the commandments of God may decide our destiny. But at this moment it has not become the accurate test of loyalty that it will be in the days ahead. There are still too many people outwardly faithful to the commands of God, including the Sabbath, whose commitment is only for fair weather. When the predictions of Revelation 13 become a reality, when it is no longer convenient to obey God, the superficial hangers-on will be shaken out. And those who keep the faith even when it is a matter of life or death will be giving God evidence that they can be trusted with never-ending life. The mark of God will be in their foreheads. His mark is never received in the hand, for God accepts only that worship which comes from the heart and mind. Satan, on the contrary, doesn't care how he gets his worship. If he cannot get it by choice, he will gladly accept it by force!

The mark of God. And the mark of Satan. On the one hand a command that is based solely upon the authority of God. On the other hand a command that is based solely on the authority of men. This is the choice that is racing toward us!

Have we been weaving here a fabric of guesswork? Has there really been an attempt to change God's law? Is the challenge of God's authority about to surface openly and burst into flame? Yes. Daniel predicted it. Paul said it would come. Revelation spotlights it. And the power represented by the beast of Revelation 13 comes along and says in substance, "Yes, we did it. We're proud of it. We consider the act a mark of our authority."*

We are moving rapidly toward the day of final choices. And we are preparing for that day by the little decisions, the seemingly insignificant choices we make along the way. If in these little situations we habitually choose the easy way, the popular way, we shall find it only natural, in the crisis, to decide the same way—along with the crowd!

We shall have some surprises when we see who is strong—and who is weak. Some that we thought were strong will prove miserably weak. And some that we thought were weak will display the courage of David—and be forever marked as friends of God!

Professor D—— was no friend of God. And everybody in his five-hundred-member class knew it. In September he had told them, "During the course of this semester all who have the desire to remain in this section of Anthropology 201 will learn the truth. In learning this truth you will find every belief you have ever held about a God or religion in general will be destroyed." And in the weeks that followed he had never missed an opportunity to criticize and ridicule religion.

And now the class was meeting for the last time before Christmas vacation. Dr. D—— was giving his annual lecture "proving" that prayer is a fallacy. He had been giving this lecture for ten years, so he knew it well. It had gone off so well the first time, and was such hilarious entertainment, that he had made it an annual event.

This day, as he finished his mocking attack, he stood up. He was wearing what he always wore for this performance—jeans, sneakers, and a T-shirt that read, "Jesus is coming again, and boy, is He peeved."

He glared at the auditorium full of students and defiantly inquired, "After two months in this class is there anybody here who still believes in the ridiculous notion of religion?"

He walked around to the front of his desk and stood gloating. In his upraised right hand he held a new piece of chalk. The classroom had a concrete floor. All eyes were glued on the professor. There was utter silence.

Then with a mocking jeer he went on with the challenge he had long since memorized: "Well, if there's anyone in this classroom who still believes in religion and the so-called power of prayer, I ask you to stand up and pray. Pray that when I drop this piece of chalk from my hand it will not break. . . . I defy you and this so-called power by stating this: 'Nothing—not all your prayers, not all your religion, not even your so-called God Himself, can stop this piece of chalk from breaking when I drop it.' I defy you to prove me wrong!"

There was a slight movement near the right side of the auditorium. Every eye turned. A boy, we'll call him Jim (not his real name), stood up and walked to the aisle. Then he moved toward the front and stopped in front of his instructor. "Dr. D——," he said in clear and confident tones, "I do."

"Well, how about this? We've here before us a real, live person who claims he believes in the stupid notion that God can answer his prayer. Is that right?"

"Yes, sir. I know God will answer my prayer."

"How about this?" the professor repeated. "But I'll tell you what. Just in case you misunderstood, I'll explain to you again exactly what I am going to do."

Then he went through the sequence again—how he would drop the chalk, it would shatter into a dozen fragments, and no power in the universe could keep it from shattering. Then he chided, "Do you still want to pray?"

"Yes, Professor, I sure do."

The professor reveled in this glorious moment of victory, gloating over what was about to happen. "Isn't this something? All right, class. I want you all to be real quiet and reverent-like while this boy prays." There was sarcasm in every word. Then he turned back to Jim. "Are you ready?"

And Jim replied, "Professor, I have been preparing for this moment all my life."

"All right, then. We'll all be real quiet and bow our heads while you pray." Never were words more mocking and derisive.

Not one of the more than five hundred could take their eyes off Jim. They all held their breath. The boy just turned his face heavenward and prayed, "God, I know You are real, and I pray in the name of and for the glory and honor of Your Son Jesus. And I pray for myself, who trusts You with all my heart. If it be Your will, do not let this piece of chalk break. Amen."

The sneering smile was still on the professor's face. "Is that it?"

Jim breathed a quiet "Yes."

Dr. D—— grasped the chalk in his right hand and held it up above his head in defiance. Then he let it fall. But that day a miracle happened. As the chalk tumbled toward the floor it fell against the leg of his jeans. Then it toppled down onto his canvas sneakers, and with a muffled tinkle it rolled to a stop on the concrete floor, unbroken!

The silence was deafening! Then a student burst into laughter. Soon another joined. In seconds the entire auditorium was laughing at the red-faced professor. Someone in the back of the auditorium shouted at the top of his voice, "You did it, Jim!" He turned and smiled—a careful, humble sort of smile. Then he just pointed upward. And everyone understood. Even the professor!

Jim was not strong and muscular like the boy who herded sheep and killed a lion and a bear and a giant on the way to becoming king. Jim was slight of stature and a little scrawny. He looked as if a little wind could blow him away. But scrawny little Jim had decided that such defiance of God could not be ignored. This modern Goliath must be challenged. And God used a modern David to silence him!*

God hides the stuff of heroes in a thousand unsuspected places. And crisis always finds it. It will again!

---

*Used by permission of the author.

The Ultimate Hoax

Suppose, if you will, that you are an impostor who has decided to stage a counterfeit second coming—a counterfeit return of Christ to this planet. Just what would you have to do?

Now I know, as you know, that it isn't difficult to get a following these days. Some people seem to have no difficulty in attracting millions. With Bible literacy low and gullibility high, even a Jonestown is not impossible. In fact, it was relatively easy.

So let me reword my question. *What would you have to do to fool the man who knows his Bible?*

First of all, of course, you would need someone to play the role of Christ. And that isn't difficult, because Satan himself would be glad to volunteer. He's been practicing up for just such a role for millenniums.

Could Satan disguise himself sufficiently? Could he make himself *look* anything like Christ? Could he make himself *sound* enough like Christ to fool even a Bible-reading Christian? Absolutely. The apostle Paul says that "Satan himself is transformed into an angel of light." 2 Corinthians 11:14, KJV.

And if you need some miracles, remember that, according to the book of Revelation, demons can work miracles. See Revelation 16:14.

So far it's easy.

But wait. So far we've only seen that it would not be difficult for Satan and his demons to set up a hoax that would fool millions. But our question is this: What would you have to do, what would an impostor have to do, what would Satan have to do, to duplicate exactly the Bible description of the second coming of Christ?

Satan has a lot of power, supernatural power. He can disguise himself. He can impersonate. He can work miracles. He can fool people. But his power is limited. He can only go so far.

Listen. If any impostor, even Satan himself, wants to successfully duplicate the return of Christ, he will have to be able to get

315

up there in the sky and descend to earth in the clouds of heaven. Because Jesus said, "They shall see the Son of man coming in the clouds of heaven with power and great glory." Matthew 24:30, KJV.

Now it isn't so easy. Now it's getting tough. But let's go on.

An impostor would have to get the cooperation of all the angels of heaven, every one of them. Because they're all descending to earth along with Christ. See Matthew 25:31.

Do you think the loyal angels of heaven would ever cooperate with a rebel impostor?

But it gets more difficult as we go along. We read this about the second coming: "Look, he is coming with the clouds, and every eye will see him, even those who pierced him; and all the peoples of the earth will mourn because of him." Revelation 1:7, NIV.

Here are insurmountable problems for any impostor. It says that every eye will see Jesus as He returns. Everybody will be watching. Nobody will have to be told what is happening—or hear it on the news. And that means everybody everywhere on earth, because it says that all the peoples of the earth will be involved.

Just how our God will make it possible for everyone on earth, not only east and west but north and south as well—just how God will make it possible for everyone on earth to see what is happening, I don't know. It would seem that some manipulation of the planet itself, some turning or twirling of the globe, must be involved. Would any impostor be able to manage that?

And there's something else in the verse we just read. It says that those who crucified Jesus will see Him return in glory. This would require a resurrection of those people. It would mean bringing forth from their graves those who played a special part in the death of Jesus. Could an impostor do that?

An impostor, if he is to really duplicate the second coming, would have to have the cooperation of all nature. For listen to this: "Out of the temple came a loud voice from the throne, saying 'It is done!' Then there came flashes of lightning, rumblings, peals of thunder and a severe earthquake. No earthquake like it has ever occurred since man has been on earth, so tremendous was the quake. . . . And the cities of the nations collapsed. . . . Every island fled away and the mountains could not be found. From the sky huge hailstones of about a hundred pounds each fell upon men." Revelation 16:17–21, NIV.

Would any impostor have the power to do all this?

But there is still more. Here is the apostle Paul's description of the second coming: "For the Lord himself will come down from heaven, with a loud command, with the voice of the archangel and with the trumpet call of God, and the dead in Christ will rise first. After that, we who are still alive and are left will be caught up with them in the clouds to meet the Lord in the air. And so we will be with the Lord forever." 1 Thessalonians 4:16, 17, NIV.

Will any impostor be able to break open the graves all around the earth and call to life those who have died trusting in their Lord? Never!

And did you notice that the feet of Jesus, when He returns, will not even touch the ground? He comes no nearer than the living cloud of angels that escort Him. To be sure, He comes very near the earth—near enough for His voice to be heard by all, near enough to call the dead to life. But He does not actually set foot on the ground. *Remember this* when you hear on the evening news that Christ has returned and is out in the Arizona desert. *Remember this* when you hear that Jesus is working miracles in Times Square. *Remember this* when you hear that a being believed to be Jesus Christ has just stepped out of a UFO!

Do you see how terribly important it is to know *how* Jesus is going to return? It's our *only guarantee* against being fatally deceived!

Jesus warned that there would be many impostors, many false Christs. And He said they would work great signs and wonders— miracles—so that if possible even His own people would be deceived. See Matthew 24:24. But He added, "So if anyone tells you, 'There he is, out in the desert,' do not go out; or, 'Here he is, in the inner rooms,' do not believe it." Matthew 24:26, NIV.

You say, "Don't we have to check these things out? Don't we have to go and listen so we can decide whether it's Jesus or not?"

No. Jesus is saying to us, "Look! You don't need to bother with checking out all these people who claim to be Christ—no matter how many miracles they work, no matter how many millions may follow them. Because I have told you just *how* I will return. So you won't need to pay any attention to anyone who appears some other way."

An impostor, then, doesn't have a chance with the person who knows his Bible!

And someone says, "Satan probably has read all these scriptures, too, and knows how hard it would be to really counterfeit the second coming. So that's one thing he won't try."

No. I believe it would be a mistake to try to reason ourselves out of danger that way. There's not much of anything that Satan won't try—if it has any chance at all of serving his evil purposes. I believe he definitely will try to impersonate Christ and counterfeit the second coming. I believe he will do it for four reasons—at least four:

1. He knows that most people haven't read the Bible enough to know—and remember—*how* Jesus will return.

2. He knows that among those who do read and study the Bible there are many who, at his satanic instigation, have simply been playing games with Bible prophecy—with the book of Revelation especially. They are weaving for themselves a fabric of speculation and wishful thinking. They have figured out how they would like future events to be—and have convinced themselves that that's the way it will be. In spite of all the scriptures that describe the second coming as the most spectacular event since creation, some have decided that it will really be a secret affair that only a few will be aware of. And some are expecting things to happen in Israel that won't happen in Israel. And some believe Christ will set up a political kingdom on this earth in the near future. And some, influenced by the psychics, have decided Jesus will return in 1999 and that therefore we all have plenty of time to prepare. If only we would let the Bible be its own interpreter! How much safer we would be! One thing is certain. The future is not going to happen a thousand different ways. It will happen only *one way*— the way the Bible describes!

3. Satan knows that with his supernatural power, the impersonation will be so spectacular, so convincing, *so like Jesus* that it will be impossible by the senses alone to detect the counterfeit.

4. The fallen angel is so desperate, so determined to gain the

worship of men and women one way or another—even if only for an hour and even if by mistake—that he will go ahead with his plan even though he knows that any successes will be of very short duration. His plea to the human race, as it was to Jesus in the wilderness temptation, is this: "Worship me just once. Worship me just a little—even if you don't mean it!"

And the tragedy is that when the Lord Jesus appears in the sky, almost everybody will already have bowed down to a masquerading impostor, believing him to be Christ!

We are being conditioned for a monstrous deception that will sweep the world—a deception tailored to fit the mood of this space-minded generation. Unquestionably Satan is planning some sort of end-of-the-world extravaganza in which he will play the leading role.

And don't ever think that the big hoax will be easy to ignore. On the contrary, it will be so cleverly carried out as to be almost overpowering. Satan and his angels-turned-demons have been in this impersonating business for thousands of years. They have impersonated angels. They have impersonated dead people. They have impersonated living people. They have impersonated people from outer space. Why not go for the big one? Why not impersonate Jesus—the second coming and all? After all, Satan has always wanted Jesus' place!

Already we have witnessed a number of dry runs—rehearsals for Satan's second-coming stunt. People locking themselves in a lead-lined bomb shelter and waiting for the end of the world. People gathering on a mountaintop, expecting to be picked up by a spaceship. People selling their homes and abandoning their families, following a leader somewhere—only to be disillusioned. The world is a pushover for a counterfeit Christ—for anyone who appears able to solve our problems that are getting out of hand. The world is wired for the big hoax!

Satan has permitted his followers to stand in for him in these rehearsals. But you can be assured that when he is ready for the big show, he will play the starring role himself. And few will escape fatal deception—only those who have learned to trust the Scriptures more than their eyes and their ears!

Ellen White, many years ago, described the day of the ultimate hoax. Listen:

"As the crowning act in the great drama of deception, Satan himself will personate Christ. . . . Now the great deceiver will make it appear that Christ has come. In different parts of the earth, Satan will manifest himself among men as a majestic being of dazzling brightness, resembling the description of the Son of God given by John in the Revelation. . . . The glory that surrounds him is unsurpassed by anything that mortal eyes have yet beheld. The shout of triumph rings out upon the air: 'Christ has come! Christ has come!' The people prostrate themselves in adoration before him, while he lifts up his hands and pronounces a blessing upon them, as Christ blessed His disciples when He was upon the earth. His voice is soft and subdued, yet full of melody. In gentle, compassionate tones he presents some of the same gracious, heavenly truths which the Saviour uttered; he heals the diseases of the people, and then, in his assumed character of Christ, he claims to have changed the [law of God]. . . . This is the strong, almost overmastering delusion."—*The Great Controversy*, p. 624.

There he stands, this being of dazzling brightness. If you ask your eyes, who is it? Jesus. If you ask your ears, Who is it? Jesus. If you ask your feelings, Who is it? Jesus.

But if you ask the Scriptures, Who is it? A masquerading devil! And almost all the world will bow down, taken in by the ultimate hoax!

Friend, I commend to you the Word of God. Read it! Read it for your life!

Section Twelve
Toying With the Nick of Time

The Breath of Armageddon

Out of the Middle East comes a chilling wind. Is it only the approach of another winter? Is it just another stirring of an atmosphere so long troubled? Is it the coldness of steel, of weapons stored against one more holocaust? Is it only the perennial sensitiveness of the East caught up in the restless winds that blow our way?

Or is it the hard, driving, inescapable breath of Armageddon?

And what is Armageddon? Does anybody know?

To the journalist, it is a convenient term to describe any titanic struggle, military or otherwise. Even a coal strike has been called an "industrial Armageddon."

The author of a religious paperback may confidently describe Armageddon as a decisive and final battle to be fought on a plain in northern Israel, with the Soviet Union, China, and many other nations participating.

To some it is another name for World War III. And others are not sure. They have a vague notion of some devastating nuclear holocaust in which reality will finally outdo the fiction writers.

Armageddon! Frightening! Almost upon us! Breathing the chill of doomsday! What is this ultimate horror that will finally do our planet in?

We must turn to Scripture for the answer. For the word has its origin in the book of Revelation. And even there it is used only once. This is what it says: "For they are the spirits of devils, working miracles, which go forth unto the kings of the earth and of the whole world, to gather them to the battle of that great day of God Almighty. . . . And he gathered them together into a place called in the Hebrew tongue Armageddon." Revelation 16:14-16, KJV.

Notice that Armageddon is a battle—evidently the final battle in this world's history, for it is called "the battle of that great day of God Almighty." And evidently it is a worldwide conflict, for the nations of all the world are involved.

"A place called in the Hebrew tongue Armageddon." And right here the questions begin. Right here we are confronted with details that we do not know. For in all the world there is no place called Armageddon.

We are told that the place is called Armageddon in the Hebrew tongue. So we turn to the Hebrew for the meaning of the word. And we find that it is a combination of *har*, which means mountain, and *mageddon*, which many have connected with Megiddo, a city of Old Testament times which is now only a hill of ruins. So actually, in Hebrew, the name Armageddon is literally "mountain of Megiddo." But nowhere is there a mountain called Megiddo. It is true that the valley of Megiddo, or the Plain of Esdraelon, has a long history of military conflict. But are we to believe that the armies of all the world could be crowded into the valley of Megiddo in northern Israel?

And that is not all. For other armies, too, are involved. Listen to this: "These [nations] shall make war with the Lamb [Christ], and the Lamb shall overcome them: for he is Lord of lords, and King of kings." Revelation 17:14, KJV.

And then this: "The armies which were in heaven followed him [Christ] upon white horses, clothed in fine linen, white and clean." Revelation 19:14, KJV.

So the armies of heaven are involved in this battle as well as the armies of earth. The nations may only be fighting each other at first. It may start that way, as a military and political conflict. But ultimately the nations will be fighting against Christ and the armies of heaven. Ultimately this final battle will be an all-out showdown between God and His enemies. And certainly the little valley of Megiddo would be too small for that. The battle will rapidly escalate into a conflict involving the whole world—and heaven too!

Now sometimes, as we are all aware, a word has more than one meaning. This is the case with the Greek word *topos*, which has been translated "place"—"a place called . . . Armageddon." This Greek word is used not only to mean a geographical location, but also to mean status, condition, or situation.

Haven't you used the word *place* in that way? You've said, "That was a hard place to be in." Or, "I wouldn't want to be in the place that man is in." And you weren't talking about a geographical location at all.

A *situation* called Armageddon. That makes it easier to understand, doesn't it?

But now, if that is the case, why "mountain of Megiddo"? Why even the hint of a geographical location if it is a *situation* that is referred to?

Now the name becomes very interesting and takes on real meaning.

Suppose, if you will, that you wished to visit the ruins of ancient Megiddo. You might take a bus eastward from the port city of Haifa and follow the Carmel ridge, the western end of which drops suddenly into the Mediterranean at Haifa. Tell el-Mutesellim, the site of ancient Megiddo, stands at the foot of this ridge on its northeastern edge. And if you survey the ruins close to the mountain, it is easy to see why many have identified the "mountain of Megiddo" with the Carmel ridge. For there, looming large before you as you stand on the Megiddo mound, would be Mount Carmel. And you know what happened atop Carmel!

Yes, in the days of Elijah, Mount Carmel was the site of one of the great showdowns between God and His enemies. It was there that fire came down from heaven to demonstrate once and for all who is the true God. And the confrontation on Mount Carmel was, in many ways, a miniature of the great showdown to come in the final days.

A *situation* called Armageddon. A *situation* like Carmel. A *showdown* like Carmel!

In this sixteenth chapter of Revelation we are told of the seven frightful judgments that God will release upon His enemies at the very last. And striking similarities exist between these seven judgments and the ten plagues that fell on Egypt—the water turned to blood, the boils, the darkness, and the hail. Why ten judgments were released upon Egypt and only seven are scheduled at the last we are not told. But the number seven is often used to denote completeness. And certainly, as you look over the account of these final horrors, you will agree that seven is enough!

Another similarity stands out. At the last, as in Egypt, God will make a difference between those who serve Him and those who serve Him not. Just as the Hebrews then were untouched by the plagues, just so the child of God today is promised, "A thousand shall fall at thy side, and ten thousand at thy right hand; but it shall not come nigh thee." Psalms 91:7, KJV.

It is during the sixth, the next to the last of these final judgments, that Armageddon begins. Armageddon continues during the seventh judgment, the battle to be interrupted by the return of Christ.

The river Euphrates, mentioned in verse 12, is the river that once ran through the ancient city of Babylon. It is the river of Babylon. Babylon has long since been destroyed. But in the book of Revelation its name is used as the symbol of false worship. Since Babylon here is symbolic, its river and the drying up of the river must also be symbolic. The river would represent people (Revelation 17:15), and the drying up of the river would represent the withdrawal of the people's support for Babylon, leading to its downfall.

Then verse 13: "I saw three unclean spirits like frogs come out of the mouth of the dragon, and out of the mouth of the beast, and out of the mouth of the false prophet." Revelation 16:13, KJV.

The dragon, the beast, and the false prophet are here used to represent a threefold coalition of God's enemies—the dragon denoting paganism, the beast denoting a religious and political power that challenges God's law, and the false prophet denoting churches once loyal to God that have fallen away from that loyalty.

Now if Babylon here is figurative, if the river is figurative, if the beast and the dragon and the false prophet are figurative, would it be any surprise that God should give this final battle a figurative name? And since Babylon represents false worship all around the world and the Euphrates represents people all around the world— for we are plainly told that all the nations of the world are involved—must not the battle of Armageddon be worldwide? We can hardly reach any other conclusion. It would hardly be wise, then, to try to confine it to some precise location in the Middle East.

On the other hand, it would be a serious mistake to suppose

that Armageddon, because of all these symbols, is not a literal battle. For certainly it is. But God, in order to protect the prophecies of Revelation from His enemies, has made a liberal use of symbols. You can see that if His enemies were clearly named and their activities clearly delineated, certainly they would be stirred to destroy the Book.

The battle of Armageddon will be very, very real. There will be bloodshed beyond anything we can imagine. The large majority of those living on this planet will be slain. The prophet Jeremiah, speaking of that same time, says, "The slain of the Lord shall be at that day from one end of the earth even unto the other end of the earth: they shall not be lamented, neither gathered, nor buried." Jeremiah 25:33, KJV.

And those words are not symbolic at all. They are very, very literal!

Yes, few will escape. Just as in ancient Egypt, on that fateful night, only those homes that displayed the blood on the doorpost were spared, that blood prefiguring the blood of Jesus, just so, when the final judgments of God encompass the planet, only those who have accepted the sacrifice of Jesus, who trust in the merits of His blood, and whose names are written in the Lamb's book of life, will be spared. That sacrifice was made for all. It is free to all. But most people will reject it. And what can God do but honor their choice?

You say it is out of character for Jesus, the gentle and compassionate Healer, to destroy? Yes, it is out of character. The Bible calls it His "strange act," the act that He puts off as long as He can. See Isaiah 28:21. But haven't we ourselves asked, again and again, why He doesn't step in and set things right? And how else can He remove evil except by removing those who refuse to be separated from it?

But now notice. The three unclean spirits like frogs are said to be spirits of devils. It is these spirits of devils who lead the nations into Armageddon. It is not simply evil in the hearts of men, corruption even in the highest circles, that is leading the world to ruin. Demon activity is also responsible for what is happening all around us.

I need not tell you that spiritualism, in its seemingly limitless forms, is sweeping the world today. This generation seems to be obsessed with the psychic, with the occult. Satan worship has come out into the open. But Satan and his demon helpers also work subtly, under cover, under a thousand unsuspected labels.

Spiritualism is spreading like wildfire. It is even infiltrating many Christian churches. This should be no surprise, for we are told that Babylon, the symbol of false worship, has become the habitation of demons. See Revelation 18:2. No wonder God makes the urgent plea, "Come out of her, my people!"

And never forget that these demons, these spirits of devils, are able to work miracles. Largely through these miracles the nations are deceived and will be led into the final battle. And these miracles, the work of demons, will be very convincing. An agent of Satan will even bring down fire from heaven to convince those who look on. See Revelation 13:13, 14.

Do you see the danger? In the days of Elijah the supernatural fire was an evidence of the true God. But it will not be so in the future confrontation, for God will permit Satan to duplicate that miracle!

Someone says, "Then are people to blame if they are deceived? Aren't we just at the mercy of deception if fire was a proof then and not now?"

But I ask you, If God has plainly warned us and if the warning has been written down for centuries for all to see, then do we *need to be* at the mercy of deception? Have we no defense against the miracles of demons?

To be sure, we walk on dangerous ground these days. Every step we take is on ground that is mined by the enemy. But God's Word is both our warning and our defense. Our peril is in neglecting it. To live in the days of Revelation without reading and understanding Revelation is like presuming to operate a high-powered and unfamiliar machine without bothering to read the instructions!

It is easy to say, "I'll be OK. I'll figure it out. I'll just play it by ear." But playing it by ear is dangerous business in an hour like this. It is only as we keep close to God's Word, only as we both read and heed its warnings, that we are safe from deception. There is no safety anywhere else. And to neglect the Scriptures does not make us sophisticated. It makes us gullible!

We are approaching the final showdown. The conflict is accelerating all about us. We can feel it in the air. The participants are still the same as when rebellion first disrupted the peace and harmony of heaven. It is a war between Christ and His angels and Satan and his angels. But now every inhabitant of this planet is to be involved, enlisted on one side or the other.

The issues, too, are the same. Nothing has changed. In Armageddon, as in Eden, and as at Mount Carmel, it is the authority of God that is challenged. His government and His law are still the target of the enemy's wrath.

And sun worship? Sun worship was the big issue at Mount Carmel. And believe it or not, it will still be an issue for you and me. Loving obedience has always been the mark of allegiance to God. But Satan, through willing accomplices, will yet take a pagan holiday, a day dedicated to the worship of the sun, and make it a mark of allegiance to himself. And every man and woman and youth will have to choose. No, sun worship is not dead!

But thank God, we know the outcome of it all. The fury of men and demons will be directed against Jesus, the Lamb of God—and against those who remain loyal to Him. And the battle will be fierce. But the Lamb will overcome!

Yes, if you take a peek at the back of God's Book, you'll see that Jesus wins! He will win at the last because He won on that dark Friday when He died, alone and forsaken, on a rough and rugged cross outside Jerusalem!

It is to that cross, to the Lamb of God who died there, that I urge you to turn your eyes. It is to Golgotha's splintery cross that I invite you to nail your colors and declare your loyalty.

But there is so little time. Already we feel the chilling breath of Armageddon. The sounds of battle are not as distant as they once were. And when Armageddon has slipped out of the future and into the past, only one question will matter. What have you done with the Lamb?

Toying With the Nick of Time

For three days the long, weary hours had dragged by. Flight 316, with its sixty-eight passengers, still sat on the runway at Kennedy International Airport.

Why? Was it mechanical trouble? The weather? A hijacking? No. United States authorities only wanted to be sure that one particular passenger aboard that plane was not leaving the country against her will. Her husband had defected to the United States. He wanted her to join him. Had she been pressured, or even forced, to board the plane? That was his fear.

But now, in the presence of officials of both nations, she had said, "I love my husband. But he made his decision to stay here and I have made mine to leave."

Had she spoken freely, without coercion? Her husband's lawyer responded, "I couldn't say for sure. I wasn't able to tell. After all, she's an actress."

Actress or not, her decision had been made. And so it was that after seventy-two hours on the runway, television lights went out, reporters hurried to the telephones, watching tourists turned to less exciting drama, and Flight 316 lifted into the evening sky.

Is the ship of time being held on the runway—waiting for certain passengers aboard to make up their minds?

We read again from Revelation: "And after these things I saw four angels standing on the four corners of the earth, holding the four winds of the earth, that the wind should not blow on the earth, nor on the sea, nor on any tree." Revelation 7:1, KJV.

Winds on a leash! Angels holding back the winds of war and destruction. Holding back the flight of time. Turning aside disaster. Blunting the power of the hurricane and the flood. Restraining the winds of violence and terror. Holding the hourglass on a slant so that the last grains of sand will not escape. Forbidding history to sign out just yet. Because God is unwilling to wrap it all up until every man has decided whether or not he wants to be free!

So often we have seen it happen. We have prepared for the big disaster, even for doomsday. And somehow doomsday just didn't arrive. Now you will understand why.

Hurricane Allen was billed as the big one—the storm of the century. A whole county was evacuated. Yet its devastation was far less than expected.

Again and again a hurricane has been aimed directly at our nation's capital. Yet nearly always the storm has veered from its expected course, leaving Washington with only a fringe of steady rain.

You know now who restrains the full fury of the storm—and holds the winds on a leash!

Have you ever wondered what would have happened if the Arabs had won the Yom Kippur War? What if the Israelis had turned to nuclear weapons—as it is rumored they were about to do?

What if the Shah of Iran had been deposed twenty-five years earlier? Would the whole course of history have been changed?

Or what if that ill-fated rescue attempt had succeeded? What if there had been no dust storms that night on the Iranian desert? What if three of the helicopters had not failed? What if the flames of a burning jet had not lighted up the Iranian sky? Would the hostages have been safely rescued? Or would they have all been killed? If the well-intentioned mission had been successful, would it have triggered World War III?

I do not know. I do know that God is still in control. History, more often than we realize, has been altered by divine intervention. God has often caused the guns to fail. He has used the fog to protect men from their enemies. He works in a thousand ways that have never crossed our minds. If it were not for His restraining hand upon the winds of international terror, Armageddon would have overtaken us long ere this!

It is God who says to the winds of war as He says to the waves of the sea, "Hitherto shalt thou come, but no further: and here shall thy proud waves be stayed." Job 38:11, KJV.

But one day soon the winds will be unleashed. They will blow with a fury that defies imagination. It will not be a *county* that needs to be evacuated. It will be a whole planet!

Angels now are holding the winds—*until* God's people are sealed in their foreheads. With a visible mark? No. But thousands of men, women, and children will be so in love with Jesus that they will say, "Lord, I want to be marked as one of Your children forever!"

But other thousands—the majority, unfortunately—will say in their hearts, or by their actions, "No thank You, Lord. I know You died to save me. But I don't want to be saved. I choose to go my own way."

One day soon every man, woman, and child will have made up his mind. There will be only two groups in that day. Those who have accepted the sacrifice of Jesus. And those who have not. And there will come a day when the Saviour will know that those in one group will never stop sinning, and that those in the other group will never sin again!

Then will go forth the fateful decree found in the last chapter of the Bible, "He that is unjust, let him be unjust still: and he which is filthy, let him be filthy still: and he that is righteous, let him be righteous still: and he that is holy, let him be holy still." Revelation 22:11, KJV.

That decree will mark the close of man's probation. No changing of camps after that. Not because God wants to be arbitrary. Not because He wants to cut anyone off. Rather, the decree will reflect the fact that men and women have made their final choices. And now God will honor those choices!

Then the winds will blow! *Then* we will be ushered into a time of trouble such as this world has never known. *Then* the seven final judgments will be released upon the enemies of God. *Then* the predictions of Revelation will reach their final fulfillment. *Then* the last grains of sand will slip through the hourglass. And Jesus will return!

Are you ready for the winds to blow?

At this moment the winds of trouble and terror and all-out war have not yet been unleashed. A lighted match in the Middle East has not blown us into World War III. Doomsday hasn't happened to an unsuspecting planet—yet. But it will not long be this way.

Even now many are *toying with the nick of time!*

Today, as I write these words, the angels have not let go the winds, though they seem to be loosening their grip. Today, as I write these words, it is not too late to make your choice for eternity. But the words which are true today may not be true tomorrow. Tomorrow the roar of unleashed winds may deafen us with their fury. And once they are unleashed, once time begins its final countdown for a rendezvous with eternity, the prophecies of Revelation—those that are left—will be fulfilled with a rapidity that will take our breath away!

Time is history in motion. It creeps like a freight train, ever so slowly, out of the past. How could time ever run out? How could the slow freight ever catch up with us? But one day soon it will pass us by as if we were only a whistle stop—and the future will have become the past. *Have you ever thought what it would be like to look back at the end of the world?*

Today—toying with the nick of time. But one day soon it will be *just after the nick of time!*

Does it somehow seem incredible to you that the hour should be so late?

Let me remind you of the day God delivered His people from the tyranny of ancient Egypt. If you had visited Egypt just four months before, you would have found not a sign—not a single sign—that God was about to set an enslaved people free. Yet in the short space of four months God sent ten fearful judgments upon the and land delivered His people—just as He had promised! And it will be that way again. The final pages of history will turn more rapidly than we can focus our eyes!

In the meantime—what little meantime there is—the enemy will do his best to divert our attention from the only thing that really matters—getting ready to meet our Lord!

It was a clear, pleasant evening in late summer. Eastern's Flight 212 was approaching Charlotte, North Carolina. The flight crew was discussing politics and used cars.

Nothing wrong with talking about politics and used cars. Nothing wrong except that their words would turn out to be sand in an hourglass!

"Say, look!" An amusement park caught their attention.

The low-altitude warning signal may have been regarded as more of a nuisance than a warning. But that signal was the very last before the point of no return!

Complacency reigned in the cockpit—while the nick of time had passed!

Six seconds before the crash, the captain said, "All we got to do is find the airport."

"Yeah," said the first officer.

Both men shouted about a half second before the crash.

Ten months later, after a careful investigation, the report of the National Transportation Safety Board prompted this headline: AIR CRASH KILLING 72 LAID TO PILOT'S IDLE TALK.

Friend, don't let it happen to you!

Airlift

It was September 23, 1922. The old U.S.S. *Mississippi,* with a new owner and a new name, lay at anchor in the harbor of Mytilene—an island in the Aegean Sea. In the gray morning a young American civilian had come out to the ship in a borrowed rowboat and asked to see the captain. And now, twelve hours later, he had just delivered an ultimatum to the Greek government!

It happened this way. Not many weeks earlier a man named Asa Jennings, with his wife and family, had been sent by the Y.M.C.A. to the Turkish city of Smyrna. His assignment—to study what might be done to smooth relations between the Turks and Armenians and Greeks and Jews of that troubled city.

Things had happened fast. The Allies, you may recall, had given Smyrna to the Greeks as a reward for their participation in the war. The Greek Army had moved into Smyrna and pushed inland toward Ankara. But Ataturk had rallied the Turkish people behind him in a daring drive for independence.

The Greek Army was confident of victory. Its troops were pushing steadily toward the heart of the country—when suddenly they retreated before Ataturk. They burned and pillaged their way back to Smyrna.

The Greek troops, in their wild retreat, forced their own countrymen, as well as the Armenians, to abandon their homes and flee to the coast. Every road to the sea was choked with refugees. And then, believe it or not, the Greek soldiers, thinking only of their own safety, simply took ship and sailed away. The refugees were left to make out as best they could.

And then suddenly—no one seems to know just how—Smyrna was in flames. The great mass of refugees were pushed toward the sea, with the fire behind them.

Asa Jennings, while the city was still burning, put his little family aboard an American destroyer. But he stayed behind to see what he could do for the refugees. Somehow he arranged for food to be sent in. But this suffering mass of humanity that choked the quay, caught between fire and sea, needed more than food. They needed ships!

Now providentially, it seemed, the twenty Greek transports that had carried the Greek soldiers away to safety were anchored at Mytilene. So he lost no time in getting to Mytilene. Surely Greek ships would be willing to save Greek people. But General Frankos, in charge of the transports, was cautious and couldn't make up his mind.

It was then that Asa Jennings sighted the old U.S.S. *Mississippi* at anchor and rowed out through the early morning mist to board her. He was determined to go over the head of General Frankos and make contact directly with the Greek government in Athens.

He told his story to the captain. He then asked that a code message be sent to Athens, requesting that all ships in the waters about Smyrna be placed at his disposal. It was four o'clock in the morning.

A message came back, "Who are you?"

A natural question. He had been in that part of the world only about a month, and no one had ever heard of him.

He sent word back, "I am in charge of American relief at Mytilene." He didn't explain that he was in charge only by virtue of being the only American there.

Athens outdid General Frankos in caution. The Cabinet would have to decide. The Cabinet was not in session. The Cabinet would meet in the morning. What protection would be given the ships? Would American destroyers accompany them? Did that mean that American destroyers would protect the ships if the Turks should try to take them? And so it went.

Finally, at four in the afternoon, the young American's patience was exhausted. He wired Athens that if he did not receive a favorable reply by six o'clock, he would wire openly, without code—letting all the world know that the Greek government had refused to rescue its own people from certain death.

It worked. Shortly before six o'clock a message came through: ALL SHIPS IN AEGEAN PLACED YOUR COMMAND. REMOVE REFUGEES SMYRNA.

Those ten words meant life for many thousands. They also

meant that a young, unknown American had just been made Admiral of the Greek navy!

And so he assumed command. The captains of the twenty ships were asked to be ready to leave for Smyrna by midnight. And at that hour they were all in place. Asa Jennings, aboard the lead ship, ordered the Greek flag run down, an American flag flown in its place, with a signal that meant "Follow me." He mounted the bridge and ordered full steam ahead.

Picture the scene if you can. As the ships moved toward Smyrna, he could see from his station on the bridge the smoking ruins of what had once been the business section of the city. Directly in front, gaunt brick and stone skeletons of once-fine buildings pushed themselves up from the charred debris. And at the water's edge, stretching for miles, was what looked like a lifeless black border. Yet he knew that it was a border of living sufferers waiting, hoping, praying—as they had done every moment for days—for ships, ships, ships!

As the ships moved closer, and the shore spread out before him, it seemed as if every face on that quay was turned toward them, and every arm outstretched to bring them in. It seemed that the whole shore moved out to grasp them. The air was filled with the cries of those thousands—cries of such joy that the sound pierced to the very marrow of his bones. No need for anyone to tell them what those ships were for. They who had scanned that watery horizon for days looking wistfully for ships, did not have to be told that here was help, that here was life and safety!

Never had he been so thankful, so truly happy, as on that early morning when he realized that at last—and thank God in time—he had been able to bring hope, and a new life, to those despairing thousands!

It was Asa Jennings' son who told me the story.

I can never forget it. Nor can I forget the striking parallel that I know will happen soon. A spectacular rescue—not from the sea, but from the sky. Involving not three hundred thousand refugees on a single shore, but—if only they would be willing—every man, woman, and child on a shaking, burning, convulsing planet. Pushed to the brink—the brink of oblivion. And no way out but by airlift from the sky!

Unquestionably there will soon come a time when living on this planet is no longer desirable or safe. There will soon come a time when frantic, frightened, frustrated men will borrow the cry of the Broadway stage, "Stop the world! I want to get off!"

But God has not been caught unprepared. He has scheduled a great airlift. I never tire of the way the apostle Paul describes it: "For the Lord himself shall descend from heaven with a shout, with the voice of the archangel, and with the trump of God: and the dead in Christ shall rise first: Then we which are alive and remain shall be caught up together with them in the clouds, to meet the Lord in the air: and so shall we ever be with the Lord." 1 Thessalonians 4:16, 17, KJV.

There it is! God's airlift! Wonderful day—for those who are prepared for it. Hear them shout the glad welcome, "Lo, this is our God; we have waited for him, and he will save us: this is the Lord; we have waited for him, we will be glad and rejoice in his salvation." Isaiah 25:9, KJV.

But all will not be prepared to welcome their Lord. Some will be surprised, needlessly surprised, as were the people of Noah's day. Some will breathe the tragic words, "I knew He was coming. I was expecting Him. But I didn't think it would be so soon!" And some will call out to the mountains and the rocks, "Fall on us, and hide us from the face of him that sitteth on the throne, and from the wrath of the Lamb." Revelation 6:16, KJV.

Friend, do you love your Lord? Do you want to be with Him? Do you want to be rescued from this planet when it has become too unsafe, too hazardous, for living? Then listen once more to the words of Paul that we read only a moment ago. Let them sink deep into your heart until you feel the pull of the better land. "For the Lord himself shall descend from heaven with a shout, with the voice of the archangel, and with the trump of God: and the dead in Christ shall rise first: Then we which are alive and remain shall be caught up together with them in the clouds, to meet the Lord in the air: and so shall we ever be with the Lord."

News. Good news. Encouraging news. Comforting news. This isn't death. This is resurrection. This isn't destruction. This is survival. This isn't panic. This is rescue! Like the ships moving in toward Smyrna. It's a way off this planet. And it's in time. Just in time!

This isn't gloom. This isn't doom. This isn't something to spoil your plans. This isn't something to fear—or dread—or wish you could postpone. That is, unless you don't want to be rescued. And who wouldn't want to be rescued in an hour like that?

Who would have chosen to turn back to the smoking ruins of Smyrna—with ships in sight? And who would want to turn back to this smoking, shaking, convulsing planet with rescue on the way?

Picture it if you can. Like the ships at Smyrna. A vast mass of humanity pushed to the edge of a smoking, ruined, convulsing world. Caught between the fires of time and the realities of eternity. Desperate for a way off this planet. Scanning the skies for the first hint that rescue is on the way. Staring into space. God's people will be straining their eyes for the first glimpse of their Lord as He emerges from the corridors of Orion and rides the cloud closer and closer to the earth!

Every face is turned toward the sky. Every eye filled with tears of irrepressible joy. Every voice shouting His welcome. Every arm outstretched to bring Him in. As if the earth itself reached out to grasp its Creator!

No need to tell us why He has come. We who have scanned the heavens wistfully for days, while a planet burns behind us, don't have to be told that here is rescue from the skies. We have waited for our Lord. And now at last He is here!

This is the airlift, the rescue that God has planned. Are you ready for it? Am I? Will you and I be aboard that living starship as it begins to move—on its way back to the City of God?

That airlift has been scheduled by God Himself. And it won't be canceled. It is sure. It is certain. The only question is this: Who will get to go? And what will it cost?

How much will it cost? Just a surrendered heart. A heart cleansed. A heart changed. A proud, selfish heart made selfless and humble. A hard heart made kind. A heart that has been to Calvary—and will never be the same again. A heart made strong enough to stand in that tumultuous day. A heart that wants, more than anything else, to be ready to meet its Lord!

Think about that day. Think about it over and over. Let it give you something to live for. Could anything be more exciting to contemplate? Seeing first a small black cloud in the eastern sky. Watching it move nearer and nearer till it becomes a glorious white. A cloud like none you've ever seen before. A cloud of angels—uncounted angels. Hearing a sound like none you've ever heard before—the sound of a trumpet echoing round the world. A voice like none you've ever heard before—the voice of the Lord Jesus—calling the dead to life. The earth shaking. The tombs bursting open. Angels everywhere. Carrying little children, in the bloom of perfect health, from the broken graves. Placing them in their mothers' arms. Shouts of joy as loved ones long separated by death are reunited, never to part again!

And then, together with those happy, resurrected ones, we who have waited through the long night are caught up into that angel starship, ready for the trip home!

I like to try to picture that space vehicle. A cloud of shining angels. A cloud chariot with living wings on either side and living wheels beneath. A rainbow above it and the appearance of fire beneath. Jesus riding the cloud—and not a person missed who really wanted to make the trip. Ten thousand angels surrounding the cloud and singing the praise of their Creator. Moving up through the glittering, star-studded corridor of Orion. A living starship on the way to the City of God!

What if trouble and pain and disaster *do* crowd our days *now* and interrupt our nights? What if the wail of the siren *is* always with us—the whine of missiles, the roar of bombers, the thunder of the approaching storm?

Let these increasingly remind us that there is a better place to be, and an absolutely fascinating way to get there—the great airlift, not by jet but by cloud, to the City of our God! The incredible flight to Orion and beyond! The living starship with its cargo of committed men and women and children who want more than all else to be forever with their Lord!

Will your name be on the passenger list? It can be. There's only one requirement. It's the word *pardon,* written in the blood of the Lord Jesus, beside your name!

God's Yellow Ribbons

Victims of kidnapping are sometimes told that family and friends have forsaken them. And sometimes they are brainwashed into believing it.

How could we let fifty-two American hostages know that their country had not abandoned them?

Someone tied a yellow ribbon around an old oak tree—and yellow ribbons spread like the measles. But how would *the hostages* know? How would *they* know that eight brave men had lost their lives in an attempt to rescue them? How would *they* know that we were numbering our days by the days of their captivity? How *could* they know when bags full of mail addressed to them were left unopened—and when the few letters that were delivered were first carefully censored?

But love has a way of getting through. Militant students overlooked the value of a Valentine—in August—from a little girl. It said simply, "It's just not America without you!" And another, from a child in school, slipped past the censors. It said, "I'm awfully sorry they didn't get you out. I hope they try again."

Then there was a *Time* magazine which carried the full story of the rescue attempt. The story had been carefully removed—and then inadvertently stuffed into the back of the magazine and forgotten.

At Christmas time a visiting clergyman gave Morehead Kennedy the assurance he needed in one short sentence: "Nobody's talking about anything else!"

The fifty-two were not forgotten!

And then, on January 20, almost as abruptly as it had begun, the long ordeal was over. The fear and the hunger, the blindfolds and the isolation and the beatings, the terrible loneliness, the fake firing squads—all slipped into the past, to scar only their memory.

Four hundred and forty-four dull, dragging, seemingly endless days suddenly gave way to a tumult of joy and reunion and welcome that couldn't happen except in a dream. Yet it *was* happening—happening to fifty-two Americans who in their hours of darkness had been tempted to think nobody cared. It would take a while to sort it all out and be convinced that it was real!

Telephones! Milk to drink! No blindfolds! Moving about without asking permission! German children singing to make up for the Christmases they had missed! The Statue of Liberty lighted for the first time since 1976! Kissing American soil! Church bells ringing! Falling at last into the arms of loved ones! The memories were theirs to keep!

And each day brought more pictures to hang in memory's hall. Pictures framed by bus windows as they inched through the cheering, tumultuous crowds. The Lincoln Memorial bathed in colored lights. The President praying simply, "Dear God, thank You! Thank You for what You've done!"

The days of celebration had all the thunder of a Fourth of July, all the dignity of an inauguration, and all the pathos of a reunion that had kept them hoping for fourteen months!

Americans had not been content to tie a yellow ribbon round an old oak tree. They tied them everywhere. On trees. On cars. On planes. On gates. On buildings. They tied one completely around the National Geographic Building. And the biggest yellow ribbon in history was tied in a bow round the Super Dome in New Orleans!

Yellow ribbons were everywhere. Canyons of yellow ribbons and flags and people slowed their buses almost to a stop. Miles and miles of ribbons—beside the highways and above them. Corridors of welcome they would never forget!

It all merged into a happy blur of color and tickertape and God-bless-America that was difficult to sort into days. But did it matter? It was crowding out the past, dimming the shouts of hate that had bombarded their ears those fourteen months, shrinking the memory of their ordeal to livable proportions. Said one former hostage, "It couldn't have been better if I had died and gone to heaven!"

Americans watched it all—from the streets and from their living rooms—and wept for joy. The hostages were home! They were safe! And not one of the fifty-two was lost!

But the captives haven't all come home. Probably you are

aware that more and more reports are surfacing from individuals who claim that American servicemen, MIAs, are still being held, alive, in Vietnam—and in Laos. They have been seen in prisons, in camps, in chain gangs, at forced labor in the fields. It is said that some are held in caves. We ought to be praying that these, too, will come home!

Is the name Raoul Wallenberg familiar to you? He has been called "the lost hero of the holocaust." He was a young Swedish diplomat who, on a hot July day in 1944, arrived in Budapest on a mission that some say makes him the greatest hero of World War II. He was shy, soft-spoken, a member of an illustrious Swedish family. But he is credited with saving as many as 100,000 Hungarian Jews from extermination by the Nazis!

He accomplished this largely by issuing thousands of Swedish passports which he used to get Jews off the trains bound for the gas chambers, and to get them out of the long death marches to the Austrian border. Then he purchased or rented safe houses which flew the Swedish flag and sheltered Jews. The passports were actually worthless—but in the confusion and turmoil of war they worked!

The tragedy is that Wallenberg, at the end of the war, was arrested by troops of an Allied nation as a U. S. spy and has not been heard from since!

But it is reported anonymously that as late as 1980 he was alive, still a hostage, held in cell 77 of a certain well-known prison!

California congressman Tom Lantos and his wife Annette both credit Wallenberg with saving their lives when they were teenagers. And Lantos says, "I don't want to minimize the trauma of the fifty-two American hostages. But it is possible [that his captors] have kept him in anticipation of some meaningful exchange, and that Wallenberg is the ultimate hostage."

Yes, the hostages haven't all come home! And the truth is that some of them, at this moment, are reading these words!

Jesus said, "I tell you the truth, everyone who sins is a slave to sin." John 8:34, NIV.

Sin enslaves. It enslaves everyone it touches. And no man is more enslaved than the man who cannot see his own chains!

But Jesus came to free the captives of sin. See Luke 4:18. The chains that have bound you, that have left your life wounded and scarred, that have weakened your will, that have promised you freedom while they made you a slave—those shackles can be broken. They can be broken *now!*

Every one of us can be free from the *power* of sin, from its domination in our lives—if we choose. Says the apostle Paul, "Sin shall not have dominion over you." Romans 6:14, KJV.

But this does not mean that we are free from the *presence* of sin—sin in our environment. We are still surrounded by it, by its deceptive philosophy, and by the ruin and devastation it is causing in human lives.

We are still in enemy territory. From this point of view, every human being alive today is a hostage. This planet is still occupied by the forces of rebellion that took it over in the early morning of its history. Still held by the fallen angel who is the author of rebellion—and by the host of angels-turned-demons who chose to join him in his war against God. We are still here—for now. In that sense we are all still hostages.

The saddest day in all the history of the universe was the day the father of our race sold out to rebellion and made us all vulnerable to its infection.

Think, if you will—try to imagine—how God must have felt, how our Creator must have felt, the day it happened. It will break your heart. It broke His!

He knew what He would do. Calvary even then lay hidden in His heart. But in the meantime how could He let us know He cared? How could He let us know that the fallen angel's charges were untrue?

He sent us message after message. But the enemy did his best to jam the communication lines and to censor and distort and misinterpret the word that did get through. God sent us a long letter, full of love and assurance. But few bothered to read it.

Finally He sent His own Son to live among us. For thirty-three years He was hounded and harrassed and tempted by the enemy—just as we are hounded and harrassed and tempted. Then He was laid on a despised Roman cross and let men nail Him there—to die in our place, to die the death that should have been ours!

Love had found a way of getting through!

And then Jesus went back to His Father's house. But He left us with this promise: "Set your troubled hearts at rest. Trust in God always; trust also in me. There are many dwelling-places in my Father's house; if it were not so I should have told you; for I am going there on purpose to prepare a place for you. And if I go and prepare a place for you, I shall come again and receive you to myself, so that where I am you may be also." John 14:1–3, NEB.

A place for you. A place for me. What a promise! Not a filmy fiction on the edge of some cloud. Not a storyland. Not a dream world. *A place* as real as your own backyard. *A place* in God's country where you can build a house—and plant a vineyard. See Isaiah 65:21, 22. *A place* in the city that God has built. See Hebrews 11:10. *A place* in a city so real that it has foundations and walls and gates and streets and measurements. See Revelation 21:10–27.

A place where the blind will see, and the deaf will hear, and the dumb will sing (Isaiah 35:5, 6)—and where no one will ever say, "I am sick" (Isaiah 33:24). *A place* where there is no pain or sorrow or death—where God Himself will wipe the tears from our eyes. See Revelation 21:4. And when God wipes away the tears, they will be gone forever!

But it has been quite a while now—since all this was promised. And some are saying that He doesn't care after all, that He has forgotten us, abandoned us, that we are hostages forever.

It isn't true! But the Lord Jesus—while He waits a little longer, for reasons we will soon understand—still searches for ways to let us know we are not forgotten.

Does heaven have an old oak tree—a very old oak tree—about which God can tie a yellow ribbon?

I like to think that the stars God has hung in space, flashing against the velvet night, are God's yellow ribbons!

Think what it would be without the stars! Think what it would be like to be orbiting alone in the blackness, wondering if there is anybody out there, wondering if anybody knows we're here, wondering if there really is anybody else but us.

Thank God it isn't that way! God knows we're here. He hasn't forgotten us. His lamps are all lighted, waiting to welcome us home!

I am fascinated with the way Amahl, the crippled boy in Gian-Carlo Menotti's Christmas opera, *Amahl and the Night Visitor*,

describes the night sky. Remember how he limps indoors shriek-
ing with ecstasy, "Oh, Mother, come and see . . ."? Remember
his words?

> Oh, Mother, you should go out and see!
> There's never been such a sky!
> Damp clouds have shined it
> And soft winds have swept it
> As if to make ready for a King's ball.
> All its lanterns are lit,
> All its torches are burning,
> And its dark floor
> Is shining like crystal.
> Hanging over our roof
> There is a star as large as a window,
> And the star has a tail,
> And it moves across the sky
> Like a chariot on fire.
> And his mother says wearily,
> Oh Amahl! When will you stop telling lies?
> All day long you wander about in a dream.
> Here we are with nothing to eat,
> Not a stick of wood on the fire,
> Not a drop of oil in the jug,
> And all you do is worry your mother
> With fairy tales.

Friend, it *isn't* a fairy tale! All God's lamps *are* lighted. And
one day soon the Lord Jesus will make His way down through
that star-studded processionway of the skies to keep His promise.
And not one hostage who wants to go home will be forgotten!

I think of you heroes of Vietnam who didn't get a parade, who
didn't get any tickertape, who have reason to say, "Where are *our*
yellow ribbons?" Some of you will never walk again—until Jesus
comes to set things right. No wonder you feel abandoned and
unloved!

But you *aren't* abandoned. You *are* loved. Ask someone to
wheel you out under the stars or push your bed near a window.
Look up at those brilliant lamps, twinkling in the distance. They
are God's yellow ribbons—lavished across the night to tell you
that He cares!

Jesus is coming soon! And not one will be missed who wants to go home, who chooses to be included in His mission of rescue. Tell Him you want to be on His list. His angels will find you, wherever you are. Languishing in hospitals. Held captive in caves. Wherever. Not one will be missed!

Don't ever think that God doesn't *want* you to come home! He does, friend! He does!

Some years ago a boy quarreled with his father and left home. He said, "You'll never see me again!"

Three years passed—three tough years. He wanted to go home, but he was afraid. Would his father let him come back? He wrote his mother, told her that he would be on a certain train as it passed the house. He asked her to hang something white in the yard if it was all right with his dad to come home.

He was nervous on the train—sat in one seat and then another. A minister noticed, and asked what was wrong. He told him. They rode along together as the boy looked out the window.

Suddenly he started up excitedly. "Look, sir, my house is just around the bend, beyond the hill. Will you please look for me, see if there is something white? I can't stand to look. If there isn't anything white—you look, please!"

The train lurched a bit as it made a slow curve, and the minister kept his eyes on the round of the hill. Then he forgot his dignity as he fairly shouted, "Look, son, look!"

There was the little farmhouse under the trees. But you could hardly see the house for white. It seemed that those lonely parents had taken every white sheet in the house, every bedspread, every tablecloth, even every handkerchief—everything they could find that was white—and hung them out on the clothesline and on the trees!

The boy paled. His lips quivered. He couldn't speak. He was out of the train before it had completely stopped at the water tank. The last his new friend saw of him he was running up the hill as fast as his legs could carry him—toward the sheets that were fluttering in the wind, and *home!*

That's what God has done. He's hung out every star He had—in dazzling white—all over the sky!

I like to picture that great day—when all the hostages go home. What a procession it will be, with Jesus Himself leading the way!

With harps and crowns and in the distance flashing suns! God's yellow ribbons everywhere—as the tumultuous songs of welcome echo from world to world!

I like to think that the fifty-two will be there—and the heroes of Vietnam. Jeremiah Denton and all the POWs. And the MIAs. The captives that Jesus came to set free. The slaves of drink and drugs and smoke and sin of every stripe. All forgiven—washed clean in the blood of the Lamb!

I like to think that Raoul Wallenberg will be there. And you. And you. And you! Because you *can* be—if you choose!

In all God's universe, from His grandest galaxy to the smallest atom, will beat one pulse of harmony. No note of discord will ever mar God's vast creation. No voice will ever say good-bye. No heart will ever break. God's children, hostage so long in an alien land, will be at home forever. And the cry of this lonely planet, with its symphony of tears, will be no more!